TRAPPED WITH THE BILLIONAIRE

ERIN SWANN

ERINSWANN.COM

Cover images licensed from Shutterstock.com, depositphotos.com

Cover design by Swann Publications

ISBN-13: 979-8628459119

Edited by Jessica Royer Ocken

Proofreaders: My Brother's Editor, Donna Hokanson, Tamara Mataya

Typohunter Extraordinaire: Renee Williams

The following story is intended for mature readers. It contains mature themes, strong language, and sexual situations. All characters are 18+ years of age, and all sexual acts are consensual.

❀ Created with Vellum

ALSO BY ERIN SWANN

The Billionaire's Trust - Available on Amazon, also in AUDIOBOOK

(Bill and Lauren's story) He needed to save the company. He needed her. He couldn't have both. The wedding proposal in front of hundreds was like a fairy tale come true—Until she uncovered his darkest secret.

The Youngest Billionaire - Available on Amazon

(Steven and Emma's story) The youngest of the Covington clan, Steven, avoided the family business to become a rarity, an honest lawyer. He didn't suspect that pursuing Emma could destroy his career. She didn't know what trusting him could cost her.

The Secret Billionaire – Available on Amazon, also in AUDIOBOOK

(Patrick and Elizabeth's story) Women naturally circled the flame of wealth and power, and his is brighter than most. Does she love him? Does she not? There's no way to know. When Pat stopped to help her, Liz mistook him for a carpenter. Maybe this time he'd know. Everything was perfect. Until the day she left.

The Billionaire's Hope - Available on Amazon, also in AUDIOBOOK

(Nick and Katie's story) They came from different worlds. Katie hadn't seen him since the day he broke her brother's nose. Her family retaliated by destroying Nick's life. She never suspected where accepting a ride from him today would take her. They said they could do casual. They lied.

Previously titled: Protecting the Billionaire

Picked by the Billionaire – Available on Amazon, also in AUDIOBOOK

(Liam and Amy's story) A night she wouldn't forget. An offer she couldn't refuse. He alone could save her, and she held the key to his survival. If only they could pass the test together.

Saved by the Billionaire – Available on Amazon

(Ryan and Natalie's story) The FBI and the cartel were both after her for the same thing: information she didn't have. First, the FBI took everything, and then the cartel came for her. She trusted Ryan with her safety, but could she trust him with her heart?

Caught by the Billionaire – Available on Amazon

(Vincent and Ashley's story) Ashley's undercover assignment was simple enough: nail the crooked billionaire. The surprise came when she opened the folder, and the target was her one-time high school sweetheart, Vincent. What will happen when an unknown foe makes a move to checkmate?

The Driven Billionaire – Available on Amazon

(Zachary and Brittney's story) Rule number one: hands off your best friend's sister. With nowhere to turn when she returns from upstate, Brittney accepts Zach's offer of a room. Mutual attraction quickly blurs the rules. When she comes under attack, pulling Brittney closer is the only way to keep her safe. But, the truth of why she left town in the first place will threaten to destroy them both.

Nailing the Billionaire – Available on Amazon

(Dennis and Jennifer's story) Jennifer knew he destroyed her family. Now she is close to finding the records that will bring Dennis down. When a corporate shakeup forces her to work with him, anger and desire compete. Vengeance was supposed to be simple, swift, and sweet. It was none of those things.

Undercover Billionaire – Available on Amazon

(Adam and Kelly's story) Their wealthy families have been at war forever. When Kelly receives a chilling note, the FBI assigns Adam to protect her. Family histories and desire soon collide, questioning old truths. Keeping ahead of the threat won't be their only challenge.

Trapped with the Billionaire – Available on Amazon

(Josh and Nicole's story) Nicole returns from vacation to find her company has been sold to Josh's family. Being assigned to work for the new CEO is only the first of her problems. Competing visions of how to run things and mutual passion create a volatile mix. The reappearance of a killer from years ago soon threatens everything.

Saving Debbie – Available on Amazon

(Luke and Debbie's story) On the run from her family and the cops, Debbie finds the only person she can trust is Luke, the ex-con biker who patched up her injuries. Old lies haunt her, and the only way to unravel them is to talk with Josh, the boy who lived through the nightmare with her years ago.

Interested in FREE books?

Members of Erin's ARC-Team get early access to **FREE** copies of Erin's new releases for review purposes. Yes, you read that right – free books prior to the official release date. If you are interested in learning more about this opportunity go to https://erinswann.com/arc-team

Want to hear about new releases and sales?

If you would like to hear about Erin's **new releases** and sales, go to https://erinswann.com/subscribe to join the newsletter. We only email about sales or new releases, and we never share your information.

CHAPTER 1

NICOLE

SANDY REMOVED HER SUNGLASSES AND SCANNED THE CROWD TO THE LEFT. "THE GUY in blue you were checking out earlier is watching you."

"Pass." The broad-shouldered man in the blue polo was more than cute, but by the time I looked, Mr. Studious had his head down in his iPad, same as he'd had for most of this afternoon on the beach. He didn't seem *that* interested in me, or any of the women here, for that matter.

I forked another bite of my apple slaw salad and returned to my phone. My text this morning checking on my cousin, Lara, had gone unanswered, as had the two follow-ups this afternoon. Uncle Ernst hadn't answered my question about how his meeting with the bank had gone either. What was up with my family?

"Last night here." Sandy sucked on the straw in her mango margarita. "You don't want to let it go to waste."

Sandra Targus, bless her, was my best friend, but a little on the wild side. Her idea of a night in Barbados going to waste was not finding a man's room to spend it in. So far she'd wasted only three nights of our week down here, but she didn't want to make it four.

"Girl, I saw you checking him out again this afternoon," she added.

Now that the glow of the sunset was fading, I removed my shades as well and looked for our waiter, Diego. I caught his attention with a wave.

Sandy pointed an accusatory finger. "Don't try to deny it."

Diego hurried over, saving me from having to answer her.

I lifted my glass. "Could I get some more water, please?"

"Certainly," he replied.

"One more thing." Sandy pointed past the family with the rambunctious kids toward Mr. Studious. "Can you tell me what the gentleman in blue over there is drinking?"

Diego peered over. "He's drinking tonight's special, a green monkey. Would you like one?"

I scooped a large bite of pasta into my mouth.

Sandy pointed to me. "No. My friend here would like to order him another."

Diego smiled and backed away before I could complain.

I almost choked getting my food down. "What are you doing?"

The Evil Sandy grin appeared. "Just helping. Did you know he's glanced at you seven times now?"

Of course she was counting.

"Bull, and you're paying for the drink." That wouldn't slow her down; Sandy wasn't as tight on money as I was.

I brought my water to my mouth. "I came down here to bake the worries out of my system." Condensation from the icy glass dripped on my shorts.

"You came down here to forget about your dickhead ex."

"Well, that too." Maurice Dickman had seemed okay at first—a lesson about first impressions.

For a time, I'd written men off as a waste. They were all a bunch of lying losers who moved on when it suited them, which also meant without notice. I'd taken a chance with Mo, and he'd proven it once again—the lying sack of shit. In the end, Sandy had been right. *Dickhead, dickless,* or *dickwad* suited him better than Dickman.

While I savored another mouthful of my penne marinara, I caught Mr. Studious actually looking our direction.

Sandy winked. "That makes eight."

My phone vibrated with a text message.

Ernst: We'll talk when you get back

I laid the phone down. Pursuing it tonight wouldn't get me anywhere.

Diego returned to top off my water glass.

I ignored Sandy and took another bite of my dinner. "What time's our flight?"

"Late enough in the afternoon that you two can sleep in, if you get lucky."

Diego delivered the green cocktail to Mr. Studious with a quick point in our direction.

A smile grew on the man's face as he looked over and lifted his glass to me. The smile was a definite improvement.

Sandy kicked me under the table. "Wave."

I returned his smile and offered a quick wave before looking back at my dinner.

"Now that wasn't so hard, was it?"

"No," I admitted. Glancing up again, I couldn't avert my gaze when I caught him looking our way.

Mr. Studious took a sip of his drink and nodded at me with a pucker of his lips. Had he just thrown me a kiss? His lips moved a little more. He seemed to be asking a silent question, but what?

Lip reading was Sandy's thing, but she hadn't been looking over.

What am I supposed to do now? I could tell when some idiot driver mouthed *fuck you* through his window, but that was about as far as my talent went. I settled for a pinky wave before averting my gaze and forking the last of my salad.

"That's a good start. Just a little flirty. Keep him on the line."

"I'm not fishing, just being polite."

"It's time to get back in the saddle, girl. And besides, that one's packin'."

Leave it to Sandy to judge a guy's package from afar. Whereas my assessment usually started with a man's shoulders, hers always began much lower.

"The longer you put it off, the more power you're giving Mo. You can't let fear run your life."

"It's not the right time yet," I countered.

She called it fear; I called it patience and prudence.

"Sure it is. One last night here in paradise. Loosen up. Allow yourself to have a little fun. Get crazy, for God's sake. You'll never see the guy again. What could be simpler?"

I moved the last of my pasta around on my plate. "It's a little soon."

"Six days is soon. It's been six months since Mo walked out."

My fork dropped, and my hand went to my mouth, holding back the urge to upchuck.

Sandy grimaced. "Sorry. I shouldn't have said that."

As the spasms in my gut lessened, I took another sip of water. The image of Mo walking out of my life without a minute's notice was one I wished I could forget.

"Will you be okay?" she asked, rubbing my shoulder.

Another sip of water helped. "Sure."

"I still say the best way to forget your bad memories is to create new good ones, starting with tonight."

"If you think he's so hot, why don't you walk over and pick him up or whatever?"

"I would, but you saw him first, and I'm a better friend than that."

She truly was a good friend. And she was right on the other count. I'd made the mistake of pointing him out the first day. It was supposed to be a fun game for us, rating the guys hot or not.

That first day, he'd risen out of the ocean and walked up the sand to his lounge chair, looking like Daniel Craig in that Bond film, only taller and more muscular. Dripping with saltwater, the man had pegged the hotness meter. He'd even made toweling off look sexy. I'd averted my eyes when he laid down and picked up his iPad, but only for a few seconds. Watching him made me forget what I'd just read in my book, and I'd had to back up a few pages.

After that afternoon, I'd made sure we waited until he'd already gone to the beach. We could then pick a chair under one of the green umbrellas nearby, just one row back. Like they said in real estate: location was everything.

Sandy pulled me back to the present. "You better now?"

I took another sip of my water and pushed my plate away. "Yeah."

Diego arrived with that same green drink on his tray. "From the gentleman in blue." He placed it in front of me.

I avoided looking over and turned the straw toward me. "What's in it?"

"Rum, passionfruit juice, sweet and sour, and blue curacao." The curacao clinched it for me: the secret ingredient of my favorite blue Hawaii drink. The waiter lingered, watching me. "He wants to know if you like it."

I took a sip. "Tell him yes." Looking past the family between us, I gave Mr. Studious a thumbs up.

He lifted his glass and nodded.

I'd spent the afternoons wondering what he did for a living. He was here alone, and constantly reading, but not likely a student, given his age and what they charged for rooms at this place. And not a lawyer either, with the plastic watch he wore. I'd given up and decided on *man of mystery*. I'd never know.

"Now you're making progress, girl," Sandy said.

After another dainty sip, I offered it to her. "Try it."

She did. "Not bad, but I think I'll stick to tequila tonight."

Diego came back after a bit to clear our plates.

Settling in my chair, I sipped on my drink and took in the relaxing vibe of this place. Warm weather, a light breeze, waves lapping at the beach in the post-sunset dimness, and soft music in the background: our last dinner in paradise before returning to the work-a-day world.

"I needed this," I told Sandy. "Thanks for insisting I come along."

"What are friends for?"

Diego returned with dessert menus. His smile grew as he handed me mine.

Sandy looked down at the selections, taking her time, even though they'd been the same all week. "I'm going to change it up and try the cheesecake tonight."

He took down her order.

I set the menu aside without opening it. "I'm good."

Diego cocked an eyebrow. "I really think you should check tonight's special."

Relenting, I opened the menu. A note slipped out.

Care to join me for dessert?

It wasn't signed.

Diego nodded his head toward Mr. Studious.

Looking over, I found him watching me.

"Your answer?" Diego asked. "The tiramisu is excellent."

Sandy grabbed the note and read it. "Tell him yes," she instructed Diego.

I waited until Diego had left to argue. "Don't I get a vote?"

"It's just dessert. I'll drag you over there if I have to." And she meant it too. "I'll watch from here."

I sipped the last of my green liquid courage before hefting my purse and grabbing my phone off the table. "Here goes nothing." *It's only dessert.*

His smile mesmerized me, even from this distance.

I decided on the poolside long way around the family with loud kids—more time to chicken out.

My phone rang with a number I knew too well: the county jail.

I slowed my walk and answered the call. "Hello?"

My cousin Lara's voice came over the line. "I need you to bail me out."

Not again. I thought this was behind her…

The big kid shoved his smaller sibling right at me.

I dodged left. "What happened?"

Bad idea. I moved too far and tumbled into the water. I never got to hear Lara's answer.

I came up sputtering. "Hey!"

The little kid had also landed in the pool, but at least not *on* me. His big brother laughed his head off.

I set my drowned phone up on the cement.

"Jimmy, what the hell did you do?" yelled the dad of the out-of-control family. He started toward us.

Looking behind me, I located my purse on the bottom of the pool. Seeing no other options, I dove down to retrieve it.

Moving toward the edge of the pool, I heard a crunch as Bad Dad stepped on my phone when he extended his hand to me. "Sorry about Jimmy," he said.

I grasped the side of the pool. "You should control your kids." I picked up the poor phone—cracked all right.

"You should be careful where you walk," he shot back.

Mr. Studious appeared next to him. "Back off." He pushed Bad Dad to the side, leaned over, and offered me his hand.

I took it.

"Both hands," Studious said.

I put the phone down and added my other hand, only to be yanked up out of the water like he was Hercules.

Sandy arrived and took my soaked purse from me. "It was your damned fault," she yelled at Bad Dad.

I leaned over to get the carcass of my ruined phone.

"You owe the lady a phone," Studious told Bad Dad in a commanding tone.

"Says who?" the dad asked.

Mr. Studious was in his face. "Says me." With more than six inches on Bad Dad and a scowl that wasn't to be messed with, he grabbed the other man by the collar and backed him to the edge of the pool.

It took the smaller man all of three seconds to whip out his wallet and offer a stack of bills.

Mr. Studious sneered. "Another hundred should do it."

Bad Dad mumbled and came up with more before my benefactor let him go.

Still dripping wet, I accepted the money from Mr. Studious. "Thank you."

"Perhaps dessert another time, Nicole," he offered.

I nodded. "Another time."

He was gone before it registered that he knew my name.

Sandy helped me back toward the room. "Well, that didn't go the way I expected."

~

Josh

THE KIDS HAD BEEN LOUD AND ROUGHHOUSING ALL EVENING. THE PARENTS MADE NO effort to control them.

Making the asshole who'd allowed his family to ruin everyone else's quiet evening pay for Nicole's phone had been the right thing to do.

I should have also pushed him in for a swim.

When I lifted her out of the pool, the white fabric of her shirt and shorts turned translucent. The red of her bra and thong showed through enticingly, and it had taken all the will power I had to let her escape to her room to change.

"Another time," she'd said without a hint of surprise that I'd overheard her name at the beach.

Back at my room, I plugged my tablet in to recharge. Going over the financials of another potential target all day had drained it into the red. Settling back onto the bed, I stared up at the ceiling. I had to get this one right.

Dad's words were etched into my memory: "*A business is like a machine. It works best when all the parts operate in well-oiled unison, pulling together in the same direction.*" Obvious, but profound at the same time.

On this break, I'd consumed four different management books, looking for the person who'd uttered those words. Success had eluded me so far. Clearly I'd have to expand my search. Once I found the teacher Dad had learned from, I'd be able to master the concept well enough to impress even the great Lloyd Benson.

I got up, moved a chair closer to the charger tethering my tablet, and started the next book. Four more days in the sun and still five books to go through. If I got ahead, I'd have some time to spare for actual relaxation, and I now knew just who I wanted to relax with.

Nicole.

I closed my eyes, and her words came back to me: "*Another time*." I had to readjust my pants, recalling how delectable she looked with slicked back, wet hair and her red bra showing through her wet tank top. Tomorrow's calendar now included dessert with the green-eyed beauty, and hopefully more.

CHAPTER 2

Nicole

The next morning, Sandy slept in while I laid awake in bed, wondering what kind of trouble Lara had gotten into. There wasn't anything I could do about it until I got back. The jail didn't take messages. But that knowledge didn't keep me from worrying just the same.

I'd borrowed Sandy's phone last night to get a hold of Maro Tanaka back home, and he'd agreed to feed and look after my dog until I got back, since it seemed Lara was no longer available. She would just have to survive jail until Monday because there was no way to get back to California sooner.

I'd taken in my only cousin, Lara Martini, and given her refuge after she'd had a big fight with her stepdad, Uncle Ernst. She was Aunt Rossella's only child from her first marriage and had always been a wild one. She was three years younger than me, but at times it seemed like twenty years less mature.

I'd never had any particular problem with Uncle Ernst, but Lara called him *Creeper*, without getting any more specific than that.

The bad blood ran so deep that the second time Lara had gotten into trouble, my aunt and uncle had refused to help, and it had fallen to me to bail her out.

After that, Lara hadn't even bothered to call them. And she'd gotten herself into a string of legal troubles. But, that had stopped two years ago—or so I'd thought.

When Sandy finally got up, she and I spent our last morning down by the beach.

"Maybe he'll show up for lunch by the pool," Sandy said after my umpteenth scan of the area.

"Who?"

"Don't give me that."

I rolled my eyes. "Am I that obvious?"

"You're transparent as Saran Wrap. Let's stake out the restaurant so you can at least get his number."

We abandoned our beach chairs to stroll by the restaurant. Last night I'd agreed to dessert another night before remembering I didn't *have* another night. It seemed fitting that after visually stalking him for several days, I'd lose the chance to meet him because I hadn't gotten up the courage earlier. Now he'd be relegated to a memory of what might have been, if only I'd been bolder.

Eventually the time came, and without a Studious sighting, we headed off to the airport.

~

"WHAT'D SHE GET ARRESTED FOR THIS TIME?" SANDY ASKED AS WE WAITED OUR TURN at the gate to board the plane.

"No idea. We got cut off before I found out."

"I say leave her in jail for a while. It'll do her good." Sandy knew better than to suggest getting my aunt and uncle involved.

I understood her perspective, and this *was* getting old. "Well, she's there until I get back, I guess, but I can't abandon her. She's my cousin, and I'm responsible. You want me to let her end up like the Kings' son?"

The Kings from down the street had left their son, Jeremy, in jail a week, awaiting bail, as punishment for his DUI, and he'd ended up beaten and raped. He'd come home with a broken arm, three missing teeth, and terrible psychological scars. His parents now had to live with the knowledge that they could have prevented it.

The women's jail was probably safer, but I wasn't willing to take a chance. I'd get Lara out as soon as I got back.

"I guess not," Sandy admitted. "But she needs to learn a lesson sooner or later. How many times have you bailed her out now? Three?"

I didn't answer. This would be the fifth.

"She needs some tough love."

"That's easy for you to say," I shot back.

What Lara had needed was parental guidance before she'd gotten herself as screwed up as she had.

Our disagreement was cut short when they called our group to board.

It fell out as I retrieved the boarding pass from my purse: that damned envelope with the red and white Swiss flag in the return address corner. I folded it and put it back in my purse, but not before Sandy noticed it.

"Are you still considering your uncle's offer?" she asked as she hefted the backpack she called a purse.

"No, not really. He keeps bugging me to sell him the house, but it's more than just the memories. It's my family's legacy and not for sale, not ever."

I'd grown up in Casa di Rossi, the house my grandpa built, and Daddy had always expected me to pass it down to my kids—not let it be torn down for a bunch of condos.

Sandy led the way to get in line. "If that was true, you would have thrown out the letter already."

As always, Sandy called me on my bullshit.

I followed her. "It's just in case."

My emotional brain had forced me to tell Uncle Ernst I wouldn't sell him Casa di Rossi, but my pragmatic brain had insisted on an insurance policy, and I hadn't tossed the letter.

Sandy turned back to me. "When 'just in case' comes around, don't forget to double the price to the asshole."

Sandy had never liked my step-uncle, and I guess I didn't like him enough to ask her to stop calling him an asshole either.

The agent checked Sandy's boarding pass, followed by mine, and we walked outside toward the stairs rolled up next to the plane.

Rain had been threatening for the past hour or so, and we got up the stairs and into the plane's cabin just as large drops began to fall. Once settled into my aisle seat, I closed my eyes and blotted out the sounds of the other passengers. Last night's scene played itself back on my eyelids. The falling-in-the-pool part hadn't been great, but what had led up to it had been, and Mr. Studious' lesson to the dad had etched itself into my permanent highlight reel.

"Says me," he'd growled as he forced the guy to pay for my phone.

Josh

In the bathroom the next morning, I ignored the room phone when it rang.

After having run three fast laps to the end of the boardwalk and back, I relished my shower. It was an indulgence I wasn't willing to cut short.

Whatever the desk clerk wanted could wait.

Between the temperature and the humidity, even a *morning* run in the tropics produced a gallon of sweat to rinse off. Then there was the matter of releasing my frustration so I could concentrate today. Jerking off to the vision of soaking-wet Nicole last night with her bra showing through that shirt did the trick. With some luck, I might get to sample the real thing tonight.

After toweling dry, the blinking red light on the phone begged for my attention. I pulled on cargo shorts and a shirt before I gave in. After punching in the numbers to retrieve my message, Dad's voice boomed in my ear: "Change of plans, Josh. Need you back here pronto. You're coming home today. Hope you had a relaxing week." *Click*.

Short and to the point, even if not accurate. Leaving today meant I didn't get the whole two weeks I'd planned. And, as usual, my dad had *told* me the way things would be instead of asking.

I'd turned off my phone when I arrived, as I'd planned this to be unplugged time. The phone took a minute to power up, and when it did, it showed the success of my strategy. Being powered off had prevented it from delivering eighty-two voicemail messages to interrupt my downtime.

I punched up Dad's contact.

"What's the emergency?" I asked when he answered.

"We just closed a deal. I need you to go over and get involved right away."

I sighed as quietly as I could manage. "Why not have Tony and Harold handle it?"

"This one needs your talents."

It was more of a compliment than I usually got, and welcome, but it still meant cutting my vacation short.

I took a breath. "When's the plane arrive?"

"Our plane is in the shop, so Libby booked you commercial. See you first thing tomorrow. Gotta go. Hold on the line and Libby will give you the details." Then silence.

Love you too, Dad.

"Sorry about this, Josh," Libby said after a moment. "But he said to get you back as soon as possible."

"Yeah. Go ahead."

She read the details of my flight, leaving this afternoon with a connection through JFK. I started to gather my things. Nine days here was better than nothing, but not the two weeks I'd planned on.

Since I was the only remaining Benson son in the company, I'd expected to catch a break at some point, but I'd been wrong so far. Maybe my oldest brother Dennis's idea of splitting off a piece of the company and leaving everybody else to deal with Dad had been the right one. Vincent and Zack seemed to think so, as they had left after him, and now I didn't have the option.

I spent the morning reading in my room, away from the distraction of bikinis on the beach, and I skipped lunch at the restaurant as well. So much for the enticing Nicole...

On the way to the airport that afternoon, I looked out the window of the taxi, and the dichotomy between the housing in the countryside and the resort I'd been staying at struck me. The houses weren't mud huts or anything, but lots of them weren't complete, with rebar sticking up out of the roofs as if they hadn't been able to afford to finish the upper floor. The bright colors they chose for paint would be an embarrassment back home, but seemed a source of pride here.

My head pivoted as we passed the third coconut stand on the side of the road. "What's the deal with the coconut vendors?"

"Selling fresh coconut water. Good for the health," my driver responded. "You want me to stop at the next one?"

Calling it healthy was another bullshit marketing ploy, as far as I was concerned. "No, thanks."

"I drink one almost every day." He laughed.

After reaching the airport and enduring a long line, I handed my passport to the pretty agent behind the counter.

She held up the document, comparing it to my face. "Did you have a pleasant stay with us, Mr. Benson?"

"Yes, just shorter than I wanted."

She typed on her keyboard. "It always seems that way, doesn't it?" She hit a few more keystrokes. "How many bags will you be checking?"

"Just the one." I hefted my bag onto the scale.

A minute later, she handed me my boarding pass in a folder. "Gate ten. Boarding will begin at three-oh-five."

Only after she handed me the envelope did I notice the error. The seat assignment said 31B. I handed it back. "There must be some mistake. This should be first class."

She took it back and clacked the keys again. "I'm sorry, Mr. Benson, the flight is completely full, and it was booked as coach."

I'd never flown economy. Hell, I'd only flown commercial once as a kid, and I would definitely be having a chat with Libby when I got back.

"At the gate, you can put yourself on the wait-list for an upgrade," she offered.

I took the envelope back and headed for security. Damned Libby. What had I done to deserve this?

At the gate, the agent took my name, but the look on his face was clear: fat chance getting into first.

Since the flight was connecting at JFK instead of Miami, it would be more than five hours of torture, and a middle seat no less.

I hung out at the gate 'till the last minute, hoping one of the first-class passengers would be a no-show. No luck.

It was raining when I walked to the plane. The airport was old school, with stairs to board instead of a jetway. By the time I reached the door, I was soaked.

"I'm sorry, sir. All the overhead bins are full. Your bag will need to be checked."

I relinquished my roller bag to her, bound for the belly of the plane. When I reached my row, things got even better.

I wasn't a small guy, but I was a shrimp compared to the man in the window seat. The middle seat was going to be a tight fit.

Granny seated on the aisle got up to let me in.

Just as I buckled myself in, the window guy let out one stinker of a fart.

With the narrow seats, I was forced up against Granny's side, and my knees hit the seat in front of me as well.

Libby was definitely going to pay for this.

Granny pulled out a bag of Cheetos and started munching. "Like some?"

I declined.

Fart Guy let loose another one.

All I could do was breathe through my mouth and concentrate on reading my iPad. After we took off, the cabin cooled down considerably, and my shivering made it difficult to hold the device steady enough to read. Shutting down the overhead vent helped, but the real problem was my wet clothes, and without my bag, I had nothing dry to put on.

Fart Guy detonated again, and I had to decide between the cold and being able to breathe. I chose fresh air and opened the overhead vent again. My clothes would dry out sooner or later.

Granny seemed oblivious to the smell, and after consuming a second bag of Cheetos, she fell asleep against me.

It wasn't until later that I noticed the orange drool adorning my shirt sleeve.

I checked my watch for the bad news: another four hours to go.

CHAPTER 3

Nicole

After landing at JFK and getting through immigration and customs and back into the airline system, we located the gate for the next leg of our flight.

"I vote for Hawaii next year," Sandy said after plopping down in a seat. "This immigration and connecting-flight shit sucks."

"Pick an island. I'm with you."

"Maui, Kauai, the Big Island, I don't care. Anything that doesn't mean all day in airplanes."

Eventually our boarding time neared, and they asked for volunteers to be bumped to a later flight in return for a two-hundred-dollar travel voucher.

One of the two gate agents started calling names over the PA. "Nicole Rossi, please come to the counter."

"What's that about?" I asked Sandy.

She shrugged. "I doubt you got an upgrade."

In line at the counter, I could see it definitely wasn't an upgrade. The person in front of me threw a monster fit, and the agent called her supervisor, who I heard call security.

I stepped back until they got the situation resolved.

"Next," the agent said a moment later.

I presented my boarding pass. "Nicole Rossi."

The agent pasted on a phony smile and handed me a slip of paper. "Here's your five-hundred-dollar travel voucher, and you've been confirmed on flight seventy-three. It leaves in two hours from gate eight." She pointed to the right.

"But I didn't volunteer," I objected.

Her smile brightened. "I know. That's why you're getting the larger voucher."

"But I really need to get back."

"You'll still arrive tonight, just a little later." She moved to the side and pasted on that same fake smile again. "Next."

I shuffled back to Sandy. "I got bumped."

"That sucks. Till when?"

I blew out a breath. "Two hours—if it's not late."

"Well, that's the beauty of big companies like these airlines. They're so cheap they won't feed you anymore, and then they overbook to maximize their revenue, and at the same time ruin the customer experience. I don't think they'll ever learn."

We commiserated about the evils of airline consolidation until it was time for her to board.

I gave her a sendoff hug. "I'll be in touch as soon as I replace my phone."

"I still think you should think about how quickly you come to Lara's rescue this time."

"Sure. I'll think about it," I lied. Though Sandy wasn't exactly wrong, Lara was family, and I couldn't turn my back on her.

Sandy's boarding group got called, and she gave me a quick hug before leaving. "Get a new phone first thing."

"On my list. Fly safe." I turned and trudged off in search of a bite to eat while I waited.

Josh

After escaping the plane, I had to wait to be admitted back into the States before heading to the ticket counters.

There I inquired about first-class seats available to LAX on my next flight.

"I'm sorry, Mr. Benson," I was told.

"I'm sorry, sir," said the next airline ticket agent, followed by the same answer from the third.

Getting back through security to the gates was a uniquely unpleasant experience. I had to take my shoes and belt off, got yelled at for not taking my tablet out of my bag, was electronically frisked, and then chosen for a random pat-down. How did people put up with this shit every time they flew?

Dad would occasionally wonder if his corporate plane was worth all we paid to keep it and the crew. Today, my answer was an unqualified *yes*.

Nearly three hours later, the last few passengers were having their boarding passes scanned when I revisited the counter.

"Sorry, Mr. Benson," the gate agent said.

I got in line behind the last person and readied my boarding pass: seat 34A. At least it wasn't a middle seat.

The lady in front of me turned to hand over her sheet of paper. It was Cheetos Granny from my last flight.

At the bottom of the jetway, I pulled a sweatshirt from my carry-on and handed the bag to the agent to check. I knew now that as the last one to board, I had no hope of finding overhead space for it. I kept my small backpack and my plastic bag of dinner.

No wonder airlines had a greater proportion of unhappy customers than any other business. When dentists beat you out for the bottom of the list, you're definitely doing things wrong.

When I reached row 29, I figured out the bad news. With five more rows to go, I realized I'd been assigned the very last one on the airplane.

Granny also reached the last row and put her purse down on the aisle seat on my side of the plane. "Hello, dear," she said.

The girl in the middle seat rose. "Are you in here?"

My heart sped up. It was my almost-dessert date from last night—the green-eyed beauty—Nicole.

CHAPTER 4

NICOLE

"NO, DEAR, I'M ON THE AISLE," THE GRAY-HAIRED LADY SAID.

"I'm the window seat," the man behind her said. His lips tipped up in a smile as our eyes met. It was my rescuer from last night, Mr. Studious.

The older lady moved to allow me out so Studious could slide in.

I followed him, and my hand brushed his as we both searched for our seatbelts. The gentle shock was like a spark of static electricity.

"I think that one's mine," he said, looking at the two buckle ends in my hands.

The spark of his touch had short-circuited my brain. "Oh, yeah, sorry." I traded the buckle for the tab end he held.

When my eyes rose to meet his, he smiled again. "Recover okay from your swim?"

Heat rose in my cheeks. "Yes…and thank you. That was embarrassing."

He offered his hand. "Josh. Josh Benson." His pale blue eyes held me captive.

I shook with him. "Nicole Rossi, but you already know that."

The spark from our previous touch returned in force and ran up my arm. His grip was warm and strong, reminding me of the ease with which he'd hauled me out of the pool last night. I was no featherweight, but he'd lifted me like I was nothing.

The jet lurched slightly as we started to move back from the gate.

I pulled my hand away and forced myself to look forward, lest I be paralyzed by the strength of his gaze. His eyes had peered deep into me, almost hypnotic in their pull. From a distance on the beach, I'd taken in the breadth of his shoulders, his washboard abs, and those massive arms. I hadn't been close enough to notice the eyes, or the slight scar on his chin that only made his face more interesting.

The overhead speakers began the safety announcements, but the whir of the engines soon made the words hard to understand.

"And the lavatories for the main cabin are located at the rear of the plane," she said at the end—a reminder that we'd have the pleasure of people hovering in the aisle waiting to use the facilities later in the flight. Ah, the joys of sitting in the last row of the airplane.

The aisle-seat lady tapped my shoulder. "Would you like some Cheetos?" She offered an open bag.

"No, but thank you."

She pulled out a few with orange-crusted fingers and popped them in her mouth, mumbling something about them being better than Twinkies.

Josh leaned over. "Granny has an endless supply of those things."

Every time I looked out the window as we taxied, I caught sight of his chin, and that profile. The man up close was even better than from afar.

"How are people supposed to fit in this space?" he asked after a moment. "I've never been in a seat this small." His knees banged against the seatback in front of him. But these seats were just like every other airline: crappy.

"First time back here?" He looked like a first-class-only guy.

"Only my second airline flight. How'd you guess?"

So, not first-class, but novice flyer.

"After a while, you get used to being treated like crap instead of a paying customer."

"I guess. But I don't know how I'd ever get used to this." He opened his iPad with a huff and started scrolling, just as he had at the beach each day I'd seen him—okay, more like watched him, or spied on him. A shiver shot through me as I realized that was akin to being a stalker.

He finger-swiped to the next page, and I looked over again.

Bad girl.

I took his concentration on his tablet as a signal that he didn't want to talk—

so much for the friendly guy who'd wanted to have dessert last night. I checked the movie selections on the screen in front of me. In the end, though, I left the screen set on the map of our progress. I pulled out the romance paperback I'd finished on the beach. The story was still a good one, even if I knew the ending, and worth reading again—anything to make this trip go by faster.

The turbulence as we climbed through the clouds was probably only moderate for a seasoned flier, but it rated as severe on my anxiety scale. I closed my book in my lap. The bumps kept forcing me up against Josh's solid arm. The warm contact provided an oddly calming effect.

He kept reading, ignoring the bumps that forced the tablet back and forth enough that it would have had me airsick.

At altitude, the ride smoothed out, and the seatbelt sign went off.

Josh stowed his iPad and leaned forward to reach something at his feet. "Excuse me."

"Sure," I said, pulling my book out of the way.

With the seatbacks in our faces, and as tall as he was, he had to contort himself over toward my lap to reach, which only gave me a view of rippling back muscles straining against his shirt. He came up with two bags, the first a plastic bag labeled *Papa's Pastaria*.

"You brought dinner?"

"Sure." He showed me the second bag, from Dunkin' Donuts. "Sorry. They didn't have any tiramisu."

I laughed. "So when you said another time, you meant on this flight?"

He shook his head. "No. I got called back to work early. My stay was supposed to last another four days."

"That sucks. It's terrible that your boss would do that to you."

"Yeah, I guess."

"You should've refused."

"You wouldn't say that if you knew my dad."

Ah. He wasn't the international man of mystery I'd presumed, but in business working for his father.

"I get it. I work in a family-run company too," I told him.

Now I understood his predicament. People had the misconception that working for family members made it easy, but the opposite was true. Uncle Ernst wouldn't hesitate to ask me to do something he'd never in a million years expect a non-family employee to do.

Josh nodded with raised brows, but didn't pursue the question. The bag of

Italian food he opened had well-sealed plastic containers instead of those leaky Styrofoam boxes.

The delicious aroma hit me as soon as he popped the lid. Fettuccine with marinara and small meatballs, topped with a sprinkling of parmesan.

He held up the container. "Want some? I've got plenty."

"No, thanks. I ate." I said no, but my salivary glands disagreed. I swallowed to keep from drooling. The cardboard sandwich I'd gotten at the airport had lasted only a single bite before I tossed it, and my survey of the surroundings had found all the decent restaurants closed up for the night. Apparently I hadn't gone far enough to find real food.

"You sure?"

I nodded, afraid my voice would betray me if I verbally declined.

He shrugged. "Your loss."

In an attempt to keep my growling stomach at bay, I opened my book and started reading.

Before long, he'd consumed about half of his pasta, interspersed with mouthfuls of Caesar salad from the second container. At one point, he held up his fork for a second. "Hold on."

I looked over and couldn't help but stare at that beautifully imperfect chin. I wondered how he'd gotten the scar.

He brought a lone noodle to his lips. "So, you had to leave early too?" He sucked in the noodle.

I sighed, wanting to be that noodle. "No. I could only get away for a week, and time's up. Now I wish I'd made it ten days instead."

He waved the fork. "So, let me understand. Last night when you agreed to join me for dessert another time, you planned on standing me up?"

I could almost feel the blood draining from my face. "No. Oh, no. I'm sorry. I was just so flustered after making a fool of myself, I answered without thinking."

"So you *did* want to join me?"

"Of course. I was walking over, wasn't I?"

He ate another bite of salad. "In that case, the offer to split dessert tonight is still open."

"Donuts?"

"Only one. But I'm still offering to share. You like chocolate?"

An easy question. "Who doesn't? It's one of my main food groups."

After closing his dinner containers, he spread his legs to drop them to the floor. The warmth of his thigh against mine was more noticeable than it should have been. He kicked the plastic under the seat in front of him and opened the Dunkin' Donuts bag. He split the donut in half. "Pick one."

I chose the piece that looked smaller, as Mamma had taught me. "Thank you." I decided she would have declared Josh a gentleman. I held a hand under my mouth to catch the sprinkles that fell when I bit into the delicious morsel. I'd learned the hard way how sitting on sprinkles could result in stains. "This is good," I mumbled after a mouthful.

"Only the best for a beautiful lady."

I felt my blush rising to a low-grade fever.

He wiped his fingers with a napkin after the last bite and pulled out his iPad again.

"You sure read a lot."

"Work," he replied. "I'm behind. I expected to have all week, and like I said, it got cut short." He pointed at the book in the seat pocket in front of me. "You've been reading too."

"True. But I'm reading to relax."

"I'm envious." He lifted his tablet. "This book is on business strategy."

"Sounds pretty dry." I was happy to be done with books like that.

"It is," he said tilting the tablet my way.

I made out the title and author. It was one I'd been assigned in school, and *dry* only began to describe it. *Sleep-inducing* was more like it. "You might try one by Porter instead. At least it would be easier to stay awake."

His brows lifted, and his eyes narrowed. "Porter, huh? The Harvard prof?"

I shrugged. "Dunno." I'd already said too much.

He shifted to look more directly at me, and his pale blues held me in their tractor beam. "You've read this one?"

"It sounds familiar," I admitted.

A smile followed his nod like he'd hooked a fish. "Tell me more, Nicole."

"Nothing to tell."

"Did you go to Harvard?"

I shook my head and took in a breath to admit the truth. "Stanford." That was always enough to have my dates change the subject.

"Impressive." He almost sounded like he meant it. "Undergrad?"

I nodded with a sigh.

He pointed a finger at me. "And that's not all, I bet." He rubbed his chin. "MBA as well. Nobody else would willingly read a book like this." He lifted his iPad.

Busted.

I nodded. "Yeah. How about you?" It was time to turn the tables.

"USC. Sort of a family-expectation kind of thing."

"And now you work for your father?"

"Yeah, my older brothers got away before I did, so I'm stuck with it."

"You don't want to be in the family business?"

"You wouldn't understand. It's not an option."

He was right. I didn't understand that at all. Being part of the business my family had built was a natural fit for me, and I couldn't imagine being anywhere else.

"I sort of like it, the family aspect," I said, soft-pedaling it.

"You're lucky," he said as he turned back to the tablet. "Let me work my way through more of this, and I'll probably have some questions for you."

That was my cue to let him read in peace, so I picked up my novel, opened it to the dog-eared page, and started reading.

Granny downed more Cheetos.

"Careful, she drools," Josh whispered, pointing to an orange stain on his shirt sleeve.

Yuck.

I compensated by leaning into him. He didn't complain.

Slowly, I got used to the warm contact, and it went from provocative to comforting. It had been a long time since I'd leaned on a man—either figuratively or literally. Maybe Sandy was right, and it *had* been too long.

An hour later, Josh and I were still reading. A line for the bathroom had formed, and I self-consciously avoided eye contact with the constant stream of strangers.

The PA came on again. "We're diverting north to avoid some weather ahead," the captain said. "It will add some time to our trip, but I hope it will be a better ride." The seatbelt light came on again. *Better ride* and *hope* likely didn't mean smooth air, and I prepared for a bucking bronco.

The flight attendants shooed all the people in the restroom line back to their seats, and the jostling began. The airplane became the puppet as the weather gods yanked the strings.

Granny woke with a start after the second or third big bump.

A big air pocket that felt like going over the top of a roller coaster had my heart racing. How strong did they build these airliners, anyway?

I put my book away to keep from needing the airsick bag. "What was that?" I asked Josh, hoping a conversation would keep my mind from wondering how much it took to break an airplane.

"Nervous?" he asked.

"What gave it away?"

He pointed. "Your death grip."

I'd missed that I had a white-knuckle grip on the armrest with one hand and my thigh with the other.

He offered his hand. "Squeeze this."

"I'm fine."

"You're white as a ghost." He loosened my fingers from the armrest and placed them over his.

I gripped his hand.

"It's a medical fact that physical touch lessens anxiety."

Several even bigger bumps hit the plane and jostled me in my seat. "Really?"

"I wouldn't lie to you." His voice carried a conviction I didn't doubt. "You can trust me. Let your nervousness flow through your hand to me."

As I held on to him, my heart slowed. I closed my eyes and concentrated on the feel of my hand with his.

"Does that help?"

I opened my eyes and nodded.

"Flying's safer than driving."

That statistic had never made me feel better. "Tell that to the crash victims. I'd rather be driving."

"Why?" he asked.

That was an easy one. "Because then I'm in control, and I can avoid the potholes."

Lightning burst like a camera flash outside the window before it went back to pitch black again.

"They're downdrafts, updrafts, wind gusts, and all invisible. It doesn't mean we have a bad pilot. If you were up there, you couldn't avoid them either."

I squeezed his hand harder after the next air pocket, or downdraft or whatever.

He was remarkably calm for this being only his second time on a plane.

Bang!

The plane lurched left and then right.

I grabbed Josh's arm.

People screamed in the rows ahead of us.

A popping sound came from the left.

Long strings of fire streamed from the engine visible out our window, in sync with the noise.

I buried my head in Josh's shoulder and gripped his arm with all my strength.

CHAPTER 5

Josh

NICOLE CLAMPED ONTO ME WITH TERROR IN HER EYES.

"It'll be okay," I assured her. "I'll keep you safe. I promise."

The crying from the passengers ahead of us didn't help.

Her eyes slammed shut.

The engine soon stopped spitting flames. The pilots had shut it down.

My ears popped, and the oxygen masks dropped from the ceiling, which led to another round of screams.

I pulled mine on and cinched it tight before grabbing the center one for Nicole. I had to pry her head away from my arm to get it on her.

With eyes the size of dinner plates, she fought me, trying to bury her head against my arm.

"Breathe normally," I told her when I got the mask secured. I'd need bandages when we got on the ground from the holes her nails had dug into me.

"It's not working," she said, continuing to hyperventilate. "It's not working."

The plane pitched over and started downhill.

"It works if you breathe normally," I told her again.

Granny was having trouble, and I leaned over Nicole to help the old woman.

As I helped Granny get the yellow cup cinched to her mouth, Nicole's breaths finally slowed.

"Ladies and gentlemen," the pilot said over the PA system. "We have a slight problem with one of the engines, and we'll be making a precautionary landing shortly."

He'd been careful to not call it an emergency landing.

I held a shaking Nicole close. "It'll be fine. I promise to keep you safe."

She looked up at me in disbelief. "I'm scared."

"I told you I wouldn't lie to you, remember?"

She nodded, but repeated herself. "I'm scared."

I pulled her chin up to look at me. "You'll be fine. The only people in danger are the ones up front that might get trampled by the stampede when we get on the ground."

She managed a half-hearted laugh, but her nails still dug into me like a kitten stuck in a tree.

"Airplanes are built to handle things like this." I hoped talking to her would keep her mind from going to all the dark places it surely wanted to hide.

She tapped the yellow cone over her mouth. "Why these then?"

"When they shut one engine down, there's less air from the engines for pressurization."

This question had been answered for me when Dad had made us all go up with him in the company plane for an example of single-engine flight. It had mostly been for Mom's benefit. He'd instructed the pilot to shut one of the two engines down to show us how the plane wouldn't fall out of the sky, even if one engine failed. It had made me feel better.

Mom hadn't been as impressed. "You're an idiot, Lloyd. Taking us all up and turning off an engine. How could you be so reckless?"

I'd still thought it was cool, but it had taken Dad more than a week to live it down.

Nicole clung to me, and I held her tight. It wasn't the way I'd envisioned getting her in my arms, but I'd take it.

As the plane descended, the turbulence lessened, and most of the passengers calmed down.

"The captain has told us it is now safe to remove your oxygen masks," the attendant announced after a while.

I removed mine and helped Nicole out of hers. The scene in front of us was a mess as all the masks swayed above the passengers.

Granny kept hers on until a flight attendant came by to insist she remove it.

The ground grew closer, the flaps came down, and before long I heard the landing gear extend.

The landing was nothing special, but it generated instant applause from everybody on board.

"Welcome to Sioux City, Iowa," the captain said over the speakers. "Operations tells me they will have a plane and crew here first thing in the morning to get you on your way."

The crowd groaned, and the bitching about having to wait until morning began.

Nicole joined them. "I have to get back. Like, really have to get back tonight."

I let her out of the hug, and she slowly released her grip on me. "What's the hurry?"

She shook her head and didn't answer.

Granny produced another bag of Cheetos and offered them to Nicole. "Sure you don't want some, dear?"

Nicole and I waved Granny off.

I still had Nicole's hand in mine.

The complaints ahead of us increased while we waited for the door to open.

We were the last two to join the conga line leaving the plane, directly behind Granny.

I let Nicole go ahead and grabbed the remainder of my dinner from the floor.

The pilot shook damn near everyone's hand as they exited.

I offered mine as well. "Do we know when the replacement plane arrives?"

"Not exactly, but I would figure on a departure at around seven in the morning," he said.

"Nice job on the landing, by the way, with this crosswind."

He smiled. "Thanks."

I turned back to the attendant in the galley. "Could you spare two scotches?"

She grabbed tiny bottles from a drawer. "Sure." She handed me four.

I pocketed them and headed toward Nicole, who waited part-way up the jetway.

When I got close enough, she huddled next to me. "I need a drink. Screw that. I need a whole bottle."

I draped an arm around her, and we continued up the jetway. "What's the hurry to get back?"

She ignored my question and shivered in my grasp, still seemingly terrified by the ordeal.

"Maybe I can help."

"I doubt it."

"Try me."

She answered after a few steps. "I promised to take care of my cousin. She needs me back in LA right away. I have to bail her out of jail."

Jail?

~

NICOLE

THE FIRST WORD ABOUT MY COUSIN BEING IN JAIL, AND JOSH REACTED AS THEY ALL did. His jaw dropped open, but no words came out.

I pulled away from him and the shame he made me feel. Looking back, I saw him digging in his pockets. Being in the last group to board, I'd had to check my carry-on at the gate. At least without a bag in tow I could get away from him faster now.

The inside of the small terminal was teeming with angry people. The first ones off the plane had made a beeline for the few chairs. Another group stood in front of the Hertz counter. The rest of us were out of luck. Nowhere to sit, too small an airport to have concessions, and no escape once the dozen or so rental cars were gone. At least the place had a bathroom, so I shivered in line behind the two dozen other women with the same idea.

An airport bathroom had to be better than the filthy lavatory on the plane.

I had to pee badly. Between the cold and the adrenaline of our near-death experience, I couldn't stop shaking.

I was almost to the bathroom door when Josh spied me.

He walked purposefully my way and nodded toward the Hertz counter. "Come with me."

"No." I managed the words with only minimally chattering teeth.

Somehow he didn't understand that simple answer. He leaned close and whispered, "If you want to get home tonight for your cousin, you have to trust me and come along right now."

Blondie behind me heard him. "I'll take that offer, if she won't."

I turned to catch Blondie batting her fake eyelashes at Josh.

I nodded toward the restroom door. "I have to go."

"I can solve that too."

I shouldered my purse and left the line. "Driving won't be faster."

He walked ahead briskly. "Didn't I tell you to trust me?"

I tried to keep up and followed him past the rental counter and toward the security setup. "You lied to me."

He stopped and turned. "No way. I didn't know I was getting called back to LA today."

"Not about that. You told me it was only your second flight, but you know all that stuff about planes."

"Only my second *commercial* flight. Now, come on; we have to go."

I caught up to him and pulled at his elbow. We could debate his honesty later. "Where are we going?" I should have said *you* instead of *we* because I wasn't on board with whatever his plan was yet.

He stopped and whispered. "Not with all these people around. I'm getting you home. You'll be safe with me."

I huffed and followed him anyway.

Out the front door of the terminal, he turned left. Finally we were away from the crowd. But outside in the storm that had broken the airplane, the downpour of frigid drops quickly soaked me.

I yelled ahead. "I'm not going anywhere until you tell me what's going on."

He turned and stopped. "Our plane leaves in ten minutes. I don't plan on missing it because you want to jabber all day. If you don't trust me, you can stay here for all I care."

Jabber? I'd only asked a simple, logical question.

He started off again.

I trotted to catch up. "Why didn't you say so?"

"In front of every Tom, Dick, and Harry in there? Are you kidding?"

I had to alternate walking and jogging to keep up with the man. "What plane?"

"Charter." He checked his watch. "We don't have time for twenty questions." He started to jog.

I did as well. Luckily I'd worn running shoes on the plane.

He looked at his phone and turned in at the second building.

I followed Josh inside.

"Mr. Benson?" asked a young man with pilot epaulets on his shoulders.

At least it was dry in here.

"Yeah, plus one."

The pilot pointed to the door toward the runway. "G4 on the ramp, seven five uniform. Do you have any baggage?"

"No," Josh responded.

"Do I have time to hit the bathroom?" I asked.

"Only if you make it quick," the pilot said before heading outside.

Josh evidently decided my idea was a good one and turned toward the men's room.

A few minutes later, Josh urged me up the steps, and we ducked inside the small jet that already had one engine running. There were a half-dozen seats on one side, and a couch and a few seats on the other. I chose a forward-facing seat.

Josh plopped into the aft-facing one in front of me.

One pilot was already inside, and the other closed the door after us. "Buckle up; you know the drill. Sorry we don't have an attendant tonight."

Mere seconds later, the plane started moving.

"You lied about it being only your second time." I couldn't keep my teeth from chattering any longer.

This man of mystery, who I'd figured worked for his dad at some small company like ours, obviously had more resources than I would have guessed.

"You're cold," he said.

"Freezing," I admitted.

He unbuckled, located a blanket in a cabinet, and moved to the couch. He patted the seat next to him. "Come over here." He unfolded the blanket.

If there was a blanket involved, I was all in. I joined him.

After I found the seatbelt, he tucked the blanket around us and pulled me to his side. It wasn't the way I'd hoped to be snuggled up against him, but this would work. I desperately needed the warmth.

I shivered against him. "Now, can you tell me what's going on?"

His hand rubbed my shoulder. "It's simple really." Nothing about this looked simple. "I contacted my brother about a charter to get us back quickly. He made a call, and it turns out these guys were available, but they're almost at their duty-hour limit."

"Still Swahili to me."

"If we didn't leave right away, they wouldn't be able to get us to LA without exceeding the fourteen hours they're allowed to fly in a day. The plane was here, but without a crew to make the flight, we'd be stuck until tomorrow."

I narrowed my eyes at him. "How do you know all this stuff?"

"I fly all the time for work."

Now it made sense. Mr. Big Shot never mingled with the masses like me on regular airlines. He only flew in private jets. "And this is how you get around?"

"Normally I take the company plane."

No wonder the cramped space of a coach seat had been a surprise to him.

Sandy already thought I'd been an idiot for not talking to Josh sooner. She'd blow a gasket when she found out he was rich, in addition to good looking. The plastic watch had fooled me.

"And today you were slumming with the rest of us, because…?" I asked.

The engines spooled up as we began our takeoff roll. "So I could meet an incredibly attractive girl—"

I raised a finger to interrupt. "Woman." The plane's acceleration pushed me even harder into him. I welcomed his body heat.

"Woman… Let me back up. Incredibly smart and attractive woman who lied to me about wanting to share a dessert tonight."

"Point of order," I complained. "That was a misstatement under duress, not a lie."

The jet's nose lifted, and we were airborne, but the takeoff was much steeper than I was used to, and it kept me pinned against his side, not that I was complaining.

Then the jolts began, and memories of the previous airliner catching fire came rushing back. I started shivering all over again.

Josh produced a mini bottle of Dewar's scotch.

I wiggled a hand loose from my side of the blanket and grabbed for it.

He didn't let go. "You hold the bottle; I'll unscrew the cap." With one of his arms behind me and my other one trapped under the blanket, we had to tackle the task as a team.

I held the bottle like he asked, and after he twisted the cap off, I brought it to my lips. The first swig went down hot. The second swallow finished the tiny thing. The rapid warmth in my belly helped everything seem better.

We weren't very high when the bumps worsened. The first few weren't bad, but they quickly turned even worse than they'd been on the big jet.

I clung to him. "I'm scared," I admitted.

"Tell me about the girl you were with."

"Huh?" I asked.

"Don't focus on the turbulence. Tell me about your friend."

"Sandy is my best friend. We go way back." Another jolt stopped me from saying more.

"What does she do?"

"She's a photographer," I got out between bumps.

He tightened his hold around my shoulder. "What kind?"

"Underwear mostly."

He laughed at that—a pretty common reaction. "Now that's a job I might like." With guys, that was another common reaction.

The next big drop made me cringe. "This isn't working."

He brought out another bottle of scotch. "Maybe this will help."

I nodded, and we quickly repeated our cap teamwork. I downed this drink even faster than the first.

The turbulence became worse, a lot worse. I clung to him like his arm was a life preserver. "How many of those do you have?"

"Two more."

I clutched him tighter. "One for each of us?"

"You need it more than I do."

After the fourth bottle, the jostling of the plane seemed to settle down. At first I couldn't tell if it was the liquor or if the air was actually getting calmer.

"We'll fly higher than the airlines and have a smoother time of it in a little while," he told me.

His prediction came true as we eventually cleared the clouds, and the ride smoothed out.

The scotch was having a definite effect on my eyelids. "I think I need to lie down."

~

"TIME TO BUCKLE UP," SOMEONE SAID.

My ears popped, and I pried an eye open. Slowly it came to me. I was lying on the plane's couch.

The warm body spooned behind me was Josh, his arm around my midsection. A blanket lay over us.

The pressure in my ears increased again. We were descending.

"Time to buckle up back there," one of the pilots repeated from the cockpit.

I didn't want to, but I pulled loose from Josh's grasp. "Time to wake up."

He rose groggily and rubbed his eyes. "How do you feel?"

I found my seatbelt. "Better." I stretched and smiled to myself.

It had been forever since I'd fallen asleep spooning with a man. Mo wasn't much of a cuddler and had never spooned with me for more than a few minutes—just another of his defects that I hadn't recognized until after he left.

CHAPTER 6

Josh

The landing at Santa Monica was a few minutes early, and as I glanced at the girl seated next to me, I thanked my lucky stars.

Even the five-hour flight from hell to JFK, sandwiched between Granny and Fart Guy, had turned out to be worth it after meeting Nicole.

The town car rolled up to meet us as we deplaned.

Nicole pulled out her phone. "Oops. Can you call me an Uber?"

I shook my head. "No way. Door-to-door service is part of the package."

She returned the broken phone to her purse. "You've done too much already. How much do I owe you for this?"

I frowned. She didn't get it. "Nothing. The company is paying for the charter, and an extra passenger is no charge."

"But..." she started.

"Arguing will get you nowhere." I reached for the handle and opened the car door for her.

After she slid in, I rounded to the other side and joined her in the backseat.

"Where to first?" our driver asked.

Nicole looked at me.

"Your place first," I told her.

"4312 Orangebranch," she told him.

I entered it into my phone. "And your phone number?"

She rattled it off without hesitation.

I handed her my card. "I'll call you so we can schedule that tiramisu."

Her smile was genuine. "I'd like that."

The leather seats of the car were comfortable, but tonight I didn't care for them. The hard airline seat next to her, shoulder to shoulder, and spooning on the Gulfstream's couch had both been better. I slid a hand toward her on the seat. "I'm glad we got some time together, Nicole."

Her hand was warm as she took mine briefly. "Me too." There was an electric feel to the touch of her soft skin. "Thank you again for this," she said. "It means a lot."

After a few miles of silence, she asked, "So you don't like working for your father?"

I shifted in my seat. This wasn't an easy subject. "It's hard to explain."

"I know a lot can be expected of you, working for family."

That had been my experience in more ways than she could understand.

"He needs someone—the family needs someone to take over when...well, when he's ready to give up the reins. I get that I'm the last one left, but it doesn't seem fair. My brothers all have their own things to run, and I'd like that too, instead of just moving from project to project, rationalizing acquisitions."

"What's rationalizing mean?"

Soft words like that hid the ugliness of what I did. "It means I'm the one who comes in to make the hard decisions and make the operation more profitable. But even then, I still have people looking over my shoulder."

"Is that why you fly a lot?"

I nodded. "When we acquire a company, I have to be on location for a while, or at least visit their out-of-state facilities. I've seen my share of hotel rooms."

She honed right in on my issue. "But you want to run your own show."

"Wouldn't you?" *London or bust* was my motto. The plan had always been to give me control of our European operations. I'd move to London and be independent, finally have my *own show,* as she put it, to run before I took over at Benson.

She nodded. "Of course. Do you think it'll happen soon?"

"He's promised it—even written it down and signed it, all in a pretty blue folder." I shook my head, remembering the latest conversation. *Later* had turned out to be Dad's go-to word. He hadn't broken his promise because it had always been vague.

"Soon?" she asked again.

I chose honesty over optimism. "When I prove I'm ready."

"Is that why you were reading that book?"

I laughed. "And a half dozen others."

She got it, the need to work for acceptance that seemed to come with a family-run company.

She shrugged. "Fathers can be tough, but they mean well."

Nodding, I added, "Mine has decided to rewrite the definition of *tough*."

She offered her hand.

I took it, and she squeezed. "I've found it helps to not focus on it."

"That's what my mother says." Mom had a dozen sayings along that line.

The car came to a stop. "We're here," the driver announced as he put it in park.

I unbuckled and climbed out.

She did as well before I could reach the other side.

"A lady waits for the gentleman to open the door for her," I scolded.

"And who says I'm a lady?"

I rolled my eyes. "Are we really going to end today with an argument?" I moved to the sidewalk.

"Sorry." She followed, fumbling in her bag for keys.

I followed her to the large, old Victorian and up the stairs to the porch in the dim illumination provided by the streetlights. The house had seen better days, but was still a beauty of a home, from a time when craftsmanship mattered.

A dog barked on the other side of the door.

"Quiet, Echo," she said. The dog didn't bark again.

Then things got awkward. "I'll call you," I told her.

"When I get a phone," she reminded me.

"I can be patient. Your cousin comes first, phone second."

She nodded. "Thanks."

"Goodnight, Nicole." I stepped back.

She rushed forward and gave me a tight hug, her head against my shoulder.

The feel of her soft tits against me was exciting, dangerous even. Too many seconds of this and I'd be tempted to put my hands somewhere other than her back.

She quickly let go and backed away. "Thank you so much for all this."

I held her hand at a distance for a second, not letting her get away. The temptation to pull her back to me for a proper squeeze with an added kiss boiled up. I let go instead, lest I be tempted to fuck it all up by forcing something she wasn't ready for tonight. "Dinner."

Her smile was captivating. "And dessert?"

"And maybe candles." I backed up. "I'll call you."

"I'll look forward to it." She retreated to the door. As she inserted her key, the door swung open a bit.

"Stop." I pulled her back, fished out my phone, and punched up the flashlight.

The door jamb was broken. The door had been kicked in, and in the light from my phone, the broken glass of a front window was visible as well.

She gasped. "Oh my God." She pulled away and pushed open the door.

The dog rushed out.

She knelt to greet it. "Are you okay, boy?" She nuzzled the big Labrador frantically trying to lick her face.

I pulled her and the dog away from the door while dialing 9-1-1. "Wait by the car," I told her before the emergency operator answered.

She opened her mouth to object. "But I need to check."

It was always an objection with this girl.

"Now," I insisted, pointing to the street. "You can go in after the cops."

A few minutes later, an LAPD black and white arrived, with its lights flashing.

I kept Nicole by the car while the two cops cleared the house.

Officer Bendretti handed me his card after he returned to us. "You can go in your house now," he told me. "The only apparent damage is in the front room."

"It's hers," I told him, nodding to Nicole who was holding her dog by the collar.

After a few cursory questions for the officer's paperwork, they left.

Nicole and I ventured inside. Glass littered the floor near the two windows, and the words *leave or die* had been spray-painted on the area rug in the front room.

Nicole cringed visibly when she took in the scene.

~

Nicole

. . .

THE HORRIBLE WORDS PAINTED ON GRANDPA'S RUG CHILLED ME AS MUCH AS THE Iowa rain had.

"Who would do this?" Josh asked.

I shook my head without an answer.

He pulled at my elbow. "You need to come with me."

I stayed put. "No. This is my home."

"This is unsafe, is what it is. Tomorrow you can come back—when it's daylight and the door and windows are fixed." He moved back to the entrance. "Echo, come on, boy."

My traitorous dog wagged his tail and followed.

By the time they reached the porch steps, I realized I had no choice and followed. I grabbed Echo's leash from the front table and closed the door as best I could behind me.

"My place on Wilshire," Josh told the driver after the three of us were settled inside the car. He said it as if he had more than one house.

I stroked Echo's head. "You don't have to—"

"Yes, I do. I promised to keep you safe, remember?"

"It's okay. I can go to a hotel."

"No way. I'd never forgive you if you didn't let me keep my promise."

"Never?" I scoffed.

"Never," he growled.

The knight-in-shining-armor routine was corny and cute, but the guy needed to get a sense of humor.

For a moment I considered arguing, but instead leaned against him. "Thank you." He'd been the one good thing in this shitstorm of a day. His warmth flowed through the clothing between us and comforted me.

During the ride, all I could do was wonder who would attack me like that. No names came to mind. I'd told my neighbor more than once to keep his dog off my lawn in very un-ladylike language. Outside of that, I couldn't think of a single one of my neighbors I'd had a cross word with—not even the father of the kid who'd hit a baseball through my window last year.

The driver pulled into a circular drive and stopped in front of a tall, dark building. Josh got out and started around the car.

I didn't wait. I opened my own door. Fuck this lady shit. I took Echo to the nearest shrub to let him lift his leg.

As we approached the building, a doorman held the glass door open for us. Mr. Moneybags here had a damned doorman at his place. I'd never been to a building with a doorman before, unless it was a hotel.

"George," Josh said. "This is Miss Nicole Rossi. Please add her to the approved-visitors list."

Approved-visitor's list? Like you needed an invitation to get in the door? Sandy would never believe this.

"Will do, and a pleasure, Miss Rossi," the old man said as I passed him.

"You too, George," I managed.

Once inside the elevator, I expected Josh to punch the button for the top floor. Instead he hit twenty-one, one shy of the penthouse, but still sky high by LA standards.

The corridor we exited into only led to two units. Based on the size of the building, that made these units bigger than most people's freestanding homes. He slid his key into 211, and the door opened into an even more monstrous room than I'd expected.

I let Echo off his leash.

"This way." Josh waved me down a hallway and opened a door on the right. "You can sleep in here."

I stepped into the guest bedroom, which I was not surprised to see was bigger than my master at home. Echo followed me. A bathroom and a walk-in closet were to the left and a king-size bed to the right. The window overlooked Wilshire Boulevard.

Josh returned with a USC T-shirt. "To sleep in."

I accepted it. "Thanks." With both my bags in the belly of a broken plane in Iowa, anything was welcome.

"The bathroom is fully stocked. Help yourself to anything in the kitchen. I'm directly across the hall if you need anything." He stood motionless for a few seconds. "I guess that's it. Goodnight."

"Thank you," I said as the door closed.

Echo brushed against my leg to remind me I wasn't really alone. At least I'd be able to get Lara out on schedule first thing tomorrow morning, and I had my dog. I reached down to scratch behind his ears. I knew he'd never leave me.

"You can thank me over tiramisu," Josh called through the door.

"Deal."

Ten minutes later, I was under the covers, in the dark, and alone with my demons. The fire spitting from the plane's engine ran through my head. The screams of the other passengers filled my head. Putting my hands over my ears didn't help. *"It'll be okay. I'll keep you safe. I promise."* Josh's words echoed in my ears.

He *had* kept me safe. In this shittiest of all days, the only time I'd felt safe was with his arm around me.

I rolled over. The flames disappeared, only to be replaced by the awful threat on Grandpa's carpet—*Leave or die.* I rolled the other direction, and the screams began again. Shivers of fear overtook me.

"I'll keep you safe," he'd said. My island of safety in this tumultuous day had been Josh.

Leave or die, the words flashed before my eyes when I closed them again. Staring up at the ceiling didn't help. Counting imaginary sheep was even worse, as they died jumping the fence.

"Who would do this?" Josh had asked.

I wasn't any closer to an answer now than I had been at the house. I had no fucking clue—not a one, zilch, zero, nada, zippo. Visions of the flames came back again, this time with that awful phrase superimposed over them.

Getting up, I padded to the door and opened it. I should have asked Josh for a stiff drink—or three or four. Dim light from the city filtered in through the full-length windows of the great room. After a short search, I found his liquor cabinet and a small glass. Opening the fridge for a little light in the room, I rummaged through his liquor until I found a large bottle of rum. More gulps than I could count later, the buzz began. I downed another partial glass for good measure.

When I closed the fridge door, the room went dark again. I braced against the wall, which seemed to move beneath my hand. Making unsteady progress in the dimness of the hallway, I found Josh's door was ajar.

"Can't sleep?" he asked as I passed his doorway.

Safety from my nightmares beckoned.

I took the plunge and pushed his door open a few inches.

Maybe I wasn't as crazy as I thought. "I'm scared." Alcohol-fueled courage allowed me to ask the impossible. "Can you hold me?"

He didn't say anything for a moment.

I knew I'd overstepped and backed toward the hallway.

"Only if you don't kick," he said softly.

I snorted out a laugh. "Deal." With less trepidation than I should have had, I made it to the edge of his bed without stumbling, and climbed under the covers.

"How much did you drink?" he asked.

I shouldn't have been surprised by the question. The alcohol had to be obvious on my breath. "I'll pay you back." Too scared to admit how much I'd gulped down, I turned away.

"Not an issue." He pulled me against him, and for the second time today, I spooned up against this man's warm, hard body. If I hadn't almost died today, this could be sexy. I resisted the urge to wiggle my butt against him.

In the darkness, I imagined the view of the business jet cabin from the couch. This was a repeat of that. With Josh's arm over me, I was back in the safe zone, protected from my demons. My knight would safeguard me. When I closed my eyes, empty blackness replaced the visions that had plagued me earlier.

He'd vowed to protect me, and seemed overly determined to keep his promise. *"I'd never forgive you if you didn't let me...,"* he'd said. Here, up against him, safe and protected is exactly how I felt. His arm around me became my shield against everything bad out there.

CHAPTER 7

Josh

Monday morning, I woke to the scent of coconut. Nicole's hair smelled wonderfully tropical. My arm rested over her, and my hand cradled her warm tit through the T-shirt. Pulling my raging hard-on away from her, I gingerly disentangled myself and slipped off the bed.

She didn't wake—compliments of the booze, most likely.

Gathering up today's clothes, which I'd set out on my dresser last night, I snuck across the hall to the guest bedroom.

Echo got up and greeted me by sniffing my balls.

"Get some manners," I told the dog.

After a quick shower in the guest bathroom, I made it to the kitchen for a glass of OJ.

Echo followed.

The partially empty bottle of rum that I put back in the liquor cabinet attested to how much Nicole had imbibed last night.

I wrote out a quick note. I added my phone number and two Advil, but then I decided on another two lines.

Thinking of you

and tiramisu

That was as poetic as I could get. The memory of her snuggled against me this morning had blood moving south and my pants tightening.

I adjusted myself and chugged the rest of my orange juice on the way out. My first stop was the ground floor, where I filled in Oliver, who swore he'd take proper care of Nicole. This morning I chose the Lambo; it begged to be driven.

Dad hated extravagance. It would piss him off, and he deserved it for cutting my vacation short. I didn't get a lot of chances at rebellion, so I wouldn't let this one go to waste.

The engine started with a high-pitched roar. Once on the street, I pulled over for a quick call to Phil Patterson.

"Asshole, you better not be calling to tell me how fucking warm the Caribbean water is."

Phil's language was always colorful.

"No. I got called back early."

"That sucks the big one."

"Look, I need some help, stat. A friend of mine had her place broken into last night." I didn't really know when it had been, but that part of the story wouldn't matter.

"Let me guess. You want the repair to go slow so she has to bunk with you for a few days? I can handle that."

"Exactly the opposite. I need the door and windows repaired today."

He sighed. "Man, I don't know. I'm pretty backed up."

"Would a pair of Lakers tickets help with your schedule?"

The elation in his voice gave him away. "Front row?"

"Is there any other kind?" I gave him Nicole's address and drove off.

When I stopped at the third light on my drive into work, a Porsche pulled up next to me on the right. The kid driving it looked over and revved his wimpy little engine. Ah, southern California car culture at its best. It was good to be home. I smirked.

The light turned green.

I punched it, and three seconds later, he was in the rearview mirror. I put on the brakes to slow for the traffic ahead.

They never learned. My yellow rocket hadn't lost yet. Life was fun in the fast lane.

~

ARRIVING AT THE COMPANY GARAGE, I INTENTIONALLY PARKED WHERE DAD WOULD see my yellow extravagance when he came down at the end of the day.

Upstairs, the elevator doors opened to Benson Corp. just as I had left it. The place was the model of efficiency with people at their desks, very little noise, and a small group discussing something on a whiteboard in one of the conference rooms. Someday, I'd replace Dad and rule over this money-making machine. That was the plan, and I followed plans.

I turned left and entered the inner sanctum of executive offices.

Libby was at her station outside Dad's office, and she offered a smile as I approached.

I pointed a finger. "Don't ever book me on a flight like that again."

She nodded toward my father's door. "It was his idea."

"Huh?"

"I asked about a charter. He said no." She shifted back to her computer. "He's waiting for you."

I unbuttoned my suit coat and opened the door to my office instead of his.

"They're waiting for you," Libby repeated.

I waved a hand. "Got it." After setting down my bag and hanging up my coat, I went out to my father's office. Taking a calming breath, I pulled open the door.

Dad was at his desk. Tony Vignali, our integrations expert, and Harold Snyderman, company CFO, were with him.

"Enjoy your vacation?" Dad asked.

The lack of a question about the engine fire and unplanned stop in Sioux City meant my brother had kept his mouth shut about it, like I'd asked him to.

Tony looked down at his lap.

"It wasn't as long as I'd planned," I replied, keeping my snark to a minimum.

"Couldn't be helped," Dad said as he watched me take a seat. "You can reschedule after we're done with this latest project." In Dad's world, every acquisition was a project.

I looked over at Harold. "I didn't know we'd finished the due diligence to make an offer on Camper Heaven."

We'd been circling the RV chain for two months, and Harold had told me before I left that he needed at least another month for due diligence.

"Not Camper Heaven," Harold corrected me.

"This came up suddenly," Dad said. "I was approached directly, and we had to move."

I still didn't know what we were talking about. "Who, then?"

"Tuscan Foods," Tony said.

The name didn't ring a bell. "I haven't seen a file on them. What about due diligence?" I asked.

Dad opened a hand toward Harold, who answered. "The transaction is structured to be contingent on post-purchase targets and integration performance. We have to scope it out on the fly."

I turned to Dad. "And what does this have to do with me?"

He smiled. "You're going to handle this one personally."

He'd created another of his tests.

I shook my head. "Not interested. Tony can take care of it."

Tony showed no interest in rescuing me. "I'm getting ready for Camper Heaven." But his lack of eye contact said all I needed to know about whose idea this was.

Great. Dad had laid a trap in the few days I'd been gone, and obviously the guys were under orders to not give me an out.

Dad patted the file in front of him. "Like I said, this one is for you to handle personally." I didn't have an option. He slid the file in my direction. "I want you to get them integrated with Smith's as soon as possible."

Smith's was a grocery chain Dad had acquired from an old Marine buddy of his years ago. With most of its stores in southern California, it didn't have the scale it needed, and we'd discussed selling it off to a competitor rather than keeping it.

Dad stood. "They're expecting you this morning. Libby has the details."

I hadn't even opened the folder yet. "Today?" We never went into a situation blind. Thorough research ahead of time prevented surprises down the road. Dad always insisted.

"We have a three-month right of rescission on this," Harold said.

With that knowledge, the hurry up made more sense.

"Might as well dig in right away and see how leaky the boat is," he added.

And now I had an out. I'd look it over, and if it wouldn't work, I could walk away in a few weeks and move on to Camper Heaven with proper preparation and Harold's support.

I followed Tony and Harold to the door.

"Josh, one more thing," Dad called.

I stopped.

He motioned to the open door. "Please."

I closed it and turned.

"I want you to make sure this works out. It shouldn't take long, and then it's on to Camper Heaven." He tapped the blue folder containing the promise that I would handle Camper Heaven if they accepted. That project would give me national retail experience.

"And then it's London after that?" I asked.

Dad nodded. "Absolutely, like I promised."

"Thanks," I said.

Dad never reneged on his promises. I'd soon be learning how to drive on the left side of the road, but more importantly, I'd be in charge of my own operation.

"Harold didn't seem keen on this one," I noted. "What do we do if it looks like a stinker after closer examination?"

"We go ahead anyway."

I rarely questioned Dad, but this wasn't like him. "Why?"

"I made a personal commitment," he said. "The previous CEO was a friend. The rescission period was to satisfy Harold. I don't intend to use it." He sat back down. "Keep me up to date."

That was Dad-speak for *don't ask any more questions*.

I nodded. "Okay." My out had disappeared. As far as Dad was concerned, the deal had been struck, and we had to live with it. Rather, *I* had to live with it.

Nicole

My head throbbed as I pried open one eyelid. The second seemed glued shut.

Light filtered into the strange room. The sheets cocooning me were marvelously soft.

It came back in a rush. *Josh*. This was Josh's room. I rolled, but the bed behind me was empty and cold.

He'd left me.

Had I kicked in my sleep after promising not to?

I climbed down from the bed and padded into the bathroom.

Following Echo out to the kitchen, I found the note.

Nicole,

Hope you slept well.

Lock up when you leave, and give the key to my doorman, Oliver, downstairs. He'll call you a car to get you to your place. Take care of your cousin first, phone second, and don't worry about the house. I'm arranging to have your door and windows fixed today by Patterson Construction. Call me tonight to let me know how your day went.

Juice and Advil just in case.

Josh

Thinking of you

and tiramisu

I smiled at the sweetness of his note before washing down the pain tablets with the juice he'd left me. Good looking, rich, *and* thoughtful. Josh was ticking all the boxes.

After dressing, I leashed up Echo and was out after carefully locking Josh's palace behind me.

Downstairs, I found an elderly man with the right name on his uniform. "Oliver?"

He beamed me a wide smile. "Ah, you must be Miss Nicole," he said with a British accent. "Mr. Benson told me to expect the most beautiful woman in all the town."

The Advil hadn't taken effect yet, and it hurt a little to laugh. "He's too kind."

"A kinder man you'll not meet."

I handed over the key. "To his unit."

He took it and pulled a doggie treat from his pocket. "May I?" he asked, gesturing to Echo.

"He'd love it. May I walk him on the lawn out front before I leave?" I had no idea what the protocol was in this part of town. Maybe certain stretches of greenery were off limits.

"Certainly. I'll fetch the car for you."

"I can take a cab," I objected.

Oliver shook his head. "Oh, that won't do, Miss Nicole. Mr. Benson sent his car service for you. It would be my job if I let you leave any other way."

"We can't have that." I contained my laugh. Even from a distance, Josh was controlling.

"Thank you, miss." Oliver pulled out his phone. "I do need this job."

On the drive home, I looked out the town car's window and lamented having woken up alone. Last night was more than a little fuzzy. But Josh had gotten called back to LA four days early, so he probably had an early meeting to get to. Not being able to remember what he'd said last night didn't help.

Sandy was not going to believe this. I'd slept with the man without sleeping with him. She'd call me a liar, or a dumbass, or worse.

I wished I could remember more about last night. The headache was only half my problem. I went into his room, and we cuddled… Remembering that warmed me all the way through. I didn't think I'd said anything ridiculous. Fingers crossed he still considered me a rational adult.

~

AN HOUR AND A HALF LATER, ECHO AND I WERE BACK AT CASA DI ROSSI. I WAS showered and waiting for the coffee machine to finish pouring my first cup of java.

Even though it wouldn't shut or lock properly, the door appeared closed from the street. The broken windows, however, looked worse in the morning light than they had last night.

After eating, Echo was now just a yellow lump in his bed, watching me. The message light on the phone on the far counter blinked annoyingly. Marketing calls for sure—nobody else used the landline anymore. Except I was due to hear from my dentist about whether insurance would cover replacing a filling that had been giving me trouble.

In a hurry to down some caffeine, I slipped two ice cubes into the mug when the coffeemaker finished, and stirred. A quick check of the fridge yielded only a wedge of Manchego and an apple for breakfast. I bit into the tangy, hard cheese while peeling the organic label off the apple. Giving in to the blinking light, I sipped from my mug and pressed play on the phone. The first four messages warranted quick hits of the erase button. The fifth didn't.

"Nicole." My Uncle Ernst's voice boomed out of the machine. "Uncle Ernst here. You didn't pick up on your cell, so I'm calling the house to tell you that instead of starting off at the Santa Monica store, you should come into the office Monday morning. There are things we need to go over. Hope you had a relaxing week. Bye."

Things to discuss. Maybe I'd find out how the bank meeting had gone. If it'd been great, he wouldn't have been so evasive. We probably got a rate increase on our credit line that he wanted to break to me in person. Damned bankers—to them everything was numbers. Our personal banker was a waste of time. Uncle Ernst thought he was a friend, but to me he seemed like a used car salesman in a better suit.

I erased the message and bit into my apple.

Company business would have to wait. Family business came first, and that meant a visit to Three-B Bail Bonds. They'd given me a break the first time I'd had to get Lara out, and I'd dealt with them each time since. I made another cup of coffee for the road while I finished my apple and cheese.

A knock sounded from the front door.

With Patterson Construction embroidered on his cap, the bearded guy on the porch shifted nervously from foot to foot with his hands in his pockets. "Hi. Josh sent me."

Josh had been true to his word, and it settled my nerves.

"Hi." I opened the door wider and extended my hand. "I'm Nicole. Thanks for coming over."

"Phil Patterson." He shook with me. "Hey, what are friends for?"

I gave him a questioning look.

"Josh tells me to jump; I ask how high." He laughed. "Okay if I take a look?" He pointed toward the door.

I backed out of his way, wondering if all of Josh's friends were this odd. "Sure."

He examined the doorjamb.

"How much will this cost, you think?"

He turned to check the edge of the door. "You? Nothing. Josh, plenty."

"I insist on paying."

He moved the deadbolt in and out a few times. "Nope… Good solid door."

"But I want to pay."

He opened the door wide and inspected the hinges before turning to me. "How long you known Josh?"

The truth was too embarrassing to admit. "A little while."

"That should be long enough to understand." The corners of his mouth turned up. "He made up his mind, so discussion over."

I held my tongue. *Discussion over* my ass.

"I'll need to rebuild the jamb." He pulled out a knife and sliced off a chip of the wood. "We'll match the color for you."

"I have to go out. How long will this take?"

He caught sight of the rug with the ugly message, and his brow creased. "Somebody's mad."

I shrugged, not wanting to discuss it. "I guess."

Phil motioned to the guy standing by the big pickup out front. "I'll leave Tim here to watch your house and demo this while I get materials. You can go out. Your things will be safe with us. Glass man is on the way, and we'll be done and out of your hair today."

"Thank you."

"You have a beautiful house here. Love the workmanship."

I swelled with pride. "My grandfather built it."

He patted the wood. "We'll take good care of her."

Casa di Rossi was in good hands with this man. I rolled up the carpet and put it behind the couch before I left.

CHAPTER 8

NICOLE

WITH THE TRAFFIC, THE DRIVE DOWNTOWN TOOK EVEN LONGER THAN I'D FIGURED, and the second cup of coffee was taking its toll on my bladder when I finally parked at Three-B.

Inside, I waved to Celia on the way past her to the bathroom.

She smiled back. "Long time no see, Nicole."

It was pretty damned pathetic that I was on a first-name basis with somebody in the bail-bond business.

Everything about this place was incongruous to the name on the door. The bathroom was spotless. It even had a basket of travel-size toothpaste tubes, mouthwash bottles, and new toothbrushes in plastic. My first time here, I'd expected bus-stop grungy, with a urinal that hadn't been cleaned in a year and perhaps a condom vending machine on the wall.

After washing up, I made it back to Celia's desk and took the hot seat.

She perused the papers on her clipboard. "She certainly is a handful, isn't she?"

"She's had it hard. She'll come around." Having her father run off with his mistress had soured Lara on men at an early age, and then finding her boyfriend dead in my backyard five years ago had led to the downward spiral that had become her life.

"Dear, it's bad this time. You might want to consider another approach."

I shook my head. "Not yet. What is it?"

Lara had already graduated from a simple DUI the first time to worse offenses, but she was still my cousin and my responsibility.

Celia passed over the clipboard. "Good thing you're sitting down."

My mouth dropped open when I looked down.

"Bail is one hundred and ninety-five thousand. How do you want to handle that?"

She wasn't kidding.

"I don't understand."

She read off a paper on her desk. "One hundred twenty thousand for section five-oh-seven and another seventy-five for section two-eight-zero-zero point two."

I put my hand to my forehead. "That's so much."

Before, we'd been talking twenty-five thousand, and now it was just short of two hundred? How was I going to afford this?

Celia looked over her glasses. "I'm sorry, dear. Do you want a few days to think about it? The extra time locked up might help her reconsider her course in life."

I shook my head. Lara was blood, and my responsibility. "Is there any chance we can get this reduced?"

"That's a question for the lawyers, dear, but in my experience, no. These numbers are straight off the county bail schedule. You could talk to the lawyer and come back."

I took in a breath. "No, I want to post it." I smiled. "Any way I could get a break on the fee?"

She waved over at her husband in the glass-enclosed office. "That would be up to Billy."

Billy opened the door. "What's up?"

Bad Boy Billy was the three Bs in the name, and about three hundred pounds of man you didn't want to mess with. One look at him, and you'd think twice about skipping out on your court appearance.

Celia handed him the paperwork. "Do you think we could give Nicole here a break? She's a repeat customer."

"We're running a business," he responded gruffly. "Not a charity."

"Please, Billy," she added.

He sighed. "What's nine percent?"

That was a percent less than the standard bail bond rate and would save me almost two thousand dollars.

Celia's fingernails clacked on her calculator. "Seventeen-five-fifty."

"Are drugs involved?"

"No," Celia assured him.

Billy ran his hand through his thinning hair. "How's seventeen?" He looked at me for a response.

"Thanks," I answered with my biggest smile. It would max out my credit cards, but I thought I had enough left on my limits for that.

He pointed a finger at me. "Just see that she shows."

"She will." That I could be positive about, because I'd make it happen, no matter what.

Billy leaned down and kissed his wife. "How is it I can never say no to you?" He returned to his glass cage.

Celia didn't respond to that, and I didn't hazard a guess. She had him wrapped around her little finger.

"How do you want to handle that?" she asked.

I dug out my wallet. "Can I split it across two cards?"

"Up to you. How much on the first?"

"Ten."

She typed on her keyboard, and the credit card machine facing me lit up.

I slid my MasterCard in. When the tiny screen changed to say *authorizing*, I mentally crossed my fingers that I'd remembered correctly how much the card had left on it.

A ding and a green light let me remove it.

We repeated the procedure for my Visa card, and Lara had successfully torpedoed my chance at replacing my car in the foreseeable future.

"And what are we doing for the collateral?" Celia asked. She typed on the computer again. "Last time we used the house. Have you added any financing on it since then?"

"Yeah, the house," I said wearily. A hundred and ninety-five K lien on Casa di Rossi was a painful step. "I mean no. I haven't done a mortgage or anything."

A minute later she pulled several sheets of paper from her printer and walked them in to Billy for a signature.

When it was my turn to sign, the pen felt like a lead weight.

Billy emerged again while Celia was taking down my info for her notary book. "See that she shows. I'm not shy about taking people's houses if they skip, but it's a part of the job I don't like."

"She will," I assured him again.

If that was something he didn't like about the business, what was the part he did like? I didn't ask.

"I'll call it over," Celia told me. "It'll be about an hour."

I put my wallet back in my purse and pulled out my dead phone. "Is there a place I can buy a phone nearby?"

She shrugged. "No idea, dear."

I stood to leave. "Thank you again, Celia."

"That's what we're here for."

I turned before reaching the door. "What did she do to deserve that much bail?" I should have said what was she *accused* of.

"Reckless driving to evade arrest and embezzlement of over a million dollars." Celia looked over her glasses. "She should have been on a plane straight to Brazil."

I swallowed hard. Lara worked for us, the family company. If she'd embezzled, it had been from us. But it couldn't be; that wasn't Lara. She could be impulsive, self-destructive maybe, but not a thief. None of this made any sense. *A million fucking dollars?*

I left before I decorated their floor with the vomit I felt threatening.

Leaning against my car outside Three-B Bail Bonds, I worked to keep my roiling stomach under control. In this neighborhood, I'd fit right in if I barfed all over their parking lot, but I was a Rossi, goddammit, and I had to hold it together.

Embezzling from the company—my company, our company? No wonder Uncle Ernst hadn't wanted to take my calls. It wasn't about the stupid bank line of credit; it was confronting me about my insistence on hiring Lara. I was walking straight into the shitstorm from hell when I got back to the office.

What a fucking rollercoaster the last few days had been. First, I almost make it to Josh's table for my first almost-date since Mo, if you could call sharing dessert a date. Then the pool and phone fiasco, followed by getting bumped from my flight back home—only to end up sitting next to Josh on the flight to LAX and sharing a donut, until the plane almost crashed. Which led to Josh saving the day by inviting me for a magical trip on a private jet so I could get home in time for Lara. Now I find out Lara has embezzled from the company?

Josh

I closed the door to Dad's office behind me.

Libby held out a folder. "The Tuscan Foods meeting details. It's at eleven."

I took it. "I'll trade you for a cup of coffee."

She opened her drawer, pulled out one of the mugs she always had ready, and headed off.

Once at my desk, I opened the folder and started looking through the financials for Tuscan Foods.

They operated a chain of boutique grocery stores, mostly in this area, and a few up around the San Francisco Bay Area, all under the brand name of Rossi's.

Interesting coincidence: Nicole had said she worked at a family company. Just in case, I flipped to the second page and found the name of the CEO: Ernst Berg, not Rossi.

Libby appeared at my door with my coffee. "Do you want me to pass along your opinion about the flight arrangements?" she asked coolly.

"No." Bitching about the past never helped with Dad.

She set the mug down on my desk.

"Thanks."

She turned to leave.

"Libby."

She stopped at the door.

"Sorry I jumped down your throat about it. I'm tired; it wasn't a great day."

"I understand... Open or closed?" She held the door handle.

"Closed." I lifted the mug. "And thank you."

She smiled and shut the door behind her.

I hadn't been entirely truthful about the day. The first two flights had been terrible, but I had gotten to meet Nicole. The third flight, with us on the couch, and finally her in my bed last night had certainly provided a more-than-adequate end to the day. Waking up with my arms around her this morning had been even better. My cock swelled with the memory.

I opened the file on Tuscan Foods, but then put it down. I had something else to do first.

Closing my eyes, a picture of Nicole came to mind. Long, light-brown hair, wonderful green eyes, a cute nose, and a cuter smile. I composed a text to the number I'd added to my contacts last night. I sent it after changing the suggested day to tomorrow. It might take her some time to get her phone replaced.

ME: Josh here - how about dinner Tuesday? You can tell me how you ended up in that beautiful old house

I hit send. She deserved a proper date after all she'd been through, and then we'd see.

Next I called Phil again.

He assured me he'd finish the repairs to Nicole's house today, and he had a glass guy ready to roll.

Returning to the Tuscan file, things got progressively murkier as I pored over the limited financials. They carried a large debt load, which had grown over the years. That in itself was concerning. Operating cash-flow had been inconsistent, from what I could tell, but with only a few pages, there wasn't much to go on.

I could only guess that, like a lot of family businesses, they'd promoted based on nepotism rather than performance, and slowly lost their edge. Without an outside force to shake up their ways, a lot of family firms became progressively out-of-date in their methods.

I closed the folder, followed by my eyes, and imagined a dinner across from Nicole. What would she wear? I'd call her this afternoon and see if she'd gotten her phone replaced. Maybe we could move up our dinner.

Being a gentleman last night with my arm around her had been the right thing to do since she was drunk. Why was the right thing so damned hard?

CHAPTER 9

Nicole

I waited in the throng at the jail.

Lara came out the doorway of the jail and walked sullenly my way, manila envelope in hand. "You hung up on me. I was afraid you wouldn't come," she said.

"I didn't hang up; my phone died." It hurt that she'd thought I would abandon her.

She gripped me in a fierce hug. "I can't thank you enough." She sniffled. "I owe you."

She most certainly did, but this wasn't the time nor place to tell her what she owed me was to get her life straightened out so I didn't have to make any more trips to Three-B.

"I came as soon as I could." I pushed her to let me loose. "Let's get you home." I needed to know more, but not here, not with everybody around. "The car's out front."

Lara walked with me through the doors that represented a return to freedom. The look on her face as she turned it toward the sunshine was one of relief. "Two days in this hellhole. I could kill him."

"Shh," I warned her. "You can tell me in the car."

Talk of revenge with deputies walking by was a sure recipe for more trouble, not less.

She grimaced and followed me in silence.

I unlocked the car door, and she climbed in. She tore open the envelope, and her paltry personal effects from lockup spilled into her lap. She counted her money three times.

I pulled out of the parking space. "You really think they'd steal from you?"

"I wouldn't put it past them." Her phone got the same careful scrutiny before she started working her seven earrings and studs back into place. Lara wasn't one for symmetry.

I cringed when she stuck her tongue out and struggled to replace the silver ball stud she wore there.

"You know it would be easier to get hired without that."

She shrugged as she tightened the stud. "Guys like it."

"Some guys maybe," I countered. "But not bosses."

"All guys. They see it and drool, just imagining how it will feel when I blow them."

I shook my head. I didn't need that visual.

She opened up the Swiss Army knife Uncle Ernst had given her.

I'd lost the one he gave me years ago to a TSA check at the airport.

She started with the nail file on the badly torn middle finger of her right hand.

"What happened?" I asked.

"Tore it in a fight."

"Do you have any idea how dangerous that is? You've got shit for brains getting into a fight with the kinds of women who are locked up in there."

"What would you know about it? Backing down is more dangerous."

It didn't seem like an argument I was going to win. So I said nothing.

She pocketed the knife, crumpled up the empty envelope, and the real trouble began.

"I'm gonna kill him," she announced. "He's been out to get me since forever."

Him was obviously Uncle Ernst, and we'd gotten to the root of her anger.

"Slow down. Nobody's killing anybody. Now what the hell happened?"

Her mouth became a fire hose as the words spilled out. "I started noticing the money going out, and I was logging in every day—"

I grabbed her arm. "Get a grip and slow down so I can understand."

She took in a breath through gritted teeth. "Okay." She wrung her hands. "I saw money leaving the accounts, and I started to check every day to figure it out."

"When did this start?"

"I don't know. I noticed it two weeks ago," she answered.

"And who'd you tell?"

She huffed. "Like that would have done any good? Stephanie—I mean, Mrs. Quantell—was out of town. You were too busy, and then you were gone, and I'm not even allowed to talk to the creeper."

She'd never once called her stepfather anything but Ernst, or *Creeper*, although she did have the good sense to not call him Creeper to his face.

I didn't buy her excuse. Her not talking to her stepdad had been my idea, but not a real rule. It was just meant to keep the peace and keep her from getting herself fired.

Ernst had not been a fan of my hiring her, but it was my call and not his. And besides, it had been good for Lara.

"Go on," I urged.

"Late last week, Mrs. Quantell came back, and that's when I told her." Her face screwed up in anger. "She took it to Ernst. We had a meeting. I tried to explain. Two hours later they arrested me. He's always been trying to ruin my life."

"Uncle Ernst?"

"Who else?"

"So you think he took the money and set you up?"

"Of course not," she scoffed. "He's not that smart. But instead of taking the time to find out who it was, I'm the scapegoat, just like always. That's why he has to die."

I pointed a finger at her. "You say that one more time, and I'm pulling your bail."

Her eyes went wide. "I didn't really mean it."

I sucked in a breath to slow myself down before I totally lost my cool. "The real culprit is out there—the one who stole from our company, and all you can do is focus on Uncle Ernst? Get it together. Do you have any idea what kind of trouble you're in?"

The bluster had left her. "Yeah."

"I don't think you do. You could end up in prison instead of county lockup. And for years, not days."

"But I didn't do it." She slumped in her seat. "What do I do?"

"For starters, you stop threatening Uncle Ernst. For that matter, you don't talk to anybody but me about this, and we figure out who the real thief is before it's too late."

"Okay. Hey, can you take me by the impound lot to pick up my truck?"

The sign for a phone store appeared ahead. "After we stop in and get me a new phone." It was another bad sign that I knew where the impound lot was.

~

INSIDE THE PHONE STORE, I TURNED THE SHINY THING OVER IN MY HAND A FEW TIMES before committing. "I'll take it in white, and this case." I'd picked the pink case first, and decided against a clashing color for the phone.

"Are you sure you don't want the newer model?" the cheery salesperson asked.

"I'm sure." After maxing out my credit cards getting Lara back, I'd decided to save a few bucks on the phone. It was still almost three years until I'd finally be able to tap into my inheritance. Until then, this phone would do.

"I'll get one from the storeroom and be right back," the cheery clerk said.

"You should have gotten the new one," Lara said, echoing the salesperson.

I shook my head. "It's called being prudent."

Fifteen minutes later, the phone was powered up and syncing with the cloud to transfer all my old data.

After restarting, it woke with a chime: three voicemails, all from Uncle Ernst, and six new text messages. Three from my uncle telling me to get into work, two from Sandy checking on me, and one from an unknown number.

> 555-7842: Josh here - how about dinner Tuesday? You can tell me how you ended up in that beautiful old house

I smiled and updated that number as Josh in my contacts before replying. At least one thing was going right today.

> ME: Sounds like a plan - let me know when and where to meet

His reply came just after I climbed back into my car.

JOSH: Pick you up at your place at 7

I put the phone down on the console without replying. I might feel eager, but I didn't need to broadcast that to him.

Lara picked up my phone. "Who's Josh?"

"Give me that." I reached for the phone, but wasn't quick enough. "Just a guy I met on the trip back."

"Just a guy, huh?"

The question didn't merit an answer, in my book. Lara didn't need to know I'd escalated to spooning with him last night. That hazy memory sent a tingle up my spine and a smile to my lips.

She tapped on the phone's screen.

I grabbed again, but still didn't reach the phone. "Hey. What are you doing?"

"I saw that look. I'm just making sure you're being polite." She turned the phone so I could see it.

ME: Can't wait

It was too forward for my taste, but his instant reply quelled my apprehension.

JOSH: Same here

"You can thank me later," Lara said as she put the phone back on the console.

The response she'd elicited from Josh alluded to lots of post-dinner possibilities. Sandy would love to hear about this.

I smiled and pulled away from the curb. From what Lara had said, Uncle Ernst had blamed her out of spite. But I'd learned that with Lara, there was sometimes another side to the story. For her sake, I hoped that wasn't true today.

I PARKED AT THE IMPOUND LOT. "ONE MORE THING."

She unbuckled but waited.

"There are guys at the house, fixing it."

"Okay. Fixing what?"

"Somebody broke in, painted a threat on the rug, and broke a few windows."

Her mouth hung open. "What the fuck? Why?"

I shrugged, trying to keep the whole thing low key. "Who knows?"

"Whatever."

At least she wasn't freaked. "Anyway, I'll meet you back at the house tonight."

"Whatever." Lara pulled out her credit card and left to get her truck.

I owed Sandy a call, so I dialed as I headed to work.

"Hey, girl," she started out rapid fire. "I've been worried about you. How are you going to get back from bumfuck Iowa or wherever? Are they sending you another plane or what?"

I couldn't get a word in until she took a breath. "It was Sioux City, Iowa, and I'm back."

"Wow, I just saw on TV how your plane made an emergency landing, and the plane they sent to get you broke too. What a joke. I'm not flying with them again."

She was blowing smoke. If I knew Sandy, she'd fly with them again for two dollars less than the alternative.

"Josh flew me home last night," I said as soon as I could get another word in.

That stalled Freight Train Sandy for a second before she asked, "Josh?"

"The guy in blue from Barbados," I filled in.

"Not bad, girl. Now spill. How'd you hook him?"

I laughed. "I didn't *hook* him. I ended up next to him on the later flight I got bumped to."

"And?" I could hear her drooling over the phone line.

"After we landed, Josh brought me home in his charter."

"Charter jet? So the guy must be loaded."

"Don't know," I lied. "And don't care." That part wasn't a lie. I wouldn't be as crass as Sandy in judging a guy that way.

"Sure," she said sarcastically.

I flashed back to cuddling in his arms, and how concerned he'd been for my safety. "He's a really nice guy."

"And has he asked you out again?"

I answered that with silence.

Sandy chuckled. "A piece of advice, girl. Don't refuse. If you don't take the first step, you can never round the bases."

"I'm at work, and I really have to go in. I just wanted to let you know I was okay."

"More than okay is what it sounds like. Catch ya later."

"Love you." I hung up and sat back for a second. More than okay was certainly right. Tomorrow night couldn't come soon enough.

As I pulled into the company parking lot, a text arrived.

SANDY: There may be a lot of fish in the sea, but be careful throwing a good one back, because you'll never hook him again.

Once inside the familiar offices of our company, I found Uncle Ernst in his office talking with Rosa, who handled HR.

"We can pick this up later," he said.

Rosa shook her head, stood, and slid by without meeting my gaze or welcoming me back—very un-Rosa. They'd probably been discussing my errant cousin.

I closed the door behind me. Something was off about his office. It was different than I remembered, but I couldn't put my finger on it.

Uncle Ernst rounded the desk to give me a one-armed hug. "Welcome back. How was your time off? We missed you around here."

I took a chair for what was likely to be an unpleasant discussion. "Good to be back," I answered half-heartedly. I didn't know how to start the conversation about Lara, so I settled for, "It was warm and relaxing."

"Good, because things have gotten pretty hectic around here, and you're going to need all the energy you can muster."

Hectic wasn't the word I would have chosen for having his own stepdaughter arrested.

I sat back and waited for him to explain, rather than start off by accusing him.

"You know the bank was in last week to renegotiate the credit line?"

I nodded. "Yeah."

"When Stephanie told us we had money missing, that threw a wrench into everything."

I wanted to get the facts straight. "I thought—"

"Hold on and let me explain how we got to where we are."

I closed my mouth and folded my arms.

He had a way of stretching out explanations that didn't suit me. "The bank demanded that we investigate what happened and propose a solution before they'd talk further."

I jumped in. "So you pinned it on Lara?"

His brow furrowed for a moment. Seemed he hadn't expected me to know that. "Stop right there, young lady. You should listen to the whole story before passing judgment."

I clenched my teeth, holding back telling him what I thought of him for even considering it.

"The bank demanded we identify the culprit."

"So you picked Lara?"

"Stephanie thought it was her, and besides, we can always amend it if she was wrong and we find out it was somebody else."

I seethed at the suggestion that erasing an arrest like this from Lara's record would be no big deal—never mind the whole jail part.

"The bank had frozen our credit line, but then when corporate got involved, they canceled, *canceled,* goddammit, and called all our loans."

All my strength drained at those words. That was a death sentence for the business. "I told you we should have diversified our banking beyond Coastal."

"Let's not reargue that now. Jerry has been good to us."

Jerry was his banker buddy from school, and the reason he'd ignored my suggestion more than once to broaden our banking relationships.

"Your fucked-up idea that we could rely on your asshole friend Jerry is why we're in this mess," I scolded.

Ernst's face screwed up in anger. "Bull-fucking-shit," he half yelled.

I'd made the mistake of swearing, and that always loosened his tongue in response.

"Jerry is the one who helped out." He pointed an accusing finger at me like I'd been the cause of all this, even though I'd been more than three thousand miles away at the time. "Jerry was the only one who could locate a buyer for me over the weekend."

With him yelling at me, I wasn't about to go back to polite. "Buyer? What the hell does that mean?"

"It means we'd be giving everybody pink slips today if not for my friend Jerry. And that includes you."

I thought quickly about what we could have sold to get us enough cash to pay back our credit line, and the Redondo Beach store where we owned the land was all I could come up with.

"Are you ready to listen to the solution, or do you want to berate me for being here to solve our problems while you were off sunning yourself in the tropics?"

"What?" I hissed.

I'd scheduled the trip months ago and not gotten any complaints. And I hadn't gotten any fucking communication from him while I was down there.

"I called you late Saturday, but you didn't deign to answer my call, and again yesterday before I signed the papers. But oh no, your week of me-time was too important to bother worrying about saving everybody's job. I don't know how you live with yourself."

That was it. I was done listening to his ranting. "I've given more of myself to this company than you ever have. Who's the one out on the golf course three afternoons a week?"

He winced, as I'd finally scored a direct hit to his ego.

"And for your information," I yelled as I dug through my purse. "I never got any messages or calls from you." I held up the cracked carcass of my old phone. "Some asshole broke my phone while I was down there."

He put up his hand. "Be that as it may, I did what I had to. So, do you want to hear about it or just keep yelling like a hysterical teenager?"

Hysterical teenager had become his go-to insult whenever I got annoyed with him about anything. What he really meant was *hysterical woman*, but he didn't have the balls to use that again after I'd almost flattened him the first time he tried it.

"I'm listening." I tossed the phone on his desk. "Since I couldn't get any calls, you could have left a message for me at the front desk, or had them bring a note to my room," I added. The last word on this particular argument belonged to me. "What property did you sell?"

"We sold the company."

"You what?" I yelled. "You can't do that."

The difference in this office hit me. The picture of my Aunt Rossella was missing, as were his gold pen set, and his three stupid golf trophies he'd had on the credenza. He'd cleared things out already.

"It was either that," he said, "or pink slips all around today. In addition, as trustees of your parents' estate, we were duty bound to preserve the value of shares in the company."

What he really meant was that if the company went belly up and my aunt's shares became worthless, he'd have nothing and would have to go find a real job.

I couldn't decide between crying and screaming.

"I sent you a copy of the papers," he added.

"You can't be serious," I objected. "There has to be another way."

"It's done. Lloyd Benson and I inked the deal yesterday after you didn't answer your phone."

A knock came at the door, and Cynthia poked her head in. "He's here."

CHAPTER 10

Josh

I introduced myself at the front desk. "Josh Benson here to see Ernst Berg."

"Yes, he's expecting you," the cute young girl said. She rose, came around the counter, and offered her hand. "Cynthia. Nice to meet you, Mr. Benson."

"Pleasure."

"If you'll come with me." She opened the door to an open work area with a few offices around the side.

A dozen pairs of eyes followed us as we made our way to the corner.

"You what?" The yell of a very upset woman came from the office we stopped in front of.

Not surprising given the abruptness of Dad's purchase of this family-owned company. Change like this never came easily.

Cynthia hesitated before knocking.

More words came from behind the door, but now at a low-enough volume that I couldn't discern them.

Cynthia deemed it safe to knock and told the occupants I was here.

I entered, and she closed the door behind me.

A shorter, older man with close-cropped brown hair, balding on top, and a bulbous nose, rose from behind the desk. "Mr. Benson, I presume. Ernst Berg."

"Yes," I responded.

The woman in the chair facing him also stood and turned my way. Except for the red face of anger she wore, I recognized her instantly—Nicole.

I stopped, with a sudden lump in my throat. She'd been the one yelling.

Ernst shoved his hand at me. "Pleasure to meet you."

I took it and shook. "Nice to meet you… Josh, Josh Benson." My gaze didn't linger with him, but went instantly back to Nicole.

"And this is my niece and co-owner, Nicole Rossi," Ernst said pleasantly.

"We've met," she said coolly.

Ernst returned to his chair and leaned back. "Your father said he thought Rossi's would integrate well with Smith's."

My eyes, which had been glued to Nicole, searching for an emotion other than disdain, returned to the older man. "That's right. We think combining the two would yield efficiencies."

"Please have a seat, Josh," Ernst offered.

Nicole pushed past me. "I've got things to do."

"Nicole, you should stay for this," Ernst said.

The door shut behind her without a reply.

Ernst shrugged with a look as perplexed as I felt. "I should explain, I guess."

"Yes." I took the closer, still-warm seat Nicole had occupied.

"Forgive her. She's upset. I wasn't able to reach her to tell her what was happening until just now—something about her phone."

Her dead phone from Barbados lay on the desk. "I see." He didn't need to know my part in that.

The desk and the office were oddly devoid of anything personal. Nothing on the walls, none of the usual family pictures on the desk or credenza behind him. The office was beyond stark, almost like he'd just moved into a rental.

"Anyway, as you might imagine, she's quite attached to the business, and this is a terrible shock for her. Her grandfather started with a single store, and she's the third generation working at Rossi's. We'd hoped she'd be able to take over one day and pass it on to the next generation."

I glanced at a few questions I'd written down. "How many other family members are with the company?" This could be a tricky transition if they were inserted at all levels in all departments and had the same reaction as she'd just had.

"Currently, she's the only Rossi here, my brother-in-law's only child. I married into the family, and I'm the only other relative here. My wife, her aunt, was never interested in the business, and her father didn't have any other siblings, so when the time came, I took over, and it's just me and her now."

"How long ago did you take over from her father?"

His eyes cast down for a moment. "Uh... I've been in charge for the last six years."

I studied him a moment. "You said your niece is upset about the sale, yet she signed off on it?"

"No. That's probably the root of the problem—that and the shock of it all. Her shares are in trust until her thirtieth birthday. Her aunt and I are the trustees, and we signed the papers for her share of the company. I wanted to discuss it with her but..." He pointed at the phone. "Well, circumstances prevented that, and so here we are. It couldn't be helped."

He'd been put in a hard spot by Nicole's phone disaster, but if it were me, I would have found a way to contact her. A lack of communication like that wouldn't have happened in my family. This guy had the follow through of a banana slug.

I'd had a few minutes with Harold before coming over, and he'd filled me in on their unusual need to close over the weekend. Their bank had canceled all their credit and called all the loans, so they wouldn't have been able to make this week's payroll. They were completely over a barrel.

"I'll be out of your way this afternoon, and you can use this office," he said.

His eagerness to leave was unusual. "Since we haven't had a chance to come in and learn about your operations, I'm going to need some time with you to learn about the company—your direct reports, daily operational kinds of things."

He sighed. "You don't need me for that. I've only ever been a figurehead here. Nicole is the real brains of the operation."

Add eager to leave to his odd characteristics.

With a Stanford MBA, I didn't doubt Nicole was brainy, but I still felt he was probably selling himself short. "You are the CEO, are you not?"

"In title yes, but Nicole is the COO, and she handles pretty much everything around here. She'll probably tell you I spend too much time playing golf and not enough paying attention to the business." He checked his watch. "I'll leave you in her capable hands." He stood.

I'd never run into a more disinterested CEO, at a family business or otherwise. If the rest of the senior staff was like him, no wonder they'd gotten into trouble. I picked up the pad I'd written nothing on, and rose.

He came around the desk to shake again. "I wish you and your father the best of luck. I'm sure Rossi's is in good hands with you two running it going forward."

His desire to wash his hands of what was about to happen couldn't have been clearer. He went back behind his desk and picked up a box. He'd already packed his personal shit, and he really did mean to leave right fucking now and not come back.

"I need some time with you before you go," I said.

"Nicole, and Stephanie Quantell, are the two you need to talk to." He carried the box to the door, balanced it on his knee, and pulled open the door.

A moment later, I was standing in an empty office, completely baffled.

It wasn't done like this. In a normal situation, I would be getting Dad to call this jerk and get him back in here with the threat that we'd pull out of the deal if he didn't cooperate.

A middle-aged lady with a short bob and a fair sprinkling of gray hair appeared at the door. "Mr. Benson?"

I stood. "Josh, please."

She approached and we shook. "Rosa Pasquali."

"A pleasure." I gestured to the seat.

"No, I have to go out to lunch. Mr. Berg told me you're in charge now, so I thought I should give you this." She handed me a folded single sheet of paper.

I Quit as of today.
N. Rossi.

"Is this...?" I asked.

"Nicole Rossi. Yes. She was quite upset. I wanted to give you..."

I waited.

She held out a manila folder. "I mean, I need you to sign her termination paperwork, since technically, she works for you."

I took the folder and ran a hand through my hair. This was getting more fucked up by the minute. "No." I didn't bother to open the folder.

"No?"

"I'm not signing this until I talk with her."

The CEO and COO just up and leave? This wouldn't work. No way.

Nicole

I'd walked out of Uncle Ernst's office and almost upchucked my meager breakfast for the second time today.

Poof, the family company was gone? Just like that?

How could Ernst sell the company my grandparents had started, and Mom and Daddy had grown?

I'd only been gone a week and out of touch for a day or so.

Lara's opinion of Uncle Ernst was spot on today. He was a fuckhead who hadn't made more than a half-assed attempt to contact me in the Caribbean. All he'd ever cared about was how many dollars he could wring out of the company, not the legacy that had been built to pass on to the next generation.

And combine our stores with Smith's? That was a joke. There was no overlap at all. Smith's sold bulk generic food to cost-conscious buyers. We carried specialty items for discerning shoppers and supported local growers.

No wonder Josh was so rich. He and his family were a bunch of corporate vultures, buying up vulnerable businesses and dismembering them.

To think I'd been attracted to him made me want to puke. Beneath the smooth exterior, he obviously had the morals of a snake.

I refused to be a part of dismembering Rossi's, so I wrote the note I had to write and left it on Rosa's desk. The sticky note said to deliver it to Uncle Ernst when his door opened.

My tears began as soon as I closed my car door and started home. Now Casa di Rossi was where I needed to be. It would soon be all that was left of what my family had built. Three generations of work, and all we had to show for it now was an old house and six acres of orchard. I drove slowly, blinking back tears the whole way.

CHAPTER 11

Nicole

When I stopped the car outside Casa di Rossi, I used the last of my tissue stash to dry my eyes.

Lara was in the kitchen when I entered. "You got a FedEx delivery." She pointed to the purple and orange letter envelope.

"Not interested."

Echo wandered over for a quick pat before returning to his bed.

Lara looked up from the sandwich she was making. "You're back early."

"Short day," I answered, not sure how I could explain the disaster today had become.

"Who killed your cat?"

"Huh?"

"You look like shit."

I gave up on the facade. "I feel like shit. That asshole Ernst," I said, skipping the uncle moniker he no longer deserved, "went and sold the company out from under me over the weekend."

Her mouth dropped open, and the knife she held slipped off the bread and spread peanut butter onto the counter. "That's fucked up. How can he do that?"

"Your mom and fucking Ernst control my shares until my birthday."

"Can't you sue or something, and stop them?" She grabbed a paper towel to clean off the counter.

"That's not the way it works. It's done. It's too late."

She wiped up the mess. "You're wrong. When I bought my truck, I had a few days to change my mind and walk away from the deal. Some stupid law or other lets you do that."

I grabbed the envelope and tore it open. Maybe, just maybe, there was a way out of this.

Starting through the massive pile, the reading was tough going. It wasn't until page ten that I found it. The paragraph was labeled *right of rescission*.

"You're a genius," I told Lara. "There's a right of rescission."

She held up a finger while she finished the bite of sandwich in her mouth. "I'll take that compliment in writing." She came to look over my shoulder. "What's it say?"

I reread it five times to be sure. Each time I came to the same awful conclusion. "Fuck. They can cancel it, but we can't."

"So convince them it's a bad deal," she mumbled, chewing on another mouthful.

"It's not that simple. The bank canceled our credit. Without their money, everybody's out of a job tomorrow."

She wandered back to the fridge. "Well, that sucks. How did that happen all of the sudden?"

"The…" I looked for the right words. "Missing money. That kind of thing spooks banks."

Lara put her hands up. "Don't look at me. All I did was figure it out, and then get blamed by the fuckhead."

Ernst had screwed us both.

I was coming around to her view of her stepdad now. Before, he'd been pretty innocuous. He'd let me run things while he got to put CEO on his business card and hang out at his stupid country club, amusing his stupid friends with his stupid Swiss accent.

"I say we get shitfaced and forget about it all until tomorrow."

I looked up to find Lara grinning, but shot her my no-way-in-hell glare. We weren't going there—not with her history with alcohol.

She laughed. "Lighten up. It was a joke." She took her sandwich and left the kitchen.

I went back to reading the pile of papers. I could never be sure what was a joke and what wasn't when it came to Lara.

There was a lot of verbiage on conditional payments that I didn't spend time trying to comprehend. I found a sticky note in Rosa's handwriting attached to the first page of appendix two.

Sign the final page of this attachment

Maybe something about this wasn't finalized without my signature after all. The appendix was labeled *Retention Agreement*.

Flipping to the back, I could see where the final page had been signed by Lloyd Benson, and there was indeed a blank line for me to sign.

I leafed back and started at the beginning. My blood got hotter as I read what Ernst had meant to sign me up for: this said I had to work for these Benson assholes for six months. I stopped before reaching the end of the first page and picked up my phone.

"I can't talk now, Nicole," Ernst said when he answered. "I'm about to tee off—"

I interrupted him. "I need to tap into my trust a little."

"No. Your parents were quite adamant about that." He used that line every time I brought it up. His claim that Daddy hadn't wanted me to grow up a spoiled child and had insisted I work for a living without any access to my trust had been a common refrain, and sounded exactly like Daddy.

"But this is different," I complained.

"Not at all. The answer is still no."

With Aunt Rossella in Italy, it wouldn't do any good to revisit this until she returned.

I moved on to my real reason for calling. "I need to know what the retention agreement in the back of this paperwork is all about."

"They need somebody for a while who knows what's going on, and we both know that's not me."

I held back a laugh and didn't bother agreeing with him. It was true.

"It's quite a good deal for you, I think."

Somebody called his name in the background. "Hey, let's make it a thousand a hole."

"I have to go," Ernst said. "We'll talk tonight." He hung up before I could get another word in.

I was changing into sweats when my phone rang.

It was Rosa from HR at work. "Nicole, I'm sad to hear you're leaving us."

I didn't have much to say to that. "Me too."

"I'm calling to arrange your exit interview."

"Let's just skip it," I suggested.

"I'm not allowed to do that, and there are a few things to go over with you."

Paperwork was not high on my priority list. "Like what?"

"Well, there's the matter of your non-compete agreement."

Fuck me. I tried bluster. "I don't think I'm covered by that."

"Oh, you are. All the managers are."

The non-compete agreements had been another of Ernst's bright ideas two years ago.

How was I supposed to get a decent job when all my experience was in the grocery industry and I was forbidden from joining a competitor in our geographic market for six months? It wasn't like I could leave the house and move to the Midwest for a job.

I needed time to think. "I'm a little too busy to come in."

"Then I'll see you tomorrow. Just come by my office when you're free."

When we hung up, my head throbbed. So much for sliding into a job at another grocery chain.

~

THAT AFTERNOON, I WENT OUTSIDE IN THE BACK ORCHARD, TRYING TO CLEAR MY head with a little manual labor. Working with the dirt and the trees always centered me. Surely an hour of hoeing weeds would help take my mind off things—or maybe it would take two.

"Hey, Nicky, cut that out," Maro Tanaka called as he walked my way. "You know how your uncle feels about messing with his rows."

Maro had been the foreman back when Grandpa's orchard had been over a hundred acres. He lived in the little ranch house on the far corner of the property. These days, he did landscaping on the side and helped with our orchard in his spare time. In exchange for a little help, Daddy had let him stay in the quarters he'd occupied since working with Grandpa, and I'd continued Daddy's arrangement.

"I'm just taking out my frustrations on the weeds. He doesn't keep after them enough anyway." Not thinking about it, I'd turned the corner at the end of one of my rows of orange trees and started on a row of Ernst's almonds—probably a subconscious protest as much as anything else.

"It's your funeral," Maro said dejectedly.

"If he cares so much, he should replace those two. They're almost dead," I said, pointing to the two sickly ones in the middle of the row Ernst ignored.

"You tell him that. He doesn't care what I say."

I'd suggested it twice and been heartily rebuffed each time.

Maro gave up and went back toward his little house after I insisted twice more that this was something I wanted to do myself.

We all knew the rules. We had our own rows of trees to take care of, and although Ernst seemed to hate the trees and what they represented, he'd been fierce in his insistence that none of us touch his.

"Today I need the work, and he can just shove it," I said to the nearest tree as I whacked at another clump of weeds. Today was not a day to give a fuck about what Ernst did or didn't like. Not a single flying fuck. And if he didn't like it, all the better. I envisioned his face in the dirt as I scraped up the next clump.

Battling the weeds, the gophers, and the seasons to tend to the trees had always helped. Back to basics, Daddy called it—simple work without anything more than a tool in my hand and dirt under my fingernails. Years ago, life on this land had been simple. We took care of the trees, and they'd taken care of us.

Daddy had insisted that caring for the land and the animals and appreciating how food reached the table was imperative in our business. He'd been forced to omit the 'animals' part of that after the neighbors complained and made us get rid of the chickens we'd kept along the back fence.

Ten minutes later, my name rang out through the trees, "Nicole."

The voice belonged to Ernst—he who no longer deserved to be called my uncle, because true family didn't fuck you over the way he had in the last few days.

I turned, not at all amused that he'd shown up. "What?" I answered, failing at keeping the frustration out of my voice.

"Just came over to work my trees and talk since you called when I was busy earlier." The man considered golf in the category of being busy—what an ass. "And what are you doing on one of my rows?"

"Just hoeing weeds." I leaned the hoe against a tree and took a breath. "I really don't want to sell the company," I started.

He offered me a mean glare. "We've been over that, Nicole. The bank didn't give me a choice. Payroll is due tomorrow, and it was either that or close down. Anyway, what's done is done. I wish I had a better answer for you."

I wouldn't accept that. I couldn't. "I read the contract, and there's a right of rescission. We could convince them it's a bad deal and find another bank."

He sighed loudly. "No, we can't, and I'm not going to. Instead we should talk about how you can work with them for a while to make sure the transition goes smoothly and maximize our payout."

He was still only thinking about this as a sale. To him the company was a pile of money to be harvested.

To me it was my family's legacy, and I wasn't participating in its dismemberment. "I'm not working with them to destroy Rossi's."

"Don't be rash, Nicole. Have you read the retention agreement I negotiated for you? It's really quite generous."

My morals weren't for sale. "I can't be bought. Not by them, not by anybody." I picked up the hoe and headed to the house without another word.

He was a fuckhead, or worse. I agreed with Lara.

Back inside, I washed up and checked the fridge for dinner makings. When I looked out the back window, darkness was on its way to winning the war with daylight, and Ernst was gone.

~

Josh

Back home after a full afternoon at Tuscan Foods—or Rossi's as they called it—my head throbbed like I'd been butting it against a wall all day.

After going over the financials and a few operational issues, I was more confused than when I'd started. One thing was clear: Rossi's recent cash flow sucked. They had no clue what they were doing. It was a miracle they were still in business.

Several Advil and a glass of wine later, the throbbing had been reduced to a dull ache.

Dad picked up after three rings. "Hi," he answered with more cheer than I'd felt all day. "How'd the first day at Tuscan go?"

"It's a complete mess."

"They always look that way when you start. You probably don't understand them well enough yet to see the upside."

"The CFO's out for the week, but one thing's obvious: I'm going to need a cash infusion to get it stabilized."

He didn't say anything for a moment. "That doesn't make sense."

"I'll need twenty million minimum, but thirty would give me more room to maneuver."

"No."

That wasn't the word I'd expected—not by a long shot. In the past, asking for twenty would always have netted me fifteen or eighteen.

"The company is taking on water, and it needs a little help."

"They've been in business over fifty years without my help. I'm sure you can figure it out. I got the bank to reinstate their credit line and loans just as they were. It was good enough last week; it'll be good enough this week."

He was being unreasonable, and this tack wasn't getting me anywhere.

"They're no good to us if suppliers won't ship because of credit issues."

"Who is they?"

"We're talking about Rossi's, of course."

He chuckled. "It's not *they* anymore. It's you. I'm sure you'll figure it out. I have faith. Come to me with a plan, and I'll consider it. Nobody else out there is going to give you money without a plan. That's not the way the world works."

Faith was in short supply on his end of the phone line tonight.

"Your mother's getting dinner ready here, so if that's all, I'll talk to you in a few days." He hung up.

Why wouldn't he want daily updates if there were big problems?

Something had changed. I'd been dropped off the cruise liner and into a leaky dinghy in the middle of a storm, and I had no idea why. This was worse than his usual tests.

With nothing much in the fridge, I ordered a pizza and sat down with another glass of wine to go over the financials again.

Instead of focusing on the papers, my mind wandered back to last night. For the first time in my life, I'd slept with a girl I hadn't fucked first. Sure, I'd woken up wrapped around a girl before, but not with blue balls.

I wasn't a cuddler by nature, but that's all we'd done. After promising to keep her safe, I couldn't have refused her request to join me without making myself a liar, and I wasn't ever going there.

Then my mind moved to today. Nicole officially hated me after the deal Dad and her uncle had put together.

With my transfer to London looming at some point, it wouldn't matter much anyway.

Later that evening, when I gave up and turned in for the night, my bed was a cold, inhospitable place. The scared girl who'd climbed under the covers with me last night had provided a warmth that was missing now. We'd shared a different kind of intimacy.

Me, a cuddler? No fucking way in hell, so how did I explain missing her tonight?

It didn't much matter. Her look when she'd walked out today had said it all. She hated my guts. Good thing there hadn't been any sharp objects within reach.

CHAPTER 12

Nicole

I got up Tuesday morning almost as exhausted as when I'd climbed between the sheets. Even turning up my sound machine hadn't drowned out the words that ran through my mind all night: "*We sold the company. It was either that or pink slips all around.*" Ernst's words had stabbed me in the heart.

Lara had been right. I'd given him the benefit of the doubt too many times. This shitfest was entirely of his making. He'd refused to diversify our banking. And, to have his own stepdaughter arrested on embezzlement charges without any proof? Who could do that? I wasn't sure fuckhead was strong enough for him.

Between being pissed at Ernst for selling out in the blink of an eye, it occurred to me while I was showering that Lara's situation had taken a total backseat.

She was facing serious jail time—make that prison time—and I hadn't given her a second thought last night. After reading the sale contract yesterday, Rossi's had been my only focus. She deserved better from me—a lot better, after everything she'd been through—and I was determined to help with that.

I could still remember Lara's face five years ago, the day she'd come running into the house after finding her boyfriend, Vern, stabbed to death in our orchard among the almond trees. She'd been covered in his blood, mumbling incoherently about how she shouldn't have left him alone. The drinking that had followed that day, and led later to drugs, had turned into an out-of-control spiral for a while.

It had taken time, but I'd stuck with her and pushed her to get better. The second stint in rehab had held, and she'd improved tremendously since then. Until this latest brush with the law, she'd seemed to have finally gotten herself straightened out. The job at Rossi's had provided focus and grounded her back in reality—a reality with a hopeful outlook. She hadn't mentioned Vern in over a year.

Now, without that job, what pattern would she fall back into?

Brushing aside that concern for now, I checked myself in the mirror and went downstairs.

Echo came bounding out of his bed to greet me, but I pushed at his head and kept him at a distance. Yellow Labradors were great dogs, but the shedding was a constant battle. Echo gave up his quest for more pats and trotted out the doggy door. Chasing squirrels and digging would be more fun than we were likely to be.

I'd be going into the Rossi's office for the last time today. A chat with Rosa, sign a few papers, and that portion of my life would be over.

~

THE BUILDING WAS REMARKABLY QUIET WHEN I ARRIVED. PEOPLE WERE AT THEIR desks with their heads down, working—none of the usual early-morning conversations I was accustomed to. They were probably putting on a good show for the new boss, either that or scared shitless that the monster in the corner office would reorganize them all out of a job.

Ernst's nameplate had already been removed from beside his door, and it now read Josh Benson. The door was open. I backtracked to make the approach to my office from a different angle, so I wouldn't be seen by Benson.

Having him know I was here was not on my wish list for today. It took a moment to locate the file in my desk with the stupid non-compete document Ernst had made us all sign. *"It's what all the big companies do,"* he'd said. Ten minutes of arguing about the value of the practice had gone nowhere, and I'd signed, along with everyone else. It had been the price that day of getting him out of my, *our* hair. Things always ran smoother when he wasn't around.

I'd never been able to predict whether on any individual day he'd be in a questioning mood, which slowed us down minimally, or wanting to be "helpful" with the stupidest ideas this side of Jupiter. Those days were harder because it took more time to stop stupid than it did to answer dumb.

Someone knocked on my door before I got a chance to read the file.

"Come in," I called.

It was Josh. He waltzed in and sat across from me with a smile. "I'm glad you changed your mind about staying."

I held up a hand to stop him. "I didn't."

His eyes narrowed, and he nodded thoughtfully. "Hmm... This office is reserved for the COO. I guess I'm going to have to charge you rent if you still want to use it."

"Very funny. I only came in for my exit interview."

"We really could use your help."

"I'm sure a smart USC grad from a big conglomerate like Benson Corp. can handle a tiny little backwater company such as this with one arm tied behind your back."

He grinned. "Nicole, I think I need the help of a Stanford grad."

I didn't feel like being on a first name basis with him anymore. "Look, Benson, what do you want from me? You've taken my family's company, and I have no stomach to watch you dismember it."

He leaned forward. "Let's get this straight, Rossi. I had nothing to do with the purchase of your company. Your boss came to my dad with a cash-flow problem and suggested we buy him out."

That said it all. The fuckhead had been the driver behind this.

"Be that as it may," he added after a moment. "The deal's been done, and it's up to me...up to *us* to make it work."

I saw my opening. "The only way I see for *us* to make this work is for you to exercise your right of rescission and provide bridge financing for us while we go find another bank."

"And how does that benefit me, and Benson?"

It was my turn to lean in as the aggressor. "It would keep you from failing. It would keep your company and family from being vilified for destroying a California institution, along with the lives of everyone working here."

He laughed. He fucking laughed in my face. "I don't fail, and I'm offering you a chance to be part of the success."

I rose. "Pardon me. I have an exit interview to attend. I don't work for arrogant pricks." I gathered my purse. "Or losers." I stepped around him on my way to Rosa's.

"This isn't over, Nicole," he barked.

I turned at the door. "Yes, it is, Mr. Benson." As I continued through the workspace, I felt the weight of many eyeballs on me. The offices weren't as soundproof as they should be.

Rosa's office was down the back hallway, away from the commotion I'd just been part of. Thankfully, her door was open and she was at her desk.

I closed the door behind me. "I came in as soon as I could."

"You didn't need to rush. And first, Mr. Benson wants to have a talk with you about staying on. Personally, I think you should listen to him."

I rolled my eyes, less professionally than I should have. "We talked."

"And?"

"And nothing. He talked. I listened. No change."

She looked over her glasses at me with a crease between her brows. "You're sure?"

I nodded. "Positive."

I hadn't been as positive about anything since the day I'd turned down Marty Feldstein for the junior prom. The boy's mother had fixed him sardine sandwiches with garlic mayo for lunch, and he'd smelled all afternoon, every afternoon. I knew because I had the misfortune of being his lab partner in chemistry class.

Rosa slid over a set of papers. "These are about your COBRA option for continuing health insurance."

That was another detail I hadn't considered in my admittedly rash decision to leave. The dollar numbers for individual and family coverage were pretty large. "Are these quarterly or annual payments?"

Rosa didn't roll her eyes at my mistake, but her frown told me I'd gotten it wrong. "Monthly," she replied.

I took in a breath and swallowed. "Do I need to sign this now?"

"You can take it with you. You have thirty days to decide. The next item is a bit more complicated." She handed me a folder. "The non-compete agreement. You'll want to read this carefully."

"I already signed it."

"Now you're signing that we've reviewed it and you understand everything."

I opened the file and started reading the agreement from two years ago. I hadn't remembered how restrictive it was. The sentences started out bad and only got worse.

> The employee may not accept employment with any competitive enterprise, whether for profit or non-profit, within the eighteen months following termination from the company.

That was the bad part. Somehow I'd remembered six months, not eighteen. A year and a half was an eternity to not be able to work. A worse sentence came lower down.

> This prohibition applies to employment as a statutory employee, or work performed as an independent contractor, or employment with any enterprise that performs services for a competitive enterprise.

I reread that one three times. It seemed to mean I couldn't work at a bank or accounting firm, or even a janitorial firm that did any business at all with anyone who handled food. This just kept getting worse and worse. I wanted to throttle the lawyer who wrote this piece of garbage. And the bad news kept coming.

> Any company engaged in the sale, production, preparation, or distribution of foodstuffs of any kind shall be deemed by default to be a competitive enterprise.

That threw a pretty wide net and meant I couldn't work at Walmart or Target, or even a gas station mini-mart. Or fast food, now that I thought about it. Goodbye to my one-time ambition to manage a McDonald's franchise.

The worst sentence, however, was at the bottom of the page.

> For employment at any enterprise not covered above, the employee must submit a request in writing to Tuscan Foods. The determination as to whether the proposed employment violates this agreement shall be at the sole discretion of the management of Tuscan Foods.

"This seems to say that I have to get you guys to sign off on any job I want to take."

She nodded cheerfully. "Pretty much. But Mr. Berg approved them all."

She omitted the obvious observation that Benson was now in charge.

Just great. Now I'd insulted the man who held the key to the handcuffs on my employment search.

Good going, Rossi.

"Then there's also the matter of your education loans."

I felt light-headed at the mention of the education debt I'd racked up at Stanford. It had been taken care of by the company.

Rosa slid over another piece of paper. "A requirement of the loan is that the monthly payment be an automatic bank transfer."

The outstanding balance was still huge times ten, and since it had been set up by the company with the bank, it had been short term with large monthly payments. At the time, the idea was that since the company was picking up the tab, I'd be out from under the loans quickly. Being out of Rossi's and having to pay the loan myself had never been on my radar.

There was no way I could handle this for more than a month or two without a job. And after that, it would have to be a well-paying one to stay afloat.

"You know this would all go away if you stayed," Rosa said, prodding me once more. "I think your uncle did a really good job with this."

"If he'd done a good job, we wouldn't be selling the company," I shot back.

She scowled. "That's not fair. From what Mrs. Quantell told me, we'd have run out of money this week if he hadn't persuaded the Bensons to come in. Then we'd all be on the street." She pointed at me. "And what I meant was that your uncle negotiated an exceptionally generous retention agreement for you, one you should be thanking him for."

Feeling the glare of her criticism, I replied, "I appreciate the effort. I just don't feel right staying."

"I understand, dear." She offered me a pen. "So we need to give them an account number to pull the loan payments from."

My hand shook as I held the pen over the boxes to write my bank account number.

CHAPTER 13

Nicole

Rosa tapped a finger on the retention agreement folder in front of her. "Maybe you need some time to think about your decision."

I stared at the paper with the six-digit loan balance.

"Have you read the retention agreement?" she asked.

I shook my head. "No need. I'm not staying." I put the pen to the paper and wrote the first digits of my account number.

"Did you realize that it pays off this loan for you at the end of six months?"

I pulled the pen up and cocked my head. I couldn't have heard her right. "Did you say…?"

A smile broadened across her face. "Nicole, let's go over it so you understand what you're walking away from before you dismiss it out of hand."

I couldn't be bought. It was a temptation I had to resist.

"It's what your father would have done," she said.

I looked up from the paper. Invoking Daddy was a low blow. "He never would have sold. He wouldn't want to be part of destroying what we built," I argued.

"He wouldn't make a decision like you have to make without understanding the ramifications, is what I meant."

I took a breath. "Of course. You're right." It didn't mean I was agreeing to help Benson undo everything we'd accomplished, but Rosa had a point. Daddy would have been disappointed in me if I couldn't articulate the pros and cons of a decision. "What's in it?"

"It's long, and I think you should read it through, but the short version financially is that the company will continue your current salary and benefits, including the loan payments. At the end of six months, you will receive a two-hundred-thousand-dollar bonus—"

"Cash?" I asked, interrupting her.

"Yes, cash, and the company will assume all remaining liability for your educational loans. You wouldn't owe anything after that, and your COBRA health insurance payments would also be borne by the company for an additional year."

I nodded. "That sounds like a lot."

"It is, and I know Mr. Benson would love to hear that you're agreeing to stay."

I sat back in my chair. Another thing Daddy would have told me is not to make a snap decision. "I haven't agreed, yet."

She nodded at my adding *yet* to my answer. "It also doesn't allow Mr. Benson to terminate you without cause. And this is the good part: they can't diminish your duties either."

"So they can't fire me a month early and keep me from getting the money?"

Rosa nodded. "Or getting the education loan paid off. Nicole, it's only six months."

The numbers were huge, and I was tempted. I was seriously considering selling Benson my soul. Did that mean I was the same as a prostitute of sorts? And we were only haggling about the price? What would Daddy think of that? Would he have allowed his daughter, his only child, to become a corporate whore to the Bensons?

It was too much to process. The retention agreement deserved a thoughtful reading. But I'd have to put up with Benson's idiocy for six months. Merge us with Smith's? How could anyone have a worse idea?

I rose from the chair and gathered the papers she'd given me. "I'll think about it."

"That's a good idea," Rosa replied with a genuine smile.

Josh

Rosa arrived at my open door. "Mr. Benson?"

"Please, let's make it Josh."

She nodded. "I wanted to tell you Nicole stopped in this morning."

I didn't care to acknowledge my disappointment. "And did she budge when you mentioned the retention bonus?"

Rosa had suggested yesterday that she thought Nicole might be overreacting.

"Not exactly, but I think you might be able to persuade her."

I *tsk*ed. "So far she hasn't shown a willingness to listen."

I could understand her position. I'd certainly take it personally if somebody bought out Benson Corp.

"I thought it worth mentioning—a lot of people here identify quite closely with her," Rosa added.

I nodded. This created an open threat to ongoing operations and a smooth transition if Nicole worked against me rather than for me.

My work would be cut out for me. "Thanks, Rosa, I'll try."

She nodded her head toward the door. "She's in her office now."

Nicole

Returning to my office, I ran into Gary Fontaine, our controller.

"Is it true?" he asked. "They want to merge us with Smith's?"

"I don't know," I responded. "I doubt it." Those words came more from hope than what I knew. I touched him on the shoulder. "It'll be okay."

His face didn't brighten the way it would have if he'd believed what I'd said.

"There's another problem you should know about," he added.

I backed away. "Gary, I don't have time right now. Sorry."

It hurt to see the dejected look on his face as he turned.

As if that wasn't bad enough, I ran into Jenny from marketing as well before I could reach the safety of my office door. Our conversation wasn't identical, but the concerns were.

These people had depended on me to provide a safe working environment for them. They'd given us years of service. What was I now giving them in return? Was I running away from the fight instead of giving them back the loyalty they'd given us over the years?

I assured Jenny the Smith's rumor wasn't true. That would go a long way in reassuring everyone else. Telling Jenny something was better than using a megaphone. She was queen of the gossip mill.

My office was only a few feet away when the next employee caught my eye and started toward me.

Like a coward, I turned away from her, stepped into my office, and closed the door. I couldn't lie to another one of them about how things would be okay. After rounding my desk, I collapsed into the chair.

This was so fucked up. I was fucked seven ways from Sunday—a debt I couldn't pay, a lien on my house because Lara had been accused of embezzling from the company, and a stupid non-compete agreement that Ernst had insisted upon.

I couldn't even work at a McDonald's without fucking Benson's approval. Maybe I could get a job selling T-shirts and sunglasses to tourists on Venice Beach, just so long as the shop didn't also sell soda pop or Tic-Tacs.

I ignored the knock at my door. Dealing with anybody after Gary and Jenny held no appeal.

After a second knock, the handle turned, and the door opened slightly.

"Nicole?" Josh said through the crack. "Are you decent?"

I quickly considered taking off my top to keep him out. "No," I lied. It would be a quick and dirty defense against the man, but it wouldn't last. "I mean yes."

The door opened and he slid inside, closing it quickly behind him and putting a hand up. "Just hear me out before you say anything."

I nodded wordlessly, unsure what exactly I wanted to say to him anyway. It was all such a jumble in my head—the impossibility of my position if I left, the feeling of letting everyone down if I abandoned them. How could I balance that against the pain I'd feel coming in here day after day and watching what we'd built being destroyed?

He took the visitor's chair opposite mine. "I'm not good at asking for help."

The man had all the power. What the hell did he need help with?

If I held more cards than I realized, I intended to use them. "I'm listening," I said coyly.

He leaned back in his chair and ran a hand through his hair. "How's Lara, by the way?"

"Uh..." Caught off balance by his question, I searched for the right words. "She's dealing with it."

"Embezzlement is a pretty heavy charge," he said as he steepled his hands. The balance of power in the room had certainly shifted if he knew that. "Are you two headed off to Brazil now?"

If he thought attacking my family was the right way to go, he was in for a surprise

"She didn't do it."

He nodded. "And how easy is it going to be to prove that if you leave?"

This man was a better negotiator than I could've guessed. He'd just added a major argument in his favor that I hadn't seen coming.

"I'm not sure I'm leaving." It wasn't a commitment to stay, but it was true.

"That right there's the difference between Stanford and USC."

"How so?" I asked, not sure where this was going.

He stood. "You Stanford people are all about theory, never dealing with the real world, and as a result, not ever making up your mind. At USC they taught us that indecision was by far the worst decision."

"And at USC they give you classes in *rationalizing* companies," I spit out the word with all the disdain I felt for treating people as mere statistics.

"It's not like that, and you know it."

"Isn't it?"

He took a deep breath. "Are you going to stay and have an impact? Keep me from making bad choices?"

That there was the crux of it. As much as I hated the idea of working with Mr. Rationalizer, I might be able to make some of his decisions less bad for our people.

"It's just..." I began.

He raised a hand to stop me. "*Just* is one of those weasel words. I didn't engineer this purchase, and you know that. I'm stuck here the same as you. You can either stay here and help, or leave and bitch about it. Me, I plan on making this work for everybody."

I opened my mouth, but his finger pointed right at me stopped me from speaking.

"And exactly what have I done to make you doubt me?" he asked with an accusing glare.

"I just haven't read the retention agreement," I answered, tapping the papers in front of me.

"There's that weasel word again. You Stanford grads are all alike." He walked to the door and opened it before turning back to me. "Remember Sioux City? My actions should tell you all you need to know about me. In five minutes I expect you in my office ready to get to work." He checked his watch. "If you're not, your actions will tell me everything I need to know about you." The door closed behind him, and I was alone with nothing but a dilemma staring me in the face.

I shivered in my chair. The man had laid down a challenge with all the subtlety of a rhinoceros.

If I didn't stay, not only was I abandoning the people here, he'd insinuated I wouldn't be doing all I could to clear Lara. Those were fighting words.

His question about what he'd done to make me doubt him answered itself. There was nothing except my anger at the situation. He could have left me in Sioux City; instead he'd gone out of his way to bring me home so I could rescue Lara from county lockup. He'd kept me safe Sunday night after my house had been broken into. He'd kept me from freaking out during the plane emergency. What was not to trust—except that the man worked for a company that wanted to dismantle mine.

Josh

I CLOSED THE DOOR TO NICOLE'S OFFICE BEHIND ME. HARD.

I moved down the hallway, only to discover that Rosa had taken up residence in my office again.

"Mr. Benson—sorry, Josh, I mean. We have another problem."

Somehow that didn't surprise me. This place was nonstop problems. "What now?"

What had Dad been drinking when he'd agreed to buy this place?

"Stephanie Quantell has left, and she's not coming back."

I sat down, trying to control the steam that was probably coming out of my ears. "Does nobody around here understand the concept of giving two weeks' notice?"

First Rossi, and now whoever Quantell was.

Rosa's sheepish expression made me regret my tone. "Sorry. I don't mean to take it out on you. Who is Ms. Quantell, and what does she do for us?"

"She is…was the CFO."

The bad news kept getting worse. When I looked up, Nicole was at my door.

"Stephanie?" Nicole asked.

Rosa turned in her seat to address Nicole. "She called to say she's not coming back in."

Nicole walked in to join us. "That's a bullshit thing to do." She threw her retention agreement on my desk. "Signed."

I slid it across to Rosa without bothering to check the back page for her signature. "File this, please."

Rosa picked up the papers. "With pleasure."

"And I'd like a copy as well," Nicole added.

Rosa stood. "I imagine you two have a lot to talk about."

A few seconds later, the door closed behind Rosa, leaving me alone in the office with Nicole.

At last I'd caught a break.

Nicole

Josh had tried to hide it, but he'd breathed an obvious sigh of relief when my papers landed on his desk.

Now I knew something about him I hadn't known before. He wanted me to stay, but was a bit of a poker player. His bluster in my office a few minutes ago had been part playacting. That was something I'd have to file away for another day. I might have more leverage than I'd guessed.

Quiet enveloped the room after Rosa left, and the two of us sized each other up.

If there was one thing Daddy had taught me about business, it was not to show weakness. Josh had started the staring contest, but I wasn't backing down.

I held those pale blues with my own gaze until a slight curve appeared at the ends of his lips. I'd won the initial contest.

"So how's this going to work?" I asked.

He placed his elbows on the desk and leaned forward. "I'd say the first order of business is to keep the ship from sinking. I'd like this Quantell lady to be the last departure."

"Her name was Stephanie, not Quantell lady, and she's a friend of mine. You've rocked the boat in a pretty big way and made everybody nervous."

"And it's your job to reassure them."

"My job?"

"They work for you, don't they? Most of them, at least?"

This was going to be a big problem if he kept referring to everybody here as *them*.

I gritted my teeth. "This isn't some case study like in your pretty little business strategy books. Those are real people out there, a real organization. In assigning tasks, shit may flow downhill to the little people, but company morale is one of those responsibilities that floats to the top." I pointed at him. "And that makes it your problem." I stood and paced to the door.

"Where are you going?" he asked.

I turned. "To do my job."

"You do that, while I work on the minor problem of making sure the bank account doesn't run dry tomorrow." His voice dripped with sarcasm.

"And, to reassure *our* people that you're not about to fire them all." I reached for the door handle. "I can tell them that, right?"

"Business as usual."

I shut the door behind me.

Every eye in the room found mine.

Jenny's eyes pleaded with me, and I strode in her direction. She'd be my first stop.

I gave her a genuine smile and a thumbs up before I reached her.

The relief that grew in her expression was the payoff I needed.

My *business as usual* message would percolate fastest if she and a few others were the first to hear it.

"I'm staying," I started. "Nothing's changing." I didn't add the obvious words—*for now*. Nothing in business was ever completely static.

Her face lit up.

Now I was irrevocably committed. Changing my mind with Benson wouldn't bother me. But recanting after assuring these people, my extended family, that I was staying would not be happening.

CHAPTER 14

Josh

First things first: plugging the financial holes in the leaky ship. I opened the door to my office to find an older redhead sitting outside at the desk that had previously been unoccupied.

She stood and extended her hand. "You must be Mr. Benson."

I took it. "Josh will do."

"Sorry, Mr. B. I was out yesterday and this morning. Tommy, that's my grandson, had a fever, and his mother couldn't watch him. Mr. Berg said it was okay."

This wasn't getting me anywhere.

"And what do you do for us?"

"Oh, I'm your secretary, Deandra. But everybody just calls me Dee. I mean, I'm yours and Nicky's, but of course you come first. And I don't mind the term. I grew up with it and actually prefer it. These days the girls want to be called personal assistants, but that sounds to me like somebody who helps you get dressed in the morning. I don't want somebody thinking I help you tie your shoes, if you know what I mean."

I nodded. "I see the problem, Dee." I rubbed my chin and lowered my voice to a whisper. "But secretary is a bit outdated. How about we call you a PO instead of PA. Personal Organizer."

A broad smile grew on Dee's face. "PO. I can live with that. Mr. B's PO. I like the sound of that."

"And Nicky's too. Can't forget Nicky. And no shoe tying. I promise."

Dee nodded. "Right. Phone?" She held out her hand. "I'll add everybody's numbers for you."

I handed over the device. "I'm told Stephanie Quantell has left us, and I need to talk to whoever is most senior in finance now."

Her smile betrayed her when I said Quantell had left. Quantell hadn't been universally liked. There was a story there somewhere.

"That would be Gary, Gary Fontaine. He's the controller."

"Could you round him up for me, please?"

"Sure, Mr. B."

I squinted at her. "Josh."

"I'm old fashioned, Mr. B."

I wasn't going to win this one, so I nodded before retreating to my office. "Thanks, Dee."

Nicky. I'd have to decide if I liked that nickname for Nicole or not.

An almost teenage-looking guy arrived scarcely a minute later. "You wanted to see me?"

"Gary?"

"Yes, sir."

I tried to keep my disappointment from showing. He'd likely only started shaving last year and was clearly not seasoned enough to step into the CFO role. Meeting him mid-room, we shook. "Josh will do." Correcting them all on what to call me was going to be routine here, it seemed. "Nice to meet you, Gary. I need to know what our cash position is."

He grimaced. "Before or after payroll?"

"After."

"Twenty-three thousand in the bank."

"And what else do we have?"

He shook his head. "That's it."

"Credit line?"

"It maxed out last week."

I collapsed into my seat. "This place can't run with that little." A company this size running on fumes would collapse in a second if any of the suppliers found out the till was that empty.

His chest puffed up as if I'd awarded him a medal. "That's what I've been saying."

"To who? Saying to who?"

"My boss. Mrs. Quantell. But she—"

I stopped him. "She's gone."

His brows rose in disbelief. "Gone?"

She apparently hadn't bothered to tell any of her staff—not a classy move.

"You fired her?"

"She quit."

"What do we do now?"

This kid was certainly not cut out to run the finance operation.

I opened my bag and pulled out my checkbook. "I'll get somebody to fill in. Until then, bring me anything important that you can't handle. In the meantime…" I wrote a check to Tuscan Foods. "I want you to deposit this at the bank right now." I signed the check, tore it out, and handed it over.

"Two million?" he asked with wide eyes.

"Not enough?" I asked.

"No, this is good," he said, rereading the check.

"Get going, then, and don't worry, it's good."

He scurried toward the door.

"One more thing, Gary."

He turned.

I opened my mouth but shut it in time. "Nothing important. Let's go over last quarter's numbers when you get back."

I'd considered asking him what he knew about the embezzlement issue with Nicole's cousin, but decided against it for the moment.

"Sure. I won't be long."

Dee entered as Gary left. "All done," she announced, handing me my phone.

"Thanks." I closed the office door after her for my call back to the mothership.

"Are we having fun yet?" Harold Snyderman asked when he picked up.

"Loads." I didn't care to waste any time getting to the point. "The CFO has left, and I need somebody to replace her."

"Personally, I'd have her show either the controller or treasurer the ropes as acting CFO so you can conduct a proper search for somebody permanent. The CFO is your most important hire."

As a finance guy, himself, it made sense he'd see it that way, but the marketing and operating people would have a different view.

"She's already gone, and the controller is too wet behind the ears for the job. I need to borrow somebody from Benson."

"I'll have to think about who has the time."

I knew who I wanted. "I'll take Sandman for a while."

George Sandman and I had worked well together in the past.

Harold's sigh over the phone told me he knew I'd escalate this to Dad if I needed to. "He probably makes the most sense. I'll call him and get back to you."

I thanked Harold, and we got off the phone without me having to admit I'd written a personal check to keep the company afloat this week. That would have had him advocating exercise of the rescission clause I'd been specifically told not to use.

Moving to the slit of a window in this office, I pulled back the curtain. The view of parked cars a dozen feet away was a far cry from my vista twenty stories up at the Benson building. I closed the curtain again.

My next call was to Dad.

"What's up?" he asked upon answering.

"I'd like to talk again about a capital infusion for this place."

"No need."

I let out a breath. I'd finally caught a break. "Good. I think I can make it work with twenty."

"No, there's no need to discuss it again. I already gave you my answer. Make it work with what you have. I'm sure you can handle it. It's a small business, just like what I started with. Small businesses like that are the backbone of this country. They're what make everything go. Feel free to ask Harold or Tony if you need advice."

Bringing up that I'd commandeered a CFO from Harold wasn't the right move right now, lest it get countermanded.

A few seconds later he was off the line, and I was left unsure what I'd done to deserve this treatment. It wasn't like I'd forgotten his birthday or anything.

No resources and a platitude that small businesses were the backbone of the country. If that was true, the country needed a back brace.

Nicole

. . .

I'D SPENT THE MORNING MOSTLY SHORING UP MORALE WITH CHATS AROUND THE building when my phone alarm went off. It was time.

Dee was back at her desk, and Josh's door was closed.

"Who's he got in there?"

"Just Gary."

I knocked, and when his muffled response didn't sound like *go away*, I opened the door.

Gary and Josh were huddled over reports at the small conference table.

Josh looked my way.

"Time to go," I told him.

He checked his watch with a quizzical look. "I wasn't aware we had anything scheduled."

"You said business as usual," I responded.

"It's Tuesday," Gary told him. "You have lunch with Nicole."

Josh didn't look any less confused.

"Second Tuesday lunch," I explained. "You want everything to run as it has been. This is part of the schedule. Let's get going."

Josh gave up the battle and stood.

I tried to hide my smile.

Gary stood. "I'm available after lunch if you want to continue this."

"I'll let you know," Josh replied as he wiggled into his suit coat.

Gary left us.

"You won't need the coat, and you might want to lose the tie," I advised him.

"I'm fine, thanks."

As we left, Josh told Dee he'd be back after lunch.

"Sure, Mr. B," she replied with her usual cheeriness.

"Josh," he said.

"Sure, Mr. B," she said again.

We left the building, and he turned right toward employee parking. "Why can't I get her to call me Josh?"

"Looks to me like you made an impression. She insisted on calling Ernst 'Mr. Berg.' She hasn't called anybody by an initial since she called my father Mr. R.

"I'm honored." He checked his watch.

"You should be." I stopped by my car. "This is mine. I'll drive."

He eyed my rust bucket. "How about I drive you?" He urged me on with a hand at the small of my back. His touch almost made me jump.

I gave up and moved along. "What, don't trust a woman driver?"

His huff told me I'd hit the nail on the head, which wasn't hard. No guy liked being driven around.

"Call it boss's prerogative," he said.

I walked with him in silence, still feeling the lingering heat where he'd touched me.

He took my hand for a second and pulled me to a stop by a white Cadillac Escalade. "This is it."

His touch left me speechless. The car fit him—big, imposing, and muscular. But I wasn't focused on that. Instead, it was that electric feeling again.

He unlocked the beast.

After a deep, calming breath, I climbed up into the passenger seat. The vision of him at the table in Barbados, looking my way as I answered the call from Lara, ran through my consciousness. If I hadn't fallen in the pool that night, would I have felt his touch earlier? Where would I have felt his touch? He'd pulled me through the airport in Sioux City, but today it felt different. Was California the difference?

"Which way?" he asked, pulling me out of my reverie.

He'd started backing out of the parking space, and my mind was fifteen seconds behind, still caught up in my daydream.

I looked toward the street, avoiding his gaze for fear I'd freeze up again. "Right, and left at the light."

"You okay?"

I got up the courage to look at him and smile. "Yeah."

"Thinking about Lara?"

Unable to tell him what I'd actually been thinking, I went with the lie. "Uh-huh. She's had it tough."

"Want to talk about it?"

I fidgeted for a second. "Maybe later." Somehow we'd gone from business to personal, and I didn't know how. "What do you care, anyway?"

His jaw clenched.

I looked away. My big mouth had gotten me into trouble. Where was my brain-to-mouth filter when I needed it most?

He pulled to the curb after the next intersection.

I looked away, half expecting to be told to get out for being so rude.

He cut the engine. "Look at me."

I turned.

"I thought we got past this, but apparently not," he growled. "What, exactly, is your problem with me?"

"It's not you exactly. It's what you're doing."

"Then what, *exactly,* am I doing?" he demanded.

"The company is my family, and my parents' legacy. It's all I have."

"I get that."

I took a bigger breath. "You and your family are taking it from us, and it's not fair."

There, I'd said it. The unfairness of it all is what grated on me the most. Ernst had fucked everything up.

"That's bull, and you know it."

"Is it? We had a perfectly stable company, and all of the sudden it's gone, and you're talking about merging it with Smith's. Smith's? That name shouldn't even be used in the same sentence with grocery."

"If we hadn't come in this week, the company would be shutting down today. You went to business school. No cash, no business—it's as simple as that."

"We have cash," I spat. I'd checked a few months ago, and two million was available and ready for the Redondo store remodel, after we finished the Pasadena store. Ernst had told me the issue was with the bank.

"*Had* cash. But not anymore. This morning there was only twenty-seven thousand in the bank."

My mouth dropped open. It wasn't possible. "You're wrong. That has to be wrong."

"I wrote a two-million-dollar personal check this morning to keep the company running."

"You what?" I asked softly.

He slapped his forehead. "Are all you Stanford girls hard of hearing? The bank account was down to empty, and I wrote a check to keep things running."

Processing this was impossible, and I only had one response that fit. "Thank you."

He started the engine again. "Now, are you going to help me save the Rossi's chain, or do I have to do it by myself?" He pulled away from the curb.

How could that much money go missing? "I don't understand."

He gunned it through the next light. "Simple. Your uncle—"

"Step-uncle," I corrected him, which, judging by his expression, hadn't been wise.

"Whatever… He flew too close to the flame and got burned. He was stupid."

I wasn't going to argue with that.

We passed another intersection.

I pointed. "It's two blocks up on the right."

"Which restaurant?"

"Park in the Rossi's parking lot."

We pulled in and parked.

I unbuckled and slid out of my seat as soon as he stopped.

"Wait up," he said as he shut down the engine.

"Yes, boss." I closed my door and tapped my foot while waiting by the side of the car.

After locking the big ride, he walked around to meet me.

"It's this way."

He put a hand against the car, blocking my path. "Hold it."

I glared up at him. "What now?"

He returned my stare with equal intensity. "As much as I enjoy correcting a Stanford grad, this needs to be the end of it."

"End of what?" I asked, transferring my weight after making the mistake of shifting my gaze for a moment to that scar on his chin.

He moved forward, backing me against the car, until there were mere inches between us. "Of you questioning my motives. If you want to walk away, fine. But if you stay, we're a team with a capital T, both working for the good of Rossi's. You need to back me up, not cut me down. I'll always be honest with you and always work for the good of the company. That's a promise."

The words were cold, harsh, but his breath against me was hot. Those pale blue eyes held mine.

He moved an inch closer. "Well?"

I searched his eyes for deception or malice. I had to decide if the man I'd clung to in Sioux City was truly on my side. "I just thought…"

His face hardened. He caged me with a hand on either side and moved even closer. "No wishy-washy filler words, Stanford. You trust me or you don't. I'm in this to make things right. You're either with me or you're not. Make up your mind."

CHAPTER 15

Josh

"I trust you," Nicole said. The scared eyes of a moment ago had shifted to calm and determined, almost happy eyes. She bit her lip, placed a hand on my chest, and pushed gently.

The electric feel of her touch against my shirt surprised me. I'd gotten way too far into her personal space, but I needed to corner her into a decision—one she couldn't back down from or put off. Damn, if the girl didn't make me want to get even closer.

I backed away. "Good. We're a *team*. Don't forget that." It would have been so easy to kiss her right then and there—so easy, and so wrong. But my sense was that she wanted it, almost expected it.

Her eyes closed momentarily as she took a slow breath—confirmation this had been intense for her as well. Had she wanted it, or feared it? She was a dangerous minx, this one, with more than a hint of desire in her eyes.

"Which restaurant?" I asked, shoving my nervous hands into my pockets.

"This way," she said as she started off.

I followed, which gave me a moment to admire her walk and the sway of her ass without her noticing.

She turned into the Rossi's front doors. "We'll start with a tour of the store."

It was larger than I'd imagined, bright and airy. "Where are we eating?"

"We'll get to that. First we'll look around a little.

The name tags they wore were my saving grace.

The store manager, Wanda, had been waiting for us and was the second person Nicole introduced me to.

"Wanda, I'm just going to give Mr. B a tour of the store before we go upstairs."

"Sure thing. I'll meet you up there," Wanda replied.

Nicole led me to the left, stopping to introduce an endless parade of people I couldn't possibly keep straight. She had taken it upon herself to decide the employees should address me the same way Dee did: Mr. B.

I went through at least a dozen *nice to meet you*s in the produce section. And I learned that the proper term was *associates*, not employees.

"The state requires stores to label the country of origin," Nicole explained. "We list both the region and the individual farm for all stateside produce."

As we passed the apples, I noticed not only more varieties than I was used to, but groupings by farm within the same variety. "Do customers care?"

Nicole's face instantly telegraphed that I'd asked an absurd question. "Our guests do."

Another lesson, this store didn't have *customers*, it had *guests*.

Silly me to think an apple was an apple.

"Look inside the door of your car," she said. "It'll tell you where it was made. Why is food any less important?"

I nodded. "Good point."

Everything was organized and displayed in a more artful fashion than mere shelves and piles.

I checked my watch as we started down the food aisles.

"Somewhere important to be?" Nicole asked with obvious sarcasm.

"I have to get back to Gary."

She waited for a shopper to pass by. "Maybe they didn't teach you this at USC, but a company is more than spreadsheets and numbers; it's people." She spun, but only got two steps before turning back to me again. "Now show your people the respect they deserve, and stop checking your watch like you can't wait to get out of here."

I took off my watch and slid it into my jacket pocket. "Happy?"

"I'm always happy," she said before waving to an associate. "Maisy, I'd like you to meet our new boss, Mr. B." Nicole's pleasant smile was back in place.

I introduced myself, while filing away that *"I'm always happy"* comment. It didn't ring true for me.

As we continued through the store, it struck me that the supermarket closest to my place had aisles barely wide enough for two carts to pass each other. These were much more spacious, and the shelving wasn't all straight-line monotony either. Curves had been integrated into some of the displays. The sheer variety of mustards we passed was way beyond what I was used to.

Nicole was in her element here, and it was a joy to watch her explain. She was animated, engaged, and more than just knowledgeable—she was happy to talk about the store. This was the girl I'd spied on the beach in Barbados, before everything had gone wrong for her. Coming into the store had transformed her, or maybe it was because we'd gotten past our argument outside the car.

I found myself paying less attention to what she was saying, and more attention to the way she said it—her animated hands, her genuine smile as she met the associates and introduced them. And, watching her boobs bounce and her ass sway with her energetic walk wasn't bad either. This was miles better than time with Gary.

So much was emanating from her visually that I missed most of the words.

"Are you ready?" she asked.

I hadn't caught the question. I shrugged and gave myself a mental slap for letting her distract me.

"For the tasting?"

"I'm sorry. Tasting?"

We'd just passed through the buffet section of the deli where customers—or rather guests—were scooping up food, and Nicole started up the stairs to the mezzanine seating area she'd pointed out.

"Yes, the food rotation," she said. "That's one of your responsibilities."

A tasting wasn't one of the responsibilities on your average CEO's task list.

Following her up the stairs, with her ass right in front of me, I lost my concentration. This wasn't me. It was something about her that made it impossible for me to compartmentalize the way I normally could. I'd always been able to keep preoccupation with a woman's body parts to after business hours.

"Can you explain that again?" I asked.

"I told you, we change up the offerings in the deli periodically, and you do a taste test to pick the ones we add."

It sounded like something I didn't want to fuck up. "Maybe you should do that," I told her.

She stopped me at the top of the stairs. "This is your job. Chef Bob would be insulted if you refused."

"We can't have that," I said sarcastically.

She poked me in the chest. "You better believe it. He's the best we have. And besides, it's all great. Whatever you pick will please the guests."

We reached the seating area, where a section had been roped off. Over a dozen smiling associates with store shirts surrounded the long table. We began another round of introductions, with name tags for backup, before Nicole ushered me to the center of one side, opposite Chef Bob.

The group sat when I did, and hushed as Bob stood.

"This week we have four different orzo salads to choose from," Bob began, pointing to the plates in front of me. "A caprese with mozzarella balls and a hint of dijon, a spinach and cilantro, a classic Mediterranean, and a mixed Greek."

Each plate had a fork in front of it. Apparently, it wasn't cool to use the same fork for the different dishes.

After making a show of tasting them, I agreed with Nicole that they were all good. "Chef Bob, I think we'll go with the Greek. I particularly like the mixture of black and Kalamata olives."

Bob beamed. "My favorite as well."

I smiled back. I'd passed my first test and won over at least one employee, er, associate.

Another tray appeared, this one with soup bowls and spoons.

"Also, we have three new chili choices," Bob announced.

They smelled great.

"The first is a two-bean with sausage, the middle one is three-bean with mini meatballs, and the last is a meatless four-bean with corn."

After tasting them, I asked, "Is the most recent one with or without meat?"

"Meatless," Bob answered.

"Then, the middle one," I told him.

Two of Bob's helpers at the end of the table started dishing out plates, and we handed them down the table. The plates each had a sandwich, a dollop of the orzo salad I'd chosen, and a cup of the chili. Apparently, runners-up weren't good enough for our meal.

Nicole elbowed me and leaned in after tasting her chili. "Good choice."

I'd done something right. The warmth of her leaning into my shoulder diverted my attention, and I missed the next question Wanda asked.

I smiled at her. "Sorry, this chili is so good, I missed that."

"When do you think we can start the remodel?" Wanda asked.

"Uh, I'm not up to speed on things like that yet," I explained lamely.

"Redondo is up next," Nicole answered. "But the scheduling is up to Mr. B." She laid a hand on my shoulder, once again slowing my brain to a crawl. It had to be pheromones or something.

I shrugged. "Give me a little time to figure things out." I had to get it together and get back into business mode.

Wanda bit her lip, probably dissatisfied with our vagueness.

The conversation around the table wasn't as reserved as I'd expected. The question I'd anticipated came up quickly. "I heard somebody say we were joining Smith's," a voice at the end of the table said.

I should have, but I hadn't prepared an answer for that one.

After a pregnant pause, Nicole jumped in. "No truth to that rumor at all." She looked to me. "Steady as she goes, right, Mr. B?"

I had zero room to maneuver here. "Yup. Steady as she goes is the order of the day."

"Rossi's has been here for fifty years, and it will be for another fifty," Nicole added.

That comment garnered a warm reaction from the crowd.

Partway through the additional comments and questions about daily operations from the group, my phone buzzed with the text.

Deanna: Gary wants to know when you'll be back?

Me: later

I let Nicole handle pretty much everything that came up, except a few questions about my background and Benson Corp. in general.

Oddly, nobody asked about the company's shaky financial situation. Berg seemed to have kept an unusually tight lid on it. Small companies like this were prime gossip mills where secrets like that were tough to hide.

Eventually Wanda checked her watch and called an end to the lunch. After a series of waves and handshakes, it was just Nicole, Wanda, and me left at the table.

"Seemed okay to me. How do you think it went?" Nicole asked Wanda.

Wanda nodded. "They were pretty nervous, but you settled them down quite nicely. They like you," she said, looking at me.

"I like them too. I think you have a good crew." That seemed like the proper reply, and it was honest.

Nicole stood. "We need to get back to the office so Mr. B here can get back to the spreadsheets he loves so much."

We said our goodbyes, and I held my tongue until we were outside the store. "You've got quite a group there."

"Yes, *we* do." Her demeanor indicated she had more to say than that, but it took a couple of steps for her to get it out. "You should've stepped in on the question about Smith's. It would've gone over better if you'd answered it."

"Probably right, but I don't want to be locked in just yet," I said.

"Right. Rationalizing." She turned away quickly.

"That's not fair."

Dad had been pretty adamant that he thought a merger was the course of action to take, but I was the one on the ground here.

Reflecting on what I'd seen so far, Rossi's was completely unlike Smith's. A consolidation might look obvious to the Harold types from a distance, but with shopping experiences as different as they were, I couldn't see much in the way of customer overlap. But this would take more than a day to figure out. I tried not to watch Nicole's ass as she walked confidently ahead of me to the car.

I failed as I remembered how her boob had felt under my hand Monday morning—warm, soft, inviting, tempting. Everything about Nicole was tempting, but it was more than that. She had a confidence today I hadn't seen before. In the store, she was in her element, knowledgeable, authoritative, and confident. She was the total package. In this business she had what it took to succeed, even if she had gone to the wrong business school.

She neared the car. "Didn't you notice anything special about Rossi's today?"

"Yes," I said before I could stop myself.

"What?"

She meant the store. I meant her, and now I was caught.

"A thoroughly competent woman." I looked back at the car coming up behind us.

"Which one?" she asked as she stopped and turned around.

Her rapid stop caught me off guard. I pulled up short, but not before closing to a less-than-professional distance.

She looked up at me.

I held her eyes with mine. "I'm looking at her."

A cute, pink insta-blush overtook her face as we stood inches from one another. "Uh…"

I didn't let my gaze wander as a flood of emotions passed between us. Silent questions about what the other felt, what we should do next, what it would feel like if we did—or at least it felt that way to me.

Her lips parted for second. Did she feel it? Her eyes said yes a hundred times over.

A car honked one parking row over. She looked that direction and stepped back.

The moment evaporated.

"Thank you," she said, turning away.

~

Nicole

I hadn't seen Josh since driving back from our lunch with the Westside store staff earlier this afternoon.

The moment in the parking lot had been electric, but we hadn't talked about it, about us, on the way back to the office. Maybe it had been my imagination.

Stopping by Dee's desk, I asked, "What's he up to?"

"He and Gary are going over things is all I know." Dee put her pen down. "Mrs. Q left in a hurry. Any idea why?"

"No, she didn't say anything to me."

"In the *Journal*, they always say it's a bad sign if the CFO leaves suddenly. It means the financials are shaky."

Ernst had considered his time too valuable to scan the *Wall Street Journal* daily. As a result, Dee had been tasked with reading the paper and picking out the occasional article that would matter to him.

"Change like this can trigger some people to make rash decisions," I offered.

"You don't say." Dee eyed me, a reminder that I'd just profiled my actions of yesterday.

I retreated toward my office and turned. "All that's changed is we traded

Ernst for him. Personally, I think it's an improvement in the company's situation."

Dee nodded. "Me too."

I closed my door for my end-of-day calls with the store managers.

When I finished, it was almost six. Josh's door was still closed, so I locked up and left.

CHAPTER 16

NICOLE

LARA WAS ON THE COUCH WHEN I GOT HOME. "HOW'S THE REPLACEMENT fuckhead?"

I closed the door behind me and set my purse down. "His name's Josh, and he's not a fuckhead."

"So says you. I never had a boss that wasn't," she complained as she turned up the volume on the TV.

"Pardon me for interrupting your television watching." I walked slowly in front of her instead of behind the couch on my way to the kitchen. "Have you worked your trees today?"

She ignored me.

I walked back in front of the screen. "Well, have you?"

She hit pause on the show. "No, I haven't, and you're not my mother."

I was not having this conversation again. My hands went to my hips. "No. But I'm the one who just bailed you out of jail. I'm the one giving you a roof over your head. I'm the one that gives a shit about you, and all I ask for in return is a little fucking respect, and a little fucking help."

Her eyes turned sheepish. "Sorry. You're right. It's just that every time I go out back, Maro yells at me that I'm doing something wrong. He scares me. I'll do it tomorrow when he's gone."

I didn't feel like falling for the sympathy play again. "He knows more about the trees than you or I ever will, so accept his advice."

She nodded. "Whatever."

I stepped out of the way, and she resumed her show. A dismissive *whatever* seemed to be the best I was going to get this evening.

"What are you going to do about work?" I asked.

"What?"

I stepped back in front of the screen. "Work. What are you going to do about getting a job?"

She paused her show again. "I'm just waiting for you to talk to the replacement fuckhead and get me back into the company."

"It's not that simple. You've been accused of stealing from us."

"But I didn't do it." She pulled her legs up to her chest. "Don't you get that?"

"You're the one who doesn't get it." I turned around and hit the power button on the TV, hard, shutting it down.

"Hey, I was watching that."

"No, you were being disrespectful. Josh is a nice guy, and you will not refer to him as a fuckhead."

Her head tilted, and her eyes narrowed. "Okay, already. What changed since last night?"

Her question jarred me more than it should have. A lot had changed since last night in the Josh Benson department.

"I spent time with him today, and he's not a bad guy." Heat rose in my cheeks as I remembered how close we'd been when he'd backed me against the car. We were a team, he'd said. That had changed everything.

She squinted at me. "You're sweet on the F-H. That's it, isn't it?"

"Get real. Do I appreciate the fact that he flew me back here Sunday night when he didn't have to so I could bail your ass out of jail first thing Monday morning? Yes. Do I appreciate that he wrote a personal check today to keep the company afloat? Yes. Do either of those things make him a nice guy? Yes. Now get a clue, Lara. You can't just sit on your ass all day and blame everybody else for your problems."

I marched to the kitchen, not wanting to continue an argument that wouldn't do either of us any good. Surveying the fridge, I chose orange juice and poured myself a glass.

Lara had resumed her show, but at least she'd turned down the volume. When was she going to get serious about her life?

The sale papers for Tuscan Foods were still on the table from last night. I shoved them back into the FedEx envelope so I didn't have to see them and be reminded of how drastically things had changed in the last few days. Sipping my juice, I thought back to that moment before lunch when I was pinned against the car, with a bare inch separating Josh from me.

I'd chosen to trust him, and what I'd explained to Lara about why had been the logic of it, but there was more. In his eyes, I saw something that drew me in. Maybe it was honesty, maybe it was determination. Maybe it was something more.

After finishing my juice, I stood wearily and opened the refrigerator again to pick out something for dinner.

When the doorbell rang, I closed the fridge and this time walked behind the couch.

Lara hadn't budged.

I opened the door to find Josh standing on my porch.

He checked his watch. "We said seven, right?"

I backed clear of the door. "Yes, come in. I, uhh…" I caught myself before he corrected me for using a filler word. "I didn't think we were still on, after everything."

I'd separated my Josh encounter into pre-takeover and post-takeover, and I'd written off his pre-takeover texts inviting me to dinner, given how I'd acted since then, and not to mention our new working relationship.

He stepped inside. "You have a fine old house here."

I closed the door behind him. "Thank you," I replied, suddenly embarrassed by the condition of Casa di Rossi.

Not expecting guests, I hadn't cleaned. The dust bunnies of dog hair along the floorboards and the mess on the hall table I hadn't noticed until now were suddenly all too obvious.

Josh's eyes narrowed on me, mercifully avoiding the mess around us. "I said I would take you to dinner, and I was brought up to follow through on my commitments."

The sound of Lara's TV show in the other room went quiet.

This whole situation had caught me off-guard. "I…"

Lara bounded up, interrupting me, "Hi, I'm Lara."

"Josh," he said, accepting her energetic shake. "Nicole tells me she's very proud of you."

A bright blush rose across Lara's face as she cast me a look of kindness I didn't deserve. "Really?"

"We should get going," I told Josh, returning his smile.

"Really proud," Josh assured Lara. He extended a hand to me. "Hungry?"

I moved to the door. "Not really." I couldn't remember a single thing I'd told Josh about Lara that fit in the 'proud' category.

Josh opened the door. "Nice meeting you, Lara."

She put on a wicked grin. "Have a fun date."

I shot her a keep-your-mouth-shut glare before walking down the steps to escape my prying cousin's eyes.

Josh caught up to me.

"Proud of her?" I asked under my breath as we walked to the street.

"She's family. She deserves your support—our support," he said as he opened the car door for me.

My heart swelled up at the kind spirit of his words.

I lifted up on my toes to brush a kiss against his cheek as I climbed up into the car. "Thank you for that." He'd done me and Lara several kindnesses.

He touched his cheek. "For that reward, I'll do it every day." He waggled an eyebrow at me as he closed the door.

I watched him walk in front of the car to his door. Barbados Josh was back in spades, and his pull was undeniable.

He climbed in and buckled up behind the wheel.

"That was very nice of you," I said, adding to my thanks.

His smile was magnetic. "Don't act so surprised. I told you, we're a team."

He extended his hand across the console. "Team?"

I took it. My body's reaction to his simple touch and gentle squeeze short-circuited my brain. "Team," was the only response I could muster.

But Team Rationalizer was not a label I wanted.

He took back his hand to steer the car.

I settled into my seat, already missing his touch. The tingle that lingered in my fingers had me wondering how his hands would feel if they roamed elsewhere. I closed my eyes and imagined us by the pool back in Barbados, dancing in the moonlight. What would it have felt like to have his hand roam up my side to my breast. My nipples hardened at the thought…

"Is Italian okay?" he asked.

Jerking my eyes open, I realized my mistake. Barbados Josh had been a mirage, and I couldn't date Josh the Rationalizer. "I'm not up for a meal. How about just coffee?"

"Playing hard to get? I guess I deserve that." His eyes twinkled with naughtiness.

I didn't have the words to describe it. "I don't think I can…"

Barbados Josh hadn't taken over our company, Mr. Rationalizer had, and I needed to keep that in mind. *Distance*. I needed to keep distance and perspective to protect my employees.

"Coffee it is," he said, ending my search for further words.

My phone rang with Sandy's name on the screen. I declined the call with the *can't talk now* text. It rang again a minute later, and once again I declined it. Talking to her now would be rude, and my parents raised me better than that.

"You can take that if you want," Josh offered.

"She can wait."

He shot me an inquisitive look.

"It's just Sandy, my friend, the one I was in Barbados with."

I settled back and sent her a text.

ME: Going to coffee with Josh

SANDY: Call me after

Josh

I OPENED THE DOOR TO PEET'S COFFEE AND LET NICOLE GO FIRST—HALF TO BE A gentleman and half to be treated to the sway of her hips as I followed.

Coffee instead of dinner was a step back, but better than getting the door slammed in my face.

Nicole's smile as we left her house had been the one with that inviting warmth I'd seen in Barbados.

All I wanted was to reset to before she'd gotten pissed about the Rossi's situation and see where that put us. The people at the company I'd met so far had all been completely complimentary of Nicole. It's natural that they wouldn't have much negative to say about the granddaughter of the company founder, but these had been more than platitudes. Their words had come from a place of true respect.

Would the people at Benson be equally complimentary if asked about me?

When we reached the counter, the barista asked, "What will it be?"

I gestured for Nicole to respond first and caught the guy's gaze darting back to her face from her chest. I moved closer to my date.

"A mocha, please," she said. "Medium."

"I'll have the same," I told Mr. Roaming Eyes as I pulled out my wallet.

While our drinks were being prepared, Nicole looked nervously around the store, shifting from one foot to the other. She was out of her element, somehow.

After we picked up our cups, she stopped to add cinnamon to hers.

I did the same before guiding her to a table near the window, far away from Mr. Roaming Eyes.

"I like something I can sip for a while," she said as we sat.

"Me too. See? We already have something in common."

"You don't even know me."

"Something I intend to remedy."

"You always order a mocha?" she asked with narrowed eyes. "And add cinnamon?"

Busted.

Honesty was my only alternative. "Normally I might get a café au lait."

"Might?" she asked.

"Would."

"And you think mimicking my order allows us to bond?"

Damn, this girl had a chip on her shoulder.

I twisted my drink as I formulated a response. "No, not at all. I thought I'd go with sweeter tonight to match the company."

A flush rose in her cheeks. "That's nice, but you didn't have to feel obligated to do this."

I lifted my cup and took a sip while I enjoyed the color in her cheeks. It was a nice look. "Obligated?"

Her mouth quirked up. "You know, following through on your commitment… This…" She circled her finger around the room. "Not-dinner date. Wasting compliments on me and all."

That attitude hadn't diminished one bit. It was time to nip this in the bud. "A commitment is not really why I'm here. Well, it is and it isn't. I invited you to dinner because I wanted to have dinner with you, starting in Barbados and since then. That hasn't changed. I find you unique and..."

Her finger circled the rim of her cup as she waited for me to pick the right word.

"Intriguing," I added.

"I bet you find a lot of women intriguing," she said.

The color that rose in her cheeks betrayed her. She was fighting her interest.

"You'd be surprised how few," I assured her—without the sigh that would have given away how long it had been. "I think you're the exception."

She looked down at the table. "Even when I accused you of wanting to steal our company?"

"Especially then. I can't have you going around thinking I'm an ogre, before you even get to know me."

"It's just—"

"There you go again, Stanford, using the weasel words."

Her mouth formed a thin line. "Stop calling me that. You make me sound conceited."

"Well, I certainly don't mean any disrespect."

She smiled, and her brow ticked up as she found her retort. "Really? After lecturing me on how Stanford grads are all too theoretical?"

I nodded. "I did, didn't I?" I searched for a better nickname for her, but it had to be one not everybody else used.

"It's not quite ogre-level." She sipped her coffee. "But less than nice."

I found the name. "I'll endeavor to be more nice and less ogre, Nickels."

She laughed. "Nickels? Really?"

The laugh looked good on her. A grin overtook my face. "Unique, like you—with a hint of fun."

She looked down at her drink. "What makes you think I'm fun?"

I tilted my head. "A guess, and..." I watched her squirm as I dragged out my answer. I'd hit a nerve. "I think you miss it."

Her phone chose that moment to buzz. She pulled it from her purse. "Lara."

"I'll wait."

She answered it. "Slow down, Lara... He what?... Just lock the door. I'll be right there."

I stood. I didn't need to hear both sides of the conversation to know something was terribly wrong. I took her arm as she stuffed her phone away, and I urged her ahead of me toward the door.

She trotted toward the car. "It's Lara. I have to get back."

"We," I corrected her. "Team, remember?"

CHAPTER 17

NICOLE

"WHAT'S WRONG?" JOSH ASKED AS WE APPROACHED THE CAR.

"Lara is scared somebody's outside the house. I have to get back."

He unlocked the car with his key fob. "Tell her to call 9-1-1."

I snorted as I grabbed the door handle. "That's not going to happen." I climbed up into his big car.

"Then you call. It's the safe thing to do." He accelerated into traffic.

I held on and shook my head. "I can't violate her trust that way. She's scared of the police."

He pulled his phone out.

"You can't," I complained.

"I am. You can have another reason to hate my guts."

The problem was I didn't hate him—but this still wasn't right.

"What's the nature of your emergency?" came over the speaker.

"Possible prowler at 4312 Orangebranch Lane," Josh said calmly.

"Sir, are you in the house?"

I nodded when Josh looked over.

"My cousin, Lara, is in the house and scared. I'm on the way. Please hurry," he said before hanging up.

I held on as Josh weaved his way around the other cars on the road. "*Your* cousin?" I asked.

"It was quicker that way."

Something to file away for the future, a big something: Josh felt at ease taking liberties with the truth.

"I was calling for you anyway," he added.

It made more sense when he said it that way, but still didn't align completely with the truth.

"What did Lara say?" he asked.

I'd only understood part of it. "She was too scared to make any sense."

He accelerated around a van.

I braced. "It won't help anybody if we don't get there in one piece."

He shot a quick glare my direction. "Hold on, and trust me."

I rolled my eyes. The typical don't-criticize-my-driving guy response.

When we arrived at Casa di Rossi, cop cars were already outside with lights flashing.

I bailed and ran as best I could to the house in my heels.

Josh caught me before I reached the steps and bounded up them to reach the officer at the door. "We're family."

I followed Josh in.

"It's him. I know it is," Lara told the detective sitting with her, notepad in hand.

I tried to move closer.

Josh blocked me with an outstretched arm. "Let them finish."

I wondered who Lara's *him* was.

The detective looked over his shoulder at us. It was Detective Beal from years ago—the last time the police were at my house. He smiled at me.

Josh wrapped an arm around my waist and pulled me in. Did he mean to hold me close, or just keep me from barging forward?

I settled on holding me close. Up against his side, I absorbed a feeling of strength from him—solid, like leaning against an oak.

Beal turned back to Lara. "Did you see him place the note on the tree?"

"No," Lara answered. "But it's not Tanaka's handwriting."

Beal scribbled a note. "Mr. Tanaka? The man who lives out back?"

"Yeah."

"Did you see your neighbor…" He consulted his notes. "Lenz, on the property?"

Hugo Lenz? Our old neighbor? He'd left shortly after Vern was killed, and I had no idea he was back. He'd seemed weird years ago, but always in a harmless way.

Lara glanced at her shoes before answering. "No, but since he came back a few weeks ago, he's always looking out his windows with his binoculars."

"And what do you think the note means by *he knows what you did*?"

"How should I know?" Lara nearly yelled in exasperation. "The guy's a creeper."

I knew what Beal was getting at, and it tore my heart out that he would dredge up the past after all Lara had been through. I tried to step forward to tell him what I thought of this line of questioning, but Josh tightened his grip against my movement.

Beal didn't ask again and instead went over a dozen more questions about what Lara had done today and when, and our history with our neighbor.

All the while, Josh held me tightly against his side, his hand occasionally stroking my shoulder or upper arm.

I found myself reciprocating by snaking an arm around his waist and hooking my thumb in his belt. The tingles as we traded body heat made me miss a few of Beal's questions and Lara's answers. My heart rate had come down from panicked, but the closeness to Josh wouldn't let it slow below excited.

Lara's demeanor relaxed as Beal's questioning went on.

She was safe, and that's what mattered, but I was dying to see what this stupid note said. It was torture to be fifteen feet from her and not able to comfort her after what had obviously been a traumatic experience.

Beal stood. "That should do it for tonight."

"Are you going to arrest him?" Lara asked.

Beal replaced his pen in his pocket. "I'll talk to him, and we'll process the note for fingerprints first."

Lara got off the couch and headed for the kitchen. "Thanks for nothing." She threw her hands up as she reached the door. "You never believe me."

Beal shrugged as he turned to us.

Josh urged me forward with him toward Beal. "Josh Benson. I called this in, and this is Nicole Rossi, Lara's cousin."

"We've met," Beal said, glancing at me before taking his pen out again. "And your interest in this?" he asked Josh.

Josh's eyes crinkled. "I'm a friend of Nicole's."

Beal's brow went up just a hair as he looked between us. "Benson with a B?"

"That's right," Josh answered.

"What are you doing here, Jim?" I asked Beal. It had been five years.

Josh's mouth quivered.

"I heard the call and thought I'd check in to see that Lara was okay."

I wasn't buying a bit of that line. "What's this about a note?"

Beal produced a piece of paper in a plastic bag and offered it to me.

I shivered as I read it.

I know what you did.
I will see that you pay for your crime.

Two chilling sentences—not specific, but threatening.

He took the note back. "Your neighbor, Mr. Lenz, has he threatened you in any way in the past?"

"No," I answered. "I didn't even know he was back."

"He hasn't communicated in any way?" he asked.

"I told you, I didn't know he was back."

Beal took a note. "Do you know what your cousin is supposed to have done that would make somebody write this? Other than the incident five years ago with Parker, of course."

I shook my head. I wasn't dredging up the history he knew all too well. "Nothing I can think of."

Beal looked at Josh. "Anything happen with Lara recently? Anything she could have done that would have somebody mad at her?"

Josh's lips parted, and for a second I worried he'd mention the recent embezzlement bullshit, but he kept silent.

I sighed inwardly and answered. "No. Nothing."

Beal trained his gaze back on me with a knowing smile. "Well, okay then."

Had he already known when he'd pulled up? Cops had computers in their cars. Had he checked Lara's history since our last encounter and now knew I was lying?

"I'll talk to your neighbor, but as I told your cousin, this doesn't rise to the level of an actionable threat." He fished in his pocket and pulled out a card. "You can *still* call me anytime if you want to talk." He held out the card as his knowing smile broadened.

~

Josh

I moved forward and snatched the card. "Thanks. We will." Pocketing it, I stepped back and pulled Nicole to my side. I wasn't letting this fucker hit on my date.

Nicole didn't resist, but rather melted into me—the reaction I craved.

Lara looked on from the doorway to the kitchen, shook her head, and retreated.

Beal's gaze stayed on Nicole. "Call if you need anything."

His emphasis on the word *anything* was too obvious to ignore. *Jerk.*

"We will," I replied again before Nicole could answer.

I followed him to the door and latched the deadbolt after he was out.

Nicole and Lara were in the kitchen when I returned.

The girl had obviously had a rough night. She started the microwave.

"Anything we can do?" I asked Lara.

"Yeah, shoot my neighbor so I don't have to deal with this anymore."

An attitude like that wasn't doing her any favors.

"Saying shit like that doesn't help," Nicole lectured.

Lara pulled a teabag out of the bin on the counter. "He's a creeper. He deserves it."

"Did you do anything to provoke him?" Nicole asked.

"Of course not," Lara sneered. "Now it's my fault?"

I didn't point out that we didn't really know who had left the note.

The microwave dinged, and Lara pulled a mug out. "I haven't done a thing except hang out here." She turned to Nicole. "I worked your stupid trees like you wanted, and I found that fucking note when I went back out to put away the tools."

Nicole glared at Lara, hands on her hips. "And what else?"

Lara added the teabag to the mug. "Nothing else."

"Then what is the note about?" Nicole shot back.

I stayed by the doorway, not eager to enter the fray.

"How the fuck should I know? He's a creeper." She dunked the teabag a few times.

Nicole moved a step and placed a hand on her shoulder. "I'm here for you."

"Thanks," Lara said, glancing my direction. "Sorry I ruined your date with…" Her nose wrinkled. "F-H."

Now that the argument had cooled, I entered the room.

"You were scared," Nicole said.

"Whatever," Lara responded on her way out.

"F-H?" I asked after Lara left.

"Uh…" Nicole cast her eyes down momentarily. "Fun-Haver." She looked up and rolled her eyes. "It's one of her odd compliments," she added with half a laugh.

I couldn't take my eyes off her sexy ass as she walked to the refrigerator.

"Want some ice cream to follow the coffee we didn't get to finish?"

She hadn't volunteered it, so I asked. "You know that detective?"

"Yeah. What flavor do you like?"

I forced myself to look up as she turned around. "What do you have?" The questions about Detective Beal were going to have to wait.

She leaned over to open the freezer compartment. "Picky, huh?"

My eyes scanned her form as she checked. "I like to lick the simple flavors." Fuck tiramisu. Licking some ice cream off that body would be a perfect way to end the evening. If she noticed what I'd said, she didn't show it.

"Let's see… Pineapple coconut, mango, peaches and cream."

"Please, tell me you have something normal?"

She shrugged. "Lara bought these." She rummaged around. "And chocolate fudge brownie."

I walked up behind her. "Now that's what I call a winner."

She pulled it out, set it on the counter, and turned, running right into me. "Oh."

I grabbed her and didn't let go as propriety demanded.

She looked down. "Sorry."

"I'm not," I admitted.

The feel of her breasts pressed against me brought my cock to life and prevented any more intelligent conversation. I backed away and let go of her.

"Uh…" A beautiful blush grew in her cheeks—she'd felt it too, the attraction. She walked around me. "Bowls."

I turned to keep my eyes on her.

Pulling bowls down from a cupboard, she glanced back at me. Her lips turned up to tell me she'd caught me watching, and it didn't bother her.

We sat at the kitchen table after she served up the ice cream.

Nicole closed her eyes, and a low hum of appreciation escaped as she swallowed her first spoonful. "This is good."

"A lot better than mango," I agreed.

I ate slowly, but the dessert was still done sooner than I wanted.

"You know that detective?" I asked again as she cleared the bowls.

Nicole rinsed the dishes and moved them to the dishwasher before answering. "Yes."

I wasn't settling for a one-word answer. "And the incident he mentioned?"

She sat again, wringing her hands. "That was a tough time for Lara—for both of us."

I waited for her to explain at her own pace.

"There's no easy way to say this." She straightened up in her chair. "Vern Parker was her boyfriend, and he was murdered in our orchard."

That stopped my breathing for a second.

"Lara found him, and Detective Beal always thought she did it."

"Did he charge her?" I asked.

She shook her head. "Lara didn't do it. She couldn't have; she loved that boy. Beal was just focused on her because she was the only one here. I was at work when it happened. Everything went downhill for her after that."

I had to ask the obvious questions. "Do you think the note has to do with back then?"

She cocked her head and huffed out a breath. "I don't know. After five years, I doubt it."

"And the carpet message?"

She stood, clearly upset by the questions. "I don't know. None of it makes any sense. I should go up and talk to Lara."

"Right." I rose and wandered slowly to the door, debating what to say. "I had a good time tonight…with you, I mean."

She followed me to the door. "Me too." She stood back as I walked out onto the porch. "Thank you for the coffee."

"You still owe me a dinner," I reminded her.

"Maybe next week," she said. "See you tomorrow."

Making the hard choice, I turned and walked down the steps without trying for a kiss. Lara needed her tonight, and it would be selfish of me to cut into that time.

Next week, though, I wasn't settling for maybe.

CHAPTER 18

Nicole

Wednesday morning I was fixing myself breakfast when my new phone rang with Sandy's name on the screen.

"Hi," I answered.

"You never called back last night."

I'd flat-out forgotten. "Sorry. It was a hectic night, and I forgot."

"Josh kept you busy all night? This I want to hear about."

Sandy's mind was constantly in the gutter. If anything had a possible sexual innuendo, that's where she went first.

"No, it wasn't like that."

"I thought you said he was nice."

"No… I mean yes, he's nice, but no that wasn't what made it a crazy night." I spent the next five minutes recounting all the terrible things about last night with Lara and Beal and the note.

"Girl, between falling in the pool, being in a plane crash, and now this, you sure are attracting a shitload of trouble."

"It wasn't a crash, just a…" I recalled the pilot's phrase for it. "A precautionary landing."

"Whatever you say. Now, let's get back to the hunk. Why didn't you have dinner with him? You playing hard to get?"

Josh had made the same assumption, but that hadn't been my intention.

"No, it just didn't feel right."

"Then give me his number, and I'll test drive him to see if he feels right or not." She laughed at her own joke.

"Right," I said with as much sarcasm as I could put on the word. Then I realized my feelings didn't at all fit with how I'd treated him last night. "Look, I have to get ready for work. Talk later?"

"Sure, run away from the hard conversation."

"I really gotta go. Catch ya later."

"Chicken. Bawk, bawk, bawk."

I hung up before she made me even later.

Then I did the one thing that would shut her up. I texted her Josh's contact information.

~

AT THE END OF THE DAY, I TRUDGED UP THE STEPS AND IN THROUGH THE DOOR OF Casa di Rossi. It had been a long day with a trip down to the Redondo Beach store to go over the planned renovations.

A glass of wine called my name, and then it would be an early night to bed. Last night I hadn't slept well at all between fretting over the note Lara had found and wondering what to do about Josh wanting a dinner date.

He was tempting as hell, but all wrong at the same time. The man had been sent to destroy everything my family had built, hadn't he? Fraternizing with the enemy—that's what that was called.

When I walked into the kitchen, Lara pointed to the far wall. "For you."

A smile overcame me as I noticed the magnificent vase of flowers on the counter. It was a beautiful mix of colors, and as I reached it and breathed in, the scent was fantastic as well.

Lara leaned against the counter. "From the new F-H, I'm guessing, and before you ask, no, I didn't read it."

I opened the card.

Looking forward
to our dinner.

If you show up
I'll be a winner.
-JB

Lara had scooted up behind me to peek. "Aw, that's so sweet," she cooed sarcastically.

"Mind your own business," I snapped, closing the card.

"Too bad he didn't send you red roses."

I didn't respond to her goading. No, it wasn't red roses. It was a more appropriate assortment of pink roses, lavender carnations, two sizes of poms, and a purple flower I didn't know the name of. The flowers were a perfect end to a long day, even if they were from the Rationalizer.

I popped a frozen dinner in the microwave, then poured and quickly finished a large glass of wine.

Eventually Lara tired of hassling me about Josh and went upstairs. I intended to follow after dinner.

I shooed Echo out the back door to do his business and picked up my phone.

ME: Thanks for the flowers

His response was immediate.

JOSH: I was hoping you would like them.

ME: They are beautiful

JOSH: Just like their recipient.

I didn't immediately text back to that. This was getting too hot too quickly, and the line had to be drawn somewhere.

ME: Goodnight

JOSH: What night would you like to have dinner?

ME: I said maybe

JOSH: I can be patient.

JOSH: How about Friday?

ME: No

ME: Don't you understand maybe?

JOSH: See you tomorrow

I took in the fragrance of the flowers. I knew the man was trying to wear me down, and the flowers were truly thoughtful. They made me feel shitty about what I'd just typed. I should be able to say no without being mean about it.

ME: Thank you again

JOSH: I thought you could use some cheering up

Why did he always have to get the last word?

I decided to let him. I put the phone down, opened the door, and called for Echo to come in.

Upstairs ten minutes later, my phone vibrated on my nightstand.

JOSH: If Friday doesn't work for you, I have Saturday free.

I ignored it.

JOSH: Have I told you green is my favorite color?

JOSH: Eye color that is.

If I was ever going to get to sleep, we had to finish this, so I selected his contact and hit call.

He answered the phone, "Have I?"

I didn't want to go down this route. "No."

"I'm glad you called."

"Look, I'm really tired, and I thought this way I could answer your questions faster and we could get to bed sooner."

"I accept," he laughed. "I'll be right over."

My poor choice of words had walked me right into that one.

I hazarded a guess. "Have you been drinking?"

"A little," he admitted. "But green is still my favorite color."

"How little?"

"Enough."

I laughed. "From here it sounds like more than enough."

"You didn't answer my question."

"No, I'm not free Saturday," I lied. "When I said maybe next week, what I meant was definitely not this week."

"And the other question?"

At least he couldn't see me blush over the phone. "No, you didn't tell me that." I wasn't sure how to end this call. "Josh…"

"Yes, Nickels?"

The nickname sent heat rushing through me. "The flowers were very sweet, and I'm very appreciative, but—"

"I get it," he said, cutting me off. "I still have to work myself out of the ogre category."

"I didn't say that."

"Then cut the crap, Stanford. Make up your damned mind for a change."

Somehow I'd lost control of the conversation. I'd made my choice—*maybe next week*—but no, that wasn't good enough for Mr. Decide Right Fucking Now. He'd put himself out multiple times for me in the last week, and all he was asking for was dinner. What was so unreasonable about that? Turning him down the same night he'd so thoughtfully sent me flowers seemed like a bitch-of-the-year move after how nice he'd been.

"Getting together next week sounds good," I finally said, giving up my insistence on being in control.

"I'll hold you to that."

"I know you will."

I'd removed the maybe because it was the right thing to do after all he'd done for me—for us.

"On one condition," I added.

He sighed. "Which is?"

"You stop calling me *Stanford*."

"Sure thing, shnookums."

"Eww, that's worse."

"Snugglebunny?"

"No way," I objected.

"Sugar lips?"

"Cut it out."

"Sweet cheeks?"

If we were going through every word starting with an S I had to stop this before we got to sweetheart. "No, and you're not letting me get to sleep."

"Goodnight, Nickels. I'll see you tomorrow."

"Goodnight."

After I settled under the covers, sleep didn't come as quickly as I'd expected. A dose of Josh was like a hit of adrenaline, keeping me awake thinking about the what-ifs. And now, instead of dialing things back, I'd committed to a next step.

I could cut back after that. The dinner would be my payback for his kindnesses, and it would end there. I'd be done with Barbados Josh, and free to turn down Mr. Rationalizer in the future.

Sandy wouldn't understand, but maybe having given her his number would solve both our problems.

CHAPTER 19

Josh

Friday morning, I stood under the hot water, leaning against the shower wall. My legs went weak as I finished with a grunt, painting the wall with my cum as I had each of the last few mornings.

After turning under the spray to rinse off, I splashed water on the wall to eradicate the evidence. The last thing I needed was to have my cleaning service find cum stains on the wall.

In the kitchen after getting dressed, I danced in front of the stove to oldies while I tried a variation of my mocha French toast, with more cinnamon than last time. Each time I sat down to this in the morning, it brought back a vision of Nicole across from me at coffee. I didn't know how long it would take, but she'd be my girl. She just didn't realize it yet.

Dee had just left, and the door to my office was closed. It was a little after ten in the morning when I dialed Harold.

"I was just about to call you, Josh," he said when he answered.

Skipping the pleasantries, I got right to it. "Good, does that mean you have good news for me on Sandman?" We needed a CFO over here in a bad way.

"Afraid not. He's pretty tied up at the moment, but I'm looking around for a suitable candidate for you. Don't want to stick you with somebody too junior who would need a lot of your time."

It sounded reasonable, except the part about Sandman.

"I wanted to know how the Smith's-consolidation planning was coming along," he continued.

I straightened in my chair and kept my answer brief. "That may not be the smart move."

"Of course it is," he shot back.

I knew my answer wouldn't sit well with him, and it wouldn't be smart to start a battle right now. "I said *may* not. I'm still assessing the situation."

"Planning these things takes time."

I rapped my knuckles on the desk. "Got somebody at the door, Harold. Gotta go. Let me know when Sandman's going to be available."

"Sure," he said before I ended the call.

He was being a turd for some reason. I'd heard through the Benson grapevine that Sandman was bored stiff in his current slot, and if I knew George, he'd jump at the opportunity to come over here.

~

NICOLE

SUNDAY AFTERNOON, I STARED AT THE SECOND BOUQUET OF FLOWERS FROM JOSH. IT had arrived yesterday. The card had been pure Josh again.

> I've been thinking about
> dinner just us two.
> And I'll bet money
> you have too.
> -JB

"Goofball," I said out loud. It's a bet he would have won.

Echo lifted his head and just as quickly dropped it back to his bed.

Lara strode in from the hall. "Talking to yourself is a bad sign, you know." She continued to the fridge and pulled out a Diet Coke. "Want one?"

"Sure."

She brought one for each of us and sat at the table with me.

I popped the top on mine and took a swig.

"Is this guy for real?" she asked, lifting her can toward the flowers in front of me. "He needs poetry lessons. That shit is bad."

"Uh-huh. Bad." It was, but in a cute way. Why did I find it endearing?

She pushed against the table and leaned her chair back. "So you gonna?"

"Stop that. You're going to break the chair." The chairs were old, and leaning them back on two legs loosened them.

She brought the front legs back to the floor with a thud. "Geez, get a grip. They should have been replaced years ago." She didn't appreciate the history of the things in this house. "Well? Are you going to?"

"What?"

"Dinner."

I sucked in a long breath. "I have to. I owe him…" I didn't want to list the reasons I owed Josh. It was embarrassing.

"When are you gonna learn? You don't owe nobody shit. Take care of number one first." She got up.

That argument wasn't worth it with her. "Just dinner."

She left the room. "The head says no, but the pussy says yes," she called from the hallway, laughing. "I'm not betting on the head."

CHAPTER 20

Nicole

It was another Monday morning in the office as I nursed my usual cup of Peet's coffee. So far we'd survived a week since Josh's arrival without any of the layoffs I'd feared. People were loosening up after the shock of the Benson takeover, and my repeated recitations of "steady as she goes" were having the desired effect.

Mr. Rationalizer had instead turned out to be very interested in learning about how we ran, and his vibe was completely supportive. The best news was that he'd shown no interest in exploring a combination with Smith's as he'd mentioned that first day. Every time an employee had brought it up since, he'd been quick to reassure them. Maybe my comment after lunch at the westside store had gotten through to him. Or he'd changed his mind, but that wasn't a conversation I wanted to reopen.

The hardest part for me had been keeping my mind from straying whenever we spent time together. The man oozed a magnetic appeal I noticed every time he entered the room. The thought of what could have been if I'd approached him while we were both on vacation filled my fantasies at night. I had to keep my guard up and remind myself that Josh was here to *rationalize* us and make what he called the *hard* choices. Those fantasies were just that, fantasies.

After a few hours reviewing next week's suggested produce-delivery adjustments, my phone rang with Lara's name on the screen.

"Do you have an answer yet?" she asked.

"I haven't had a chance to talk to him," I lied. "I'll try to catch him this afternoon." The timing hadn't been right yet.

"Yeah, whatever. Why don't you just say you don't believe me and you don't want me there?"

I walked around my desk. "Stop that. You know that's not true." I closed my door. The rest of the building didn't need to hear this.

"He was my grandfather too. I belong there just as much as you do," she shot back.

She was right, and her words hit a sore spot.

I'd been born to Grandpa's son, and she'd been born to his daughter. It had only been the old man's patriarchal beliefs that had my parents running the company while hers were kept out. If our parents had been reversed, I'd be the one on the outside, and she'd be in my office.

That Daddy had brought me into the company so eagerly was a testament to his break with Grandpa's beliefs. I'd gotten Lara into the company over Ernst's objections by throwing a complete fit about it. One thing I'd learned about Ernst was that he backed down from a serious fight, at least most of the time.

"I should be able to get some of his time this afternoon," I told her.

"Whatever."

That was a word of dejection she needed to learn to use less often.

"You might need to meet with him too," I told her.

A sharp intake of air came over the line. "No way. I'll handle the computers. You handle the new F-H."

I counted to three in my head before answering her. "You call him that one more time, and the deal is off."

"Okay, all ready. You don't need to go ballistic. I get that you're hot for the guy."

We'd been through this, but apparently it needed repeating. "I work with him, and he's been very helpful. That's all."

"Does he have a big dick?"

I huffed. "I don't know, and I don't care!" I shouted loud enough that even the closed door wouldn't hide it. "If you want the job, you're going to drop it. Do you understand me?"

She was silent, most likely to piss me off. This was why she'd lost her last two jobs before joining us. She couldn't keep from acting out and pushing people's buttons.

"Well?" I repeated.

"Of course. I was just messing with ya." Her remorse didn't ring true.

After we hung up, I stuck two of my purchase requisitions inside a folder and gathered up my courage.

I'd been by Josh's office first thing this morning, but instead of asking him about bringing Lara back like I'd promised her over the weekend, I'd chickened out. By now, everybody had heard of Lara's arrest and the charges.

Folder in hand, I walked down to Josh's office, only to find it empty—a reprieve, but only a temporary one.

"He went to the Benson building for a meeting," Dee told me. "Do you need him?"

The truth was too embarrassing to admit, even to Dee. "I've got two purchase reqs I need him to sign."

She held out her hand. "I'll see that he takes care of them as soon as he gets back."

My bluff had been called. I handed over the folder. "When do you think that will be?"

"No idea. Sorry." She opened the folder and perused the two reqs I'd included. A small smile tugged at her lips. "I'll tell Mr. B you want to see him about something urgent as soon as he's back."

The purchase reqs hadn't fooled her. "Thanks, Dee," I said as I left.

~

Josh

I walked into the Rossi's office a little after noon.

Dee was at her desk, eating a sandwich. "Nicky came by looking for you. It seemed important."

"Thanks." I turned toward her office.

"She went to lunch, though."

I shrugged and reversed course. "Not that important, I guess."

"I know where she eats lunch on Mondays," Dee said.

"Okay. I'll bite."

The Dee smirk made an appearance. "She might like it if you stopped by."

Dee didn't miss a lot, and this was encouraging. All last week, Nicole had been around and in meetings with me, but she'd avoided much alone time for us, and this might be a chance to remedy that.

"You think so?" I asked innocently.

She nodded. "Taco Bandito opened up a place three blocks south. She likes the walk."

"Thanks." I waved as I turned and headed back out of the building.

As she'd said, the Taco Bandito sign appeared on the third block.

The hair gave her away. Nicole was seated, her back toward me, at one of the outside tables under an umbrella. She was hunched over, but as I got closer, I realized she had a notepad in front of her, but no food.

"Care for some company?" I asked as I came up to the table.

She looked up, startled.

"Dee recommended this place," I added. A true enough statement.

She motioned to the chair opposite her. "Be my guest."

"You're not eating?"

She stood. "I was about to go in and order."

I set my sunglasses down on the table to save the seat and followed her inside. "What's good here?"

She moved up to the counter. "I like the chicken tacos, but everything I've tried is good."

Between glances at her, I perused the choices, but in the end I followed her lead and ordered chicken tacos and a Coke.

She picked up the tray of chips with two salsas while our order was being prepared, and once we had our food, we returned to the table outside.

"Freshest chips in town," she said as she selected one from the basket.

Fresh was right—the chip I picked up was still hot.

She dipped hers in the green salsa, while I eyed the red.

"You might prefer the green," she said with a sly grin.

Salsa wasn't meant to be green, so I scooped up a dollop of red with my chip. "Dee said you had something important for me." I bit into the chip.

"I do," she said, watching me intently.

As soon as I chewed the chip, her warning became clear. I quickly swallowed and sucked on my Coke. My sister's three-alarm chili was hot, but on that scale, this salsa was ten-alarm torture.

"It pays to read." She pointed to the writing on the paper liner of the tray the chips and salsa came on. *A free burrito to any customer who can finish an entire dish of red salsa.*

"Very funny," I said as I sucked in more Coke and swished it around my mouth. "Wow, that's hot." My nose was starting to run. I pulled one of the napkins to dab at the sweat forming on my brow. I sipped more Coke.

She laughed. "Rapid decisions aren't always the best."

"I'm going to need another drink." I took a mouthful of ice water and swished it around before swallowing.

She lifted her taco. "I made the same mistake the first time I was here."

Somehow that didn't make me feel better. Deciding the taco might cool down my burning tongue, I took a bite. Ten seconds later, the heat had lessened from painful to merely uncomfortable.

"What did you want to talk about?" I asked before taking another mouthful.

She set her food down. "I'd like to ask a favor."

"After you tried to kill me with that hot sauce?" I gulped more Coke.

She tried unsuccessfully to hold back a laugh. "I warned you, as I recall."

Seeing her laugh made the mouth-burning exercise almost worthwhile. My taste buds had finally recovered enough to enjoy the food. "Pretty lame warning, I'd say."

She shrugged. "I guess... It's about Lara." Her finger made a circle on the top of her Coke as she pondered her words.

"Is she all right?" I didn't want to ask if she was in trouble again.

"Yes and no."

I bit off another mouthful of taco, waiting for her.

"It would be good for the company too. It's just..."

Whatever it was, she was uncharacteristically reluctant to mention it.

"No," I said firmly. "Absolutely not."

~

Nicole

THE GALL. TO REFUSE WHAT I WANTED JUST BECAUSE IT WAS ME?

I'd just decided he was fun to kid with, the way he'd taken his salsa error in stride, and then he went and showed me his evil side.

Huffing loudly enough that he'd get the message, I pointed out the obvious. "I didn't even ask you yet."

He nodded and smirked.

The ass *smirked*, like it was funny.

"That's the point. If you don't have the guts to ask for it, you can't have it," he said. "Another thing they obviously didn't teach you at that school."

I put down the taco in my hand lest I throw it at him. "When are you going to stop lecturing me?" I'd had enough of him putting down Stanford. My school was ranked higher than his, and that was a fact.

He lifted his Coke. "As soon as you learn to be decisive. It's a lesson you need if you're ever going to run the company."

His statement floored me. "What do you mean?"

"I thought you wanted to run the company?" He chewed another bite of his lunch, nonchalantly waiting for me.

I'd never considered it anything but my destiny. Daddy had taken over for Grandpa, and as the only child, I'd been expected to follow in his footsteps, just as Josh was following in his father's.

"Well, I am a Rossi."

"Do you want Rossi's to be the best it can be?"

The question was so insulting it almost didn't deserve an answer. "Of course."

"So do I, and that means you need to be the best you can be. And I'm suggesting you could be more decisive."

As his words rattled around in my brain, I smiled. What I'd taken as an insult had been his stupid way of trying to be helpful.

"Thank you."

"No need. It's just my opinion of course."

Direct and decisive it would be, then.

"I want to bring Lara back on board." There, I'd said it.

His brows drew together. "Why? You know what everybody thinks of her."

"We need to find the real embezzler, and she's the one who uncovered it in the first place."

"You think it's worth the risk?" He picked up his drink and sipped on his straw.

"It's just that..."

His eyes narrowed at me.

I got the message faster this time. *No weasel words, no filler words, be decisive.* "I think it's well worth the risk for both her and us. The cops have stopped even looking for anyone besides Lara, so without finding the identity of the true culprit ourselves, she'll be convicted. And, if we don't find out who it is, he or she could start up again later. If you really believe Lara's to blame, isn't there a saying about keeping your enemies close? This way you can keep an eye on her."

Josh tilted his head quizzically. "Okay. I didn't say I thought it was Lara."

"Okay what?"

"Okay, bring her in starting tomorrow."

I'd come here for lunch to figure out my arguments on paper, expecting it to be a difficult conversation. The ease of convincing him surprised me. I said the only appropriate thing, "Thank you."

"Thank you for suggesting it."

This man constantly surprised me. "You're an enigma."

I'd thought him a jerk when he yanked me out of the airport in Sioux City. I'd thought him a jerk a minute ago for telling me *no* without even listening to my question, and both times he'd meant to be helpful.

He raised his drink. "Dinner tomorrow night and we can fix that." He raised a brow in invitation. "You did say this week."

"Okay, but just coffee—two coworkers getting to know each other a little better."

"We didn't have any luck with coffee last time. It should be dinner," he insisted.

"If I say no, will you stop asking?"

He chuckled. "Of course not, I'll ask Jenny to relay my dinner invitation to you."

That was low. He knew Jenny's reputation as our queen of gossip, and I'd never live it down.

"Every day," he added.

"Okay, already. Dinner tomorrow."

Having Jenny spread it far and wide was the last thing I needed.

"I'll pick you up at seven."

I rolled my eyes. "Right."

On the walk back to work, my insides did backflips as I thought about tomorrow night. When I looked over at him, I noticed that scar on his chin again, but I held back the question.

"What?" he asked, catching my stare.

Drawing us into a personal conversation right now would be a bad idea. I needed to keep my distance to make cutting it off easier. "Nothing."

"Spit it out, Nickels."

That tickled me every time he said it. "I was thinking you went a whole conversation without calling me *Stanford*."

"The things I sacrifice for you," he mused.

His words brought home how minor that was in the list of things he'd done for me, for me and Lara.

We walked on in silence.

It was just going to be a casual dinner tomorrow to repay his kindness, right? No commitment to anything more. How hard could that be?

CHAPTER 21

Josh

Yesterday over lunch, Nicole had agreed to dinner, and tonight I was collecting.

I felt the spark again as I guided her through the front door of Aldolfo's with a hand at the small of her back. My mind raced, wondering what her skin would feel like as I traced a finger down her neck to the swell of her breast and then...

"How many in your party?" the young hostess asked, pulling me back to reality.

I held up two fingers.

She nodded and picked up menus. "Right this way."

I let Nicole go first and was treated to the sway of her ass as I followed. I could watch that walk all day long.

Nicole's smile as she took a seat across from me had that same inviting warmth I'd seen just before she got dunked in Barbados.

Our waiter arrived, poured water, introduced himself, and asked, "Can I start you off with something to drink?"

I gestured for Nicole to respond first.

"A glass of house chardonnay, please," she said.

"I'll have the same," I told him.

"Red sometimes gives me a headache," she admitted after our server left.

"Me too. See? We already have something in common."

"You always order chardonnay?" she asked with narrowed eyes.

Busted. Again.

"No. Normally I would have a pinot grigio or sauvignon blanc, but tonight I'm trying the bonding routine you suggested."

"I don't think I exactly suggested it," she said.

"Is it working?"

That pulled a smile out of her. "At least your effort is appreciated."

"Now that it's been a week or so, have I managed to climb out of the ogre category?"

She cocked her head. "Did I ever call you that?"

"Maybe not in so many words."

Our wine arrived a minute later, but she hadn't actually answered my question.

"Any appetizers tonight?" the waiter asked, looking at me.

"What do you think about an order of shrimp bruschetta to start?" I asked Nicole.

She closed her menu. "Sorry. I'm allergic."

"The shrimp?" I asked her.

"Shellfish in general." She pulled out what I recognized as an Epi-Pen. "That's why I carry this."

"Can we do bruschetta then, without the shrimp?" I asked the waiter.

He nodded. "Certainly, sir."

After he left I raised my wine. "To getting to know each other."

She repeated the toast with a coy smile and gingerly clinked her glass to mine. After a sip she asked, "Is this where you lay some corny pickup line on me?" Her phone buzzed, but she ignored it.

"So what was it like falling from heaven?"

She couldn't contain a small laugh. "That's bad."

"I seem to have lost my phone number. Can I have yours?"

Her head tilted. "That's pretty bad too."

"Is your name WiFi? Because I'm sensing a real connection."

She shook her head. "That's even worse. If that's the best you've got, the women in this town are safe."

I clasped my hands over my heart. "Oh, that hurts."

Nicole's phone buzzed in her purse for the second time. She glanced toward it.

I sat back and marveled at my luck to be sitting across from her tonight. "Go ahead. I know you're itching to check it."

She pulled the pesky device out and read the name on the screen to me. "It's Lara—again."

"Are you sure you want to risk it?"

She hesitated, and then put the phone down.

"Just kidding. Go ahead. I've got all night." I put my fork down. "For you." And boy was I looking forward to the rest of the night.

Her face heated to a delectably edible pink as she tapped the phone to answer. "Hi." Concern grew on her face as she pressed the phone to her ear. "What?" she asked loudly. "What's happening? Where are you?" Her voice went up an octave. "Blood? What blood?"

I stood and yanked my wallet out. Anything having to do with blood meant we were done here. I threw bills on the table and tilted my head toward the door. I regretted even having joked about not answering the phone.

Nicole stood as she listened.

The couple at the next table looked over, eyes wide. Frantic questions and the word *blood* didn't mix well with polite dinner conversation.

"Where are you?" Nicole asked again.

Whatever Lara's issue was, the panic in Nicole's voice said we were going to move quickly.

Nicole rounded the table to me. "We're on the way."

We weaved through the restaurant and past concerned looks.

"Home," she said to me as we speed-walked to the door.

"Lara?" Nicole repeated several times before pulling the phone away from her ear.

I pushed open the door to the street. "What's wrong?"

She shook her head. "I can't believe this is happening again. She's hysterical and talking about blood."

I hit unlock on my big SUV and raced to the driver's side. I had the engine started by the time Nicole climbed in and closed her door.

Hitting the emergency button on my phone, I pulled away from the curb and punched the gas, hard.

Nicole had the phone to her ear again. "She's not answering."

I tossed my phone in the cup holder. "Keep trying."

The 9-1-1 operator came over my car's speakers. "What's the nature of your emergency?"

"There's been an accident at 4312 Orangebranch in west LA. Roll an ambulance."

"I'm sending help now," the lady said. "What's the medical emergency?"

"We're on the way now," I answered. "We got an emergency call from the resident. She's not answering her phone anymore."

"Can you tell me more?" the emergency operator asked.

Nicole spoke up. "We got a call from my cousin. She talked about a lot of blood."

"Is she safe?"

I sped around another car.

"I lost the call," Nicole said. "And she's not picking up."

"I'm sending police as well," the lady said before re-verifying the address and asking for our names and Lara's.

I ended the call with 9-1-1. The light ahead went yellow, and I accelerated into it. "What exactly did she say?"

Nicole braced herself. "She just kept saying there was blood."

I raced through the intersection and changed lanes. "What else did she say?"

"She said it's happening again."

"What does that mean?"

~

NICOLE

"THERE'S SO MUCH BLOOD," LARA HAD SAID ON THE PHONE.

I punched her contact for what was probably the tenth time, and still she didn't answer.

Josh stopped at the red light, and then floored the big SUV after a car passed from the left.

I looked right and screamed, "Look out!"

I grabbed for the armrest—not that it would do any good. If he misjudged, my side would take the hit from the pickup barreling toward us.

"Trust me," Josh said for the third time as we surged through the intersection, well ahead of the oncoming truck.

"Either slow down or let me out," I demanded.

He didn't do either as we raced for the next light. "If she's bleeding, seconds matter."

"She's not bleeding. Slow the fuck down before you kill us both."

He let off the gas a little. "You said lots of blood."

"She said there was a lot of blood, not *her* blood. Now slow down or let me the fuck out."

He slowed and stopped at the next red light without checking like he was going to run through it.

"Thank you for caring." I put a hand on his shoulder.

He'd been driving like a madman to get to Lara, to save Lara. I looked over at the face of the man I'd once thought wanted to destroy me. He'd told me he'd take care of me, and now he'd shown me again that he cared.

Warm eyes looked back at me. He didn't know Lara. All it took for him to want to help her was to know she was important to me. That he cared enough about me and about Lara to break every traffic law known to man to get us to her made me blush.

"What?" he asked.

I'd been staring and not realizing it. "Thank you for being you."

"You're weird, you know that? Now, tell me exactly what she said."

I closed my eyes for a second to recall Lara's words. "'There's so much blood,' were her words."

"And?"

"She was sobbing so hard it was hard to understand her. She said, 'It's happening again.'"

The light turned green, and Josh accelerated in a rush, but not maniacally. "What's happening again?"

"I think she means like Vern." I hoped to God I was wrong.

"She was scared, she was sobbing, and except for the lots of blood comment, that's all I understood."

He offered his hand to me. "Remember, touch lessens anxiety."

I took it. "I hope that's not what she meant."

He nodded. "I guess we'll see when we get there."

I drew strength from his hold on my hand. "I'm scared for her."

A smile grew on his face. "You can lean on me, Nickels."

As we turned the corner, the row of cop cars came into view, all with their lights flashing.

Josh couldn't park any closer than in front of Lenz's house.

I got out. The scene was horrific.

"Lara," I screamed as I started running. "Lara."

Yellow crime scene tape stretched across the entire front yard of Casa di Rossi.

Josh

A SHITLOAD OF POLICE CARS WERE PARKED IN FRONT OF NICOLE'S HOUSE, AND THE street was blocked to traffic by a fire truck.

I pulled to the curb in front of her neighbor's house.

Nicole was out and running before I'd even shifted the Escalade into park.

It wasn't until I locked the car and made it to the sidewalk that I saw what had spooked her—yellow crime scene tape like on TV.

"But it's my house," she screamed at a cop holding her back.

I made it to them and wrapped my arms around her to keep her from getting fucking arrested for hitting the cop or whatever else my crazy girl would do in this state.

"Lara's in there," Nicole pleaded. "She's my only cousin. I need to see her."

The man in blue wasn't impressed. "No one goes in—orders. Just stay back." His nametag read Milton.

"I called this in," I told him. "I'd like to talk to whoever is in charge."

That got Milton's attention. He spoke into his radio. "I need a detective at the sidewalk." He listened, we listened, no response.

"If you don't want a statement, that's fine. We'll leave," I told him and dragged Nicole back a step.

"But—" she pleaded.

I clamped her to my side and whispered in her ear. "Trust me."

I turned us toward the car. "Don't worry, honey. They don't even know our names. They'll never find us."

"Stop," Officer Milton ordered.

I looked back. "Officer, you just told us to leave."

Milton lifted the tape. "You need to come with me."

Nicole's eyes widened, and she laced her arm behind me before looking up and whispering. "Sneaky."

I kept her close as we walked under the tape and followed the officer across the yard and up the steps. "I'm sure it'll just take a second, Nickels."

"11-98, detective to the front door, now," Milton said angrily into his radio. "Wait here," he told us as he went inside and closed the door.

"I need to see Lara," Nicole said as she tried to follow him.

I held her in my grip. "Slow down."

"But she needs me."

"I got you past the tape, didn't I? Hold on until we talk to somebody with some juice around here."

The voice came from deeper inside the house. "Who called for a detective?"

"I've got someone you need to interview," Milton replied. "He says he called it in."

"Where?"

The door opened, and Milton motioned us through.

Nicole stiffened in my grasp as the detective came into view. We should have left.

"What are you doing here?" I asked.

Detective Beal sneered at me. "I show up when there's a body. What's your excuse, Benson?"

Nicole's hands went to her face. "No!"

I caught her as she crumpled. "You need to work on your delivery, asshole."

Detective Beal ignored me and approached Nicole. "Where is your cousin?" he asked her. Beal flicked his head toward me. "And take him outside," he told Milton.

I guided Nicole to the couch. I hated the idea of her facing him alone, but short of getting arrested, I didn't have any options.

CHAPTER 22

Josh

Officer Milton grabbed my elbow.

"Not until she's allowed to sit down and have some water," I told them.

Beal nodded to Milton. "Sure. Kitchen, that way." He pointed for Milton to go fetch the water.

"It's not Lara?" Nicole asked Beal.

"No. I'm sorry to have to tell you this, Nicole, but Mr. Tanaka is dead."

"Maro?"

"Yes. My condolences on your loss. Out back in your trees. Just like last time."She started to sob. "How? Why?"

Milton showed up with a glass of water, which he handed to me, and I helped Nicole sip.

"Now get him outside," Beal instructed Milton.

I put my hand on Nicole's shoulder before standing. "I'll be right outside."

She smiled at me. "Thanks."

As the door closed behind us, I heard Beal start again. "Now, where is your cousin?"

I sat in one of the chairs on the porch.

Milton waved toward the street. "You need to go to the sidewalk."

"He said outside. I'm outside."

He hesitated, as if deciding whether he should ask Beal for instructions, but he didn't.

"Am I under arrest?"

Milton shook his head. "No, not yet."

"Good. Then I'll sit here and call my lawyer." I pulled out my phone. "A little privacy, please."

He backed away.

I dialed Steven Covington's old friend Mike Salois. His office was close.

Mike picked up right away. "Hi, Josh. If you're calling about the Habitat weekend—"

I stopped him. "Mike, it's not that. I need help."

"One sec. Let me close the door… Okay, what's up?"

"A friend of mine, actually a family, needs your help, and right now if you can get here fast."

Noises came from the other end of the line. "Emily, I'm going out for a while," Mike said. "I'll call."

If Emily objected, I didn't hear it. I waited for him to speak.

"Okay, I'm headed to the car now. Where are you, and what's the situation?"

"It looks like there's been a murder," I began.

Nicole

I TWISTED THE GLASS OF WATER IN MY HAND AS THE OFFICER ESCORTED JOSH OUT THE front door.

"Where is your cousin?" Detective Beal asked again.

Closing my eyes, I willed myself to be calm and mentally counted to three before answering. "She's not here?"

He let out an exasperated breath. "No. Now, where is she?"

I told him the truth. "I thought she was here."

Beal's face became redder. "I want to talk to her. Now tell me where she is."

I shrugged. "I don't know."

"We have her phone. I know she called you just before the 9-1-1 call came in. What did she say? Did she say why she attacked him?"

I fell back into the couch. "I feel faint. I think I'm going to need oxygen." I needed to slow this down and think.

"Don't pull that crap. What did she say?"

I closed my eyes. "Can I get some oxygen?"

He gave in and called to get the paramedics.

After five minutes on the oxygen mask, the paramedic checked my blood pressure, pulse, and oxygen saturation again. He declared me ready and able to talk.

I would not let Beal intimidate me. I had the power here.

He shifted closer again and repeated the same question. "Where is your cousin?"

A policeman walked in from the kitchen. "What do we do with the dog?"

Beal turned. "Take him in."

"Hey," I protested. "You can't take my dog."

Beal waved the officer to the door. "Yes, I can. He's got blood evidence on him, and he needs to be processed by the lab guys."

My heart fell. "Blood? Is he okay?"

"You can get him back when we're done with him, and not before. Now, where is your cousin Lara?"

I have the power. I have the power, not him. This will not be like last time. "I'm not answering anything until you tell me what's going on."

His face showed the statement had set him back. "I'm investigating a murder. Are you refusing to cooperate in a homicide investigation?"

"If you're not going to tell me what's going on, then it's time you left my house."

"It's a crime scene and I'd say it's time you cooperated. We have a dead body in your backyard, just like last time. Multiple shallow stab wounds, just like last time. Someone with a connection to this property, just like last time. And, reason to believe your cousin was the last one with the victim, just like last time."

"And you think Lara did this?"

"She got away once, but that's not happening again."

A shouting match started outside the door. A few seconds later, the door opened and Josh came back in with another man and the officer from before.

"Milton, I told you to keep people out," Beal said.

The other man stepped forward with his card in hand. "Mike Salois, Miss Rossi's attorney. I'd like a word with you, Detective…"

"Beal," he filled in.

"Before Nicole answers any more questions," Mike said.

Beal ignored him. "It'll go better for everyone involved if you tell me where she went."

I clamped my mouth shut.

Mike came forward. "Don't say a thing, Nicole." He got between Beal and me. "You're done intimidating my client."

Seething, Beal backed up. "Fine. In the kitchen, counselor."

Josh sat beside me, his warmth comforting.

"Thank you," I told him.

Milton stepped back, looking unsure, and decided to return to the porch.

Josh pulled me to him. "I've got you, Nickels."

Arguing about evidence, searches, and rules for hot pursuit drifted in from the kitchen.

Beal was tough, but Mike sounded tougher.

I laid my head against Josh's shoulder and closed my eyes.

The yelling in the kitchen stopped and a quieter discussion ensued in the other room as Mike asked questions and Beal answered.

All I wanted to do was melt into Josh. *Trust me,* he'd urged, and it was clear I needed to—I had to. Josh was my rock in today's shitshow. I'd never leaned on a man in the past, but Josh made it so easy, so natural to trust him and let him bear some of the load.

"Failure to be honest would be obstruction," Beal said loudly as I opened my eyes.

Beal walked through the room to the front door. "Five minutes. That's how long she has." The door closed behind him.

Mike sat down across from us. "First, Nicole, I'm Mike Salois."

I nodded. "Thank you.

He continued. "Josh has retained me to represent you and your cousin."

I nodded again. "Both of us?"

"Unless your interests diverge, yes. If you'd like someone else, I can step back at this point."

Josh stepped in. "Mike may look young, but he knows his shit, and I trust him implicitly."

I nodded. "That's good enough for me," I told them.

"Okay then, this is the situation."

I sat up, but didn't release my grip on Josh.

"Nicole, they know Lara called you, and that within a minute, Josh called 9-1-1, alerting them to a situation here."

Situation had to be lawyer code for death.

"When they arrived, a truck was driving away that matches the description of what Lara owns."

I nodded.

"The responding officers didn't get any response from inside the house or find any sign of forced entry, and they were about to leave when Detective Beal radioed them to check the trees behind the house. Apparently, there had been an incident here recently."

I put up a hand. "Lara found a threatening note, and we called them."

"I was here for that," Josh added. He pulled his arm out from around me and scrolled through his phone. "Here's a picture of the note." He passed the phone to Mike.

"Anyway," Mike continued. "In that search, they found the body of your gardener, Mr. Tanaka. He'd been working among the trees."

I didn't bother correcting Mike that Maro wasn't our gardener.

"When they called in the body, the detective told them to search the house. They found Lara's cell phone with blood on it, which is how they know about the call."

"So, what now?" Josh asked.

Mike looked at me. "Lara is a legitimate subject of interest, given the call alerting you, which proves she was here."

"She couldn't—she wouldn't do something like this," I objected.

Mike nodded. "I understand, but see it from his perspective. The detective is convinced Lara was involved in another death here five years ago. Now we have a second murder on the same property, with the same manner of attack, and Lara was present both times."

I nodded with the pit in my stomach growing larger by the minute.

"He thinks the threatening note was just to throw off suspicion, and she planned this. What can you tell me about five years ago?" Mike asked.

"Her boyfriend was stabbed in the orchard," I said.

"Personal feelings aside," Mike said, as if taking emotion out of it when my cousin had been accused of murder was possible. "The detective is right. You need to tell him what you know about Lara's whereabouts, and lying about it is the worst thing you could do right now, for both her and you."

Josh squeezed my knee and nodded. "It's okay."

I took a deep breath. "But I don't know where she is. She was hysterical when she called and didn't say anything about going anywhere."

Mike stood. "I'm going to bring him back, and you can tell him exactly that. You don't owe him any more."

A minute later Beal walked in, seeming more controlled than before. "What do you know about where Lara is, or where she might have gone?"

Mike nodded to me.

I gathered my strength. "When she called, I told her we were on the way. I thought she would be here when we arrived, which is why I was surprised when you told me she wasn't here. She didn't say anything about leaving, or where she would go if she did."

"And where is she most likely to go?" Beal's eyes drilled into mine. "In your opinion."

This was a question I had no clue about either. "I honestly don't know. She's always stayed here since she left her parents' house. I doubt she'd go there, but it's all I can think of."

"Did she have trouble with Tanaka?" Beal asked. "Any recent argument? Did she change her mind and think maybe he left that previous note?"

I glanced at Mike, who nodded, before answering. "Not that I know of."

Lara had seemed a little scared of Maro, but only because he corrected her when dealing with the trees. Hell, Maro corrected all of us.

CHAPTER 23

Josh

Beal finally left the house after asking Nicole again about Lara's whereabouts and being told flat-out that we didn't know one last time.

"Remember the rule," Mike warned Nicole as he headed to the door.

She smiled. "Don't worry. The last thing I want to do is talk to him."

I followed Mike. "I'll walk you out."

Outside, Mike stopped at his car before getting in. "I believe Nicole about Lara, but Beal doesn't."

"No shit."

"He thinks she should have been charged five years ago. He's not looking beyond the similarities of the two cases. And I don't have to tell you how her pulling a disappearing act looks."

It was painfully obvious how bad this looked. "Lara has had a target painted on her back for a long time."

He reached for his car's door handle. "I'm sure she believes that."

"I do too." Sometimes paranoid people had good reason.

"One more thing," Mike said as he opened the door. "If she calls and tells you where she is, you won't have deniability. Keep that in mind."

I nodded. "Got it."

Back inside, I found Nicole pacing in the kitchen.

I pulled my anxious girl into a hug.

She shivered against me.

I kissed the top of her head as she molded herself to me. "I'll help you with whatever you need. You need to talk to me."

She relaxed as I stroked her back. "Don't stop—"

"You can't ever stop me from helping you, Nickels."

"Thank you," she mumbled into my shoulder. Her grip on me tightened. "Thank you."

My phone rang with Dad's distinctive ring tone.

She pushed back, but I didn't let her get away. "You should get that."

I pulled her back in. "Dad can wait. You're my priority."

The blood had drained from Nicole's face. "I worry about her," she said wearily.

I pocketed my now silent phone. Dad didn't usually call in the evening, but whatever he wanted could wait. Nicole slid down off the barstool. "It's late, and I'm tired. I'll see you tomorrow." Subtleness wasn't her style this evening. She flicked off the light in an obvious move to force me out.

That plan, however, wasn't going to fly. I took her arm and stopped her. "You're coming with me, Nickels." My condo was the only logical place tonight.

"No way. This is my house. And anyway, yours is so high I'll get a nosebleed if I go up there again." She tried to laugh in the midst of this horrible situation.

"It's not safe here. You're coming with me."

She stomped her foot with the pathetic softness of a church mouse. "I'm not leaving Casa di Rossi." Her voice carried the indignance her foot stomping hadn't.

I led her over and lifted her back up onto the barstool.

"Hey," she complained.

I stooped to look her in the eye. "You don't get it, do you? Do you think Lara killed that guy tonight?"

Her brows drew together. "Of course not. She wouldn't."

"And five years ago, did she kill Parker?"

She shook her head angrily. "How can you even ask that?"

"Answer me. Do you think she did it?"

Nicole crossed her arms. "No, absolutely not."

"The note on the tree and the message on the carpet, were those her?"

She tilted her head and narrowed her eyes. "Don't be ridiculous."

I ticked them off on my fingers as I went through the incidents. "Five years ago, there's a murder, now a maniac breaks into your house and paints a message to leave or die, then there's a note that says you'll pay, and finally someone gets killed, just like five years ago."

Her shoulders slumped.

"If none of that was Lara, there's a killer out there who's struck twice and threatened that you'll die if you don't leave. I'm not letting you stay here alone. You're coming with me."

Tears welled up in her eyes. "No." She sniffed. "I won't let someone chase me away from this house." Her stubbornness wasn't making any sense. "I won't let them win."

"That's stupid."

"Stupid?" Anger bloomed on her face.

"Sorry, bad choice of words. Let's say risky."

"If I'm stupid, you're... you're..."

"Worried," I finished for her.

"Overbearing," she said.

I moved closer. "You mean considerate and helpful."

She didn't smile. "That maniac wants to make me leave. *You* want to make me leave." She hopped down from her stool and moved around me. "What's the difference?"

I followed her. "I *promised* to keep you safe; that's the difference."

She pulled a bottle of white wine out of the fridge and closed the door. "Consider yourself relieved of your stupid promise. I'm not getting run out of my own house."

I put my hand out for the bottle. "Now who's calling who stupid?"

She scowled and handed it over.

I set it on the counter and moved toward her. "It's not that simple. You need to come with me."

She backed away. As her eyes narrowed, it became apparent I hadn't won the argument yet. "Need to? I don't *need* to do anything."

I advanced closer. "Should," I suggested. "It's the smart thing to do."

She stepped back, but the fridge halted her retreat. "What's it to you anyway?"

I caged her with a hand on either side of the refrigerator door. "You went to Stanford; you tell me."

Her breath was warm against me as our bodies almost touched.

"I'm stupid, remember?" She tilted her head up toward mine.

Even in the dim light, the evident blush filling her cheeks said she understood my meaning.

"I care about you, Nickels." I lowered my head so our noses almost rubbed. "A lot."

Her hand came up behind my neck as she pulled herself toward me. Her lips were soft as they met mine with sweet, light pressure that grew as her other hand came around me and she pulled us together. Body heat met body heat as we deepened the kiss. My tongue sought entrance, and her lips parted. We began the soft, sweet tango of lovers exploring each other for the first time. The tentative movements of her tongue became quickly more intentional, more deliberate, more assertive, more passionate.

The moan she released when I gripped her ass and pulled her against my straining cock was erotic music. She pulled at me. She was loosening the leash on the tigress within. Our kiss became needier, more primal as her nails scratched my skin and she pulled herself against me with a hunger for more—more that I was happy to give her.

My hand came up between us to caress a hot breast through fabric I was going to quickly get out of the way. Another needy moan escaped her as I circled the concealed nipple.

The coconut scent of her hair transported me to a beach. Instead of being in partial darkness with her backed against the stainless steel refrigerator, I imagined her up against a palm tree, with sand under our feet, warm trade winds in our hair, and the tropical sun beating down. The scene was one of passion unleashed.

The temperature between us rose quickly as I slipped my hand under the hem of her shirt. I pulled her away from the refrigerator door long enough to unclasp her bra with a quick pinch behind her. My hand made its way around to feel the velvety softness of her skin and the weight of her boob in my hand as I teased her nipple between my thumb and forefinger.

She responded by rocking herself into my erection.

My phone went off in my pocket with Dad's distinctive train-whistle ring tone. His timing sucked.

I ignored it. "Dad can wait."

When it sounded another time, Nicole pulled away. "You better get that," she said breathlessly.

I kissed her nose. "You're more important."

She giggled. "We've got time." She pushed at my shoulders. "Answer it."

Reluctantly, I pulled away, instantly missing the feel of her soft warmth under my hand, and swiped the screen to answer.

"Hi, Dad." I leaned back against the counter.

"Josh, there's been a change of plans."

"Change in what plans?" I asked.

Nicole took her final hand off me and carried the wine bottle to the counter.

"I've scheduled a meeting for nine tomorrow to discuss the Rossi-Smith consolidation," Dad said.

The words knocked the breath out of me. "Why tomorrow?" I walked into the other room to continue this conversation.

"Because I want to change things up and pull you off of that company."

I sat on the couch and watched Nicole take down two glasses and pour the wine. Looking at her and contemplating leaving was too much to process right now. "I'll have to see if I can make that."

"Didn't you hear me? I said we'll discuss it tomorrow."

Nicole looked my direction after pouring the second glass.

I raised a finger to have her give me a minute while I thought through the ramifications.

"You there?" Dad asked after I didn't respond.

I wasn't in a mood to be pushed tonight. "Dad, I'll get back to you on that."

"This is not a request," he said.

There it was. The same threat as always. It was always hanging over me that I had to follow his every instruction without question or else. I'd inherited the position of crown prince at Benson, which most often meant crown lackey. Do this, do that, with an unsaid *or else* at the end of every direction. Or else *what* was never a discussion we'd had. I'd always done my duty. Following Dad's instructions had become second nature.

I crooked my finger to motion Nicole over. Having her close was what I wanted tonight.

Dad breathed a sigh of exasperation. "In order to get moving on our succession plan, I need you on Camper Heaven now."

Succession plan were the words I'd always lived for. *Always* being past tense. Two weeks ago, the words would have elated me. Tonight, my gut reaction was different.

Tonight, as I looked at the girl in front of me, I had a decision to make. I'd urged Nicole to be more decisive, and now it was my turn to practice what I preached.

Nicole handed me my glass and sat next to me.

"I have unfinished work here," I told him.

Nicole took a sip of her wine and sidled up close, a very warm, very enticing hand on my chest. Her lips brushed a soft kiss on my ear.

It wasn't just the feel of her touch and the energy that flowed from it. I'd followed directions long enough. Tonight I was setting my own course, and my destination sat next to me. Leaving was not an option. Tonight, London or bust was being replaced by Nicole or bust. Somehow I knew she was worth it. If it didn't work, it wouldn't be for lack of me trying.

I gathered the strength I needed for this from her touch. "I'll get back to you. I have to go now." I hung up—only the second time in my life I could remember hanging up on Dad. The first hadn't gone well.

As I looked into Nicole's eyes, I could see my yellow brick road no longer went through London.

When my brother Vincent left the company, Dad had insisted it was time for me to join Benson Corp. I'd initially resisted, but Dad could be a force of nature when he set his mind to it, and won that battle.

This time, I would be the immovable object.

CHAPTER 24

Nicole

"I'll get back to you. I have to go now," Josh said as he ended the call. Irritation laced his voice.

I curled my fingers into his shirt. "What was that about?"

His phone rang with his father's odd ringtone again. After silencing the beast, his look softened, and he pulled me closer.

Every touch ignited sparks of possibility. Sandy was right—it had been too long for me, way too long since I'd felt like this. Just his hand at my side raised goosebumps of anticipation. This man pulled me in a way I hadn't felt before—not ever.

He put the phone away. "Dad wants me to talk to him tomorrow about another project."

"Oh… Like, another company?"

He nodded.

I stepped back. "How long would it be?"

"It doesn't matter."

I wasn't settling for a non-answer. "How long?"

"Six months or so, but I'm not doing it."

"Where?"

"Nebraska, but it's irrelevant. I don't want to go," he said emphatically.

It was happening again. Except this time I would get advance notice of the guy's departure. Josh had told me on the plane that his job sometimes entailed traveling around the country, but it hadn't clicked, I guess.

He'd been the good son. The one who'd stuck around at the company when the others left. *Don't want* to do something and *won't* do something could be miles apart, especially when dealing with orders from his Dad.

I could feel the heat of my anger in my face. "Yeah, and how many times have you told your father to stick it, huh?"

His silence answered my question. He was the one who couldn't say no. The one who valued duty above all else.

Hell, I'd felt the same way about carrying on the Rossi tradition, and still did. I'd always followed my father's directions when it came to preparing to lead Rossi's.

I stared Josh down. "Exactly what I thought."

How did I have such rotten luck that the guy I find who isn't a douche-nozzle needs to leave me? But, at least he wasn't leaving for another woman.

"But that changes today," Josh said.

I raised an eyebrow. "I heard your conversation. You didn't tell him *no*." He'd told me he was ready to break with his father, but when the words were needed, they hadn't come.

Josh turned toward me and placed his hand on my shoulder, holding my gaze. "He wasn't ready to hear it tonight, but I'm not going. That's a fact he'll have to deal with, because there's something more important."

"Which is?"

"I'm looking at her," he said with eyes that wouldn't let me go.

The pride I felt at his declaration battled the unease within me. What if crossing his father was a battle he couldn't win?

"You're saying you want to defy your father because of me?"

He sucked in a deep breath. "That's exactly what I'm saying."

"Why?"

His warm smile held me captive. "You figure it out."

Heat rose in my cheeks. But he was implying pursuing something that couldn't go anywhere. He'd be gone eventually—if not tomorrow, then in a little while, when his family duty finally weighed too heavily on him.

Needing space, I walked to the sink. I'd heard it from him on the plane—moving around the country, dealing with his father's acquisitions was his job. I understood the pressure he was under. I'd dealt with it myself. Being the heir apparent at a family company was a duty that couldn't be shirked, a skin that couldn't be shed.

He followed me and held out his hand. "Now, it's time we went to my place."

I crossed my arms. "I told you. I'm not leaving."

He went into the kitchen.

I followed. "It's my house, and I'm not leaving."

Walking over, he checked the deadbolt on the back door. "Then neither am I." He moved to the window and double-checked the latch.

I chugged my remaining wine. "I don't need babysitting."

"Of course you don't, Nickels." He wrapped me up in a hug I didn't resist. "But you do need protecting." He rubbed my back, pulling some of my stress out with each circle of his fingers.

I held back the tears that threatened while he held me, rocking slightly and rubbing my back the whole time. Neither of us was going to convince the other on this issue tonight. I couldn't leave, he couldn't stay long term, and I had to make peace with that. Until then, the safety of his embrace provided a cocoon from my shitty day. I kept my head buried against his chest, afraid that if I raised it enough to see his eyes, I'd be dragged right back to where we'd stopped.

"You can use the room on the left at the top of the stairs," I told him.

"Sure," was all he said. His hand continued the slow circles on my back. Kind motions replaced my tension with hope.

But hope was for fools. Letting this moment return to the passion of before would only make his departure more painful. I'd been broken too many times. I pushed away.

"Fine. I'm going to bed."

Any more time in his arms and my defenses might crumble. I wouldn't do it again. My heart had been ripped apart too many times already.

Josh

Dad's call had screwed things up royally. It had interrupted the kiss that might have led to much more this evening—more that we both wanted, or at least we'd wanted in that moment.

I should have taken the call in the other room. Talking to Dad in front of her had led to the obvious question of what he wanted, and lying to her wasn't an option.

Her reaction to my openness had been to pull away. Assuring her that I didn't intend to leave hadn't calmed her. The distrust in her eyes was evident. She didn't believe I wasn't going along with Dad's wishes this time, so I'd have to prove it to her.

It would take time for her to trust me, it seemed—a wait I'd have to endure because she was worth it.

After Nicole went upstairs, it took me two circuits of the old house to feel certain all the windows and doors were secure. The best weapon I could find lying around was a field hockey stick with Lara's name on it—not as heavy as a baseball bat, but it would do the job. According to my phone, it was after one by the time I slipped into the guest bedroom across from Nicole's room with my stick.

After settling under the sheets, I stared up at the ceiling with a pounding heart. My efforts to slow it were unsuccessful. Today's whirlwind of emotional interruptions ran through my head on an endless loop.

Our dinner had been interrupted by Lara's call and the murder on Nicole's property. Our kiss had been interrupted by Dad's call and his insistence that I change course once again.

Emotions normally clouded the truth, making logic harder to adhere to and the path too murky to discern, but not today. Today's events had brought out deep emotions that clarified my path. And that path led directly to Nicole.

It might take time, but I would make her understand how I felt, and I damned well wouldn't let some maniac with a knife threaten her.

Family always came first. That had been drilled into each of us Bensons and was a central part of who we were. As the last man standing working for Dad at our company, my duty had seemed clear: I needed to learn the ropes and be the best replacement for him I could be. But being true to myself came ahead of even that.

With every agonizing minute that passed, it became clearer. Nicole was my future, a future I had to try for. If things didn't work out, it wouldn't be because I'd let Dad dictate my actions.

A half hour or so later, an odd creak came from downstairs. Grabbing my less-than-lethal stick, I slipped through the door to the darkened hallway and listened. Eerie quiet filled the space, so I started down the stairs, careful to skip the last two treads at the bottom that had squeaked on the way up.

My circuit of the downstairs rooms came up empty. I ended in the kitchen, and after rechecking the back door, I turned and found myself staring at the refrigerator. A vision of Nicole's beautiful face came rushing back, and the sensations of our kiss along with it. In mere minutes, she'd ruined me for other women.

Back under the covers upstairs, I found myself further from getting to sleep than before. The extra adrenaline my downstairs hunt for the source of that noise had produced was only a part of the problem. The bigger issue was the kiss replaying in my head. The feel of her, the smell of her, the taste of her—I needed more.

Ever since Dad and I had hashed out his succession plan for me and first signed the blue folder's document, I'd wanted to get to the point of running our European operation. It had been the last step before taking over for him in every aspect.

If I got to that step, I knew in my bones that everything would work out. I'd have the autonomy I craved and be equal in all ways to what my brothers had achieved ahead of me. Being the youngest had always sucked: the last to get a driver's license, the last to graduate, and the last to get to run my own business. But being last didn't have to mean least. Our European operations were larger in revenue than any of my brothers' endeavors. It would have been my chance to come out on top for once.

London or bust had been my motto, until today. Tonight I knew London could wait. There was one thing I wanted more than London, and she was sleeping across the hall.

CHAPTER 25

NICOLE

AS I LAY AWAKE GOING OVER TONIGHT'S EVENTS, EVERYTHING WAS A JUMBLE. I'D gone from enjoying dinner with Josh to fearing for Lara, to mourning Maro, and then hating that detective. That confusing kiss with Josh had taken me full circle —a kiss I couldn't get out of my mind now.

I'd taken a chance with Mo, and he'd proven once again that I shouldn't get involved with a man. The vision of him rolling his suitcase away that afternoon had been etched into my brain, never to be forgotten. These sorts of lessons needed to be remembered so they didn't have to be painfully repeated. Wasn't that supposed to be what made humans a superior species? Our ability to learn from the past?

I had a knack for making the same mistake and expecting a different result. If I hadn't gotten home early that day, Mo's retreat from my life would have amounted to a note on the table. As it was, the short argument and bout of crying hadn't made things any easier. But because it had been harder, that made the lesson clearer.

Mo had never intended us to last. He'd said as much when I'd caught him on his way out. To him, I was merely an easy lay—a plaything to warm his bed, cook his meals, and fetch his beers.

I slammed my fist into the bed, remembering how I'd been played, how I'd missed the lies, how I'd deceived myself about his trips.

After professions of love and hints of a coming engagement, complete with a ring shopping trip, how could he just up and leave? Because he was a deceitful, lying bastard like they all were, that's how. He'd interviewed for a job in Phoenix months before without telling me. He'd planned his getaway—a trip that didn't include me—weeks ahead of time.

I'd found out later that he'd given his work four weeks' notice, timing his departure just after his annual bonus was paid out.

The skunk had lied to my face about his multiple trips to Phoenix. To top it all off, after he left, his Facebook status had never changed to single. Photos of him with another girl had only taken days to appear.

Mo had taught me that my antennae for such things sucked, and stalking him on Facebook to learn that had been the ultimate humiliation. Learning that I probably hadn't been the only girl in his life for months had me contemplating a quick trip to Phoenix for revenge.

Sandy had luckily talked me out of it. At the time Lara needed me here more than I needed revenge on Mo. An arrest in Arizona for any of the half dozen things I'd considered doing to him would've only put Lara in danger. Since then, I'd come to the conclusion that he wasn't worth it. He'd been a mistake is all, a lesson.

Josh's phone call, and the talk of him going on to another assignment had set off alarm bells for me. My antennae might not be great at this, but I could tell when something seemed familiar.

Getting into a relationship with a guy who might leave had to be a non-starter for me, and as enticing as the electric attraction between us was, Josh represented that danger in spades.

I mean, sure, he'd said he didn't intend to leave. But how did I know that wasn't just another in a long string of lies to get into my pants? A deception was a deception, and none were any better than the others. They all led down a path of heartbreak and remorse—a path I'd vowed never to walk again.

Still, something tugged at my heart. Had Josh ever really told me a lie? I dared myself to come up with a concrete example and failed. The effort only resulted in a smile in my darkened room. Hadn't he rescued me with a flight from Sioux City, which benefited Lara more than me?

Hadn't it been Josh who'd agreed to let Lara come back to the company to clear her name? Hadn't he been the one to summon his lawyer friend to my defense against that awful detective tonight?

Take that, reactive nature. Tell me what you've got besides his father's desire to put him on another assignment that Josh said he wouldn't accept.

The mental argument made me smile even broader. If I concentrated, I could still imagine the feel of Josh's hand on my boob, the taste of him on my lips, and the feel of his body up against mine.

His father's phone call had interrupted what could have been a great end to a shitty evening.

Sandy's sayings forced themselves to the front of my consciousness. "*If you don't take the first step, you can never round the bases,*" she'd told me. And another pithy text message of hers. "*There may be a lot of fish in the sea, but be careful throwing a good one back, because you'll never hook him again.*"

If I didn't have a real reason to push Josh away, what was I doing now except punishing myself and throwing back the best fish I'd ever hooked? He wasn't Mo. If anything, he'd proven himself time and again to be nothing like Mo.

Josh said I needed to learn to be more decisive.

In the dark, I slipped out of bed and found the mouthwash by my sink.

If I moved fast enough, maybe I could still salvage this.

Josh

Lying awake, I heard another noise, this one upstairs instead of down.

When the handle to the old door on this bedroom squeaked, I slipped to the floor and grabbed my trusty stick before stepping toward the entrance.

Even in the dim moonlight, I saw the door crack open. Winding up for a swing, I tensed to attack the intruder.

A short, shadowy figure squeezed through the door. "Josh," she squealed as she saw me. "What the fuck?"

I flicked on the light and blinked back the brightness. "Jesus H. Christ, what are you doing sneaking around in the dark?"

Nicole's mouth fell open as she saw the field hockey stick in my hands. "I... Uh..." She moved to the light switch and with a quick movement shrouded us in darkness once again.

I dropped the stick when her hands found me.

Her arms came around me. "I wanted to apologize."

Her soft tits pressed against me lit a fire of desire in my chest. I pulled her close and stroked her back. "No need, Nickels."

Her warm form against me said it all, and my stiffening cock would silently tell her what my words hadn't yet.

She snaked a hand behind my neck, and our lips crashed together again.

Tonight in the dark, we would let our lips and hands communicate. Moans, groans, and sighs would replace words.

It started with a soft moan when I cupped her ample boob. She wanted this as much as I did, and I wanted it more than anything in a long time.

With lips mashed together and tongues dueling for position, our arms became a tangle, searching for skin underneath the thin cotton we wore.

I won, getting her T-shirt off first, but she followed and got me down to my boxer briefs a few seconds later.

As I lifted her by the ass cheeks, she wrapped her legs around my waist and ground into me as I carried her to the bed. I leaned over to lay her down, but she refused to release her leg lock on me, and I tumbled over on top of her.

She giggled. "I got you, and I'm not letting go."

"We'll see about that." I tickled her sides.

Her legs came loose after a few giggles. "Hey, that's not fair."

"Scoot up," I urged her. "You're in my bed. I get to make the rules."

In the dim light, a devilish smile grew on her face. "Technically it's my house *and* my bed."

Moving up to straddle her, I grabbed her wrists and pinned them above her head. Hovering a few inches from her face, I asked, "Do you really want to argue tonight?" I laid a set of soft kisses down her neck.

She sighed when I pulled away.

"Or not?" I lowered my lips to her skin again and kissed my way from one shoulder down her collarbone and over to the other. "What'll it be, Nickels?" I moved lower and licked a taut nipple.

She shivered. "Maybe not tonight."

I released her wrists and shifted my hand down to cup the softness of her boob as I licked and sucked her nipple. Only after I'd wrung a few more moans out of her did I shift sides and lavish my attention on the other one.

"Definitely not tonight." Nicole's fingers pulled and scratched at my hair, my scalp, and my shoulders as I kept my attention on her marvelous chest.

Everything about her had me rock hard and ready to burst.

She pulled at my hair as I kissed my way down to her belly button. "I don't want to wait anymore."

"You deserve careful, slow and gentle."I said, lifting my lips from her skin. "But that'll have to wait. You drive me crazy, and I'm not going to last." I moved down farther and raked my chin over the curls on her pubic mound. My hands cradled the soft mounds of her chest.

A soft moan escaped her when I nudged her legs apart and dragged my tongue the length of her slit. "Like that?"

"No, not at all."

Her sharp intake of breath as I repeated it exposed the lie.

"But I'll put up with it," she panted.

She was wet as could be, and I lapped at her, delving into her channel and up to her clit, circling, teasing, working the little bud before going back to her entrance. I changed tempo and depth as I watched, listened, and felt her responses—tightening of her thighs here, an intake of breath there, moans and groans as she came closer and tugged or pushed at my scalp, guiding me.

She tugged at my hair again. "Come up here and kiss me, you fool."

I did as she asked, giving her a taste of herself and moving my hand down to take over where my tongue had been.

Her back arched as I delved a finger in.

"Yes. I want you inside me." Her hand found my cock and started to tug.

I felt for that sensitive inner spot.

She gasped as I found it and stroked.

Her hand pulled and rubbed me, bringing me too close to the edge. I released our lip lock and moved to her tits, pulling my dick away from her hand.

"That's not fair," she complained.

"My rules," I reminded her. "Tonight."

Some women enjoyed having their nipples tweaked and some didn't. Her response when I sucked hard on her nipple put her firmly in the *yes* category.

Moving my finger to her clit brought out a gasp that turned to a moan as I circled and stroked.

She tried to move lower to get at me.

I clamped her leg between mine to keep control. Increasing the tempo of my attack on her little bud brought the shudder that said she was at the edge.

I pinched her nipple and added pressure to her little bundle of nerves.

She shook, and the words poured out. "Oh... fuck... fuck... My God... Yes... Oh, right there... Yes, oh fuck..."

I slowed and then pulled her into an embrace as she melted into the mattress.

"That's not fair."

I hugged her tighter. "I want you to enjoy it enough that you'll come back."

She laughed gently. "You can count on it. But I wanted you inside me."

"You think we're done?" I asked.

Nicole

"Do you have a condom?" I asked.

He hadn't made a move for one before, so I wondered if his finger and tongue action had been because we weren't prepared.

He slid away and came back quickly. The sound of the package tearing provided my answer.

I wasn't going to ask. *Cosmo* said most men preferred doggy, so I rolled over and got on all fours. "Show me what ya got, cowboy."

It only took a few seconds for him to move behind me and urge my legs farther apart.

I put my head on the pillow and moved a hand back to guide him in.

He pushed his thick shaft in slowly. "This is what I got, cowgirl." After a quick shove, he was almost all the way in and stretching me to my limit.

I held back a yelp. This wasn't a problem I'd had with Mo.

"Too much?" Josh asked.

"You're big," I told him.

He pulled back.

I shoved back toward him. "I said big, not too big." Since he wasn't thrusting, I gyrated on him.

He grabbed my hips, and the thrusting began in earnest.

The sensations grew quickly as he went deeper, pulling me back against him as the tempo increased, along with the fierceness of his thrusts. I quickly climbed back up the hill of pleasure he'd shown me earlier. I felt every movement, every pull of his hands, every plunge.

His breath sped up and became shallow. "I warned you, I'm not going to last."

"Me either," I hissed.

The words came out between the slapping of our bodies together. "You're so… fucking tight… so wet… oh fuck… so good."

My boobs swung back and forth with our movements, and all my nerves started to fire together as he plunged into me again and again. The white light of my orgasm came quickly, and the fire in my core radiated out to my fingers and toes. My toes curled, and I fisted the sheets. My walls clenched around him, tighter than I could ever remember.

"Oh fuck." He drove into me and held there.

His cock throbbed inside me as he found his release and the spasms of my orgasm dissipated. He urged me forward, and I collapsed into the mattress.

I struggled to breathe with his weight on top of me and his cock still throbbing inside me, but I didn't care. This was how it was meant to be. Mind-blowing sex wasn't meant to be easy.

Sensing my issue, he shifted his chest off to the side, but stayed inside me. "Nickels?"

"Yeah?" I answered.

"I'm staying."

With him over and inside me, those two words meant everything.

CHAPTER 26

Nicole

The next morning, I woke and looked groggily to my right. My clock wasn't where it should have been. I was in the unfamiliar setting of the guest bedroom, but one thing was the same: I'd woken up alone.

Somehow Josh had managed to slip out without waking me—maybe not a hard task given how little actual sleep I'd gotten. Energetic sex when I'd invaded his room and again in the middle of the night had exhausted me.

After locating my nightshirt on the floor and giving up on finding my panties, I padded out to the hallway.

Faint oldies music drifted up the staircase from below.

After a pit stop in the bathroom and a bit of mouthwash, I ventured down. The enticing aroma of fresh coffee grew stronger as I got closer to the kitchen.

Josh had his back to me, dancing in front of the stove to The Beach Boys playing on his phone. The funniest part was his bare ass peeking out of the apron he'd tied around himself—and in the morning light it was a spectacular ass, with a clear demarcation from light tan to white below his waist.

Quietly, I reached for my phone on the counter and swiped up to open the camera.

He turned too soon. "Morning, Nickels. I didn't hear you come down.

Coffee's hot, and breakfast is almost ready." His brow creased as he noticed the phone I held up. He struck a pose with a flexed bicep. "Want a picture, do ya?"

I clicked off the second picture. "Thanks." I swiped between the two photos. The first hadn't caught the cute shot of his ass I'd hoped for. It was a profile of him as he turned, and you could tell he was shirtless under the apron, but that was all. I deleted it before he reached me.

"Did it come out okay?"

I showed him.

"Huh." He shrugged.

"I'll delete it if you want," I offered.

"Your phone, your choice."

I tilted my head to look at it again. The picture of him flexing for me was perfect in a goofy sort of way. "I'll keep it until I get a better one of you." I didn't intend to ever delete this picture and what it represented—the first morning-after.

He shrugged again. "Whatever."

He rushed back to the stove to tend to the frying pan, but didn't dance the way he had before.

"You always dance when you cook?" I behaved myself and passed on the second opportunity for a non-PG picture of him. The image had already been burned into my memory.

"Only on good mornings."

"Good?"

"Sorry, great."

His words sparked hope in me. Things had moved so fast last night. A guy like him had surely been with dozens of more-experienced women than me, and some guys graded, didn't they? He'd said *great*, so that had to be a B-plus at least.

I walked up and wrapped my arms around him. "I'm happy too." I peeked over his arm, and he seemed to be overcooking the French toast. "I'll take mine a little less done, if that's okay." The feel of my breasts against him brought back a surge of memories from last night—all the ways he'd kissed me, licked me, touched me, and…

"Trust me, Nickels, I know what I'm doing, and this is almost ready, if you'll get the plates. Maybe next time you can choose the menu."

Reluctantly, I let go of him, brought my focus back to this morning, and gathered up the plates and silverware.

He brought the toast over and placed a few on each plate. "My own recipe."

The slight tenting of his apron showed I wasn't the only one who'd flashed back to last night during our hug. I joined him at the table and only added a drizzle of syrup before trying a darkened piece.

It wasn't overcooked at all, and the flavors surprised me. "Mocha?"

"With a bit of cinnamon," he said with a smile.

I quickly cut another piece. "This is great."

"Only the best for the lady of the house." He forked a bite. "Now, what did you want to argue about?"

"Huh?"

We'd had a wonderful night together. Why would I want to start an argument?

He waved the fork with French toast on it at me. "I gave you the choice of arguing last night or this morning."

Except for being tired, nothing came to mind. "I don't have any complaints. So I lose a turn?"

"Just following through on a promise."

I shook my head. "You're a goofball, you know that?"

"I always keep my promises, and there's nothing funny about it."

That seemed obvious, yet it was still unexpected. I devoured my scrumptious breakfast, wondering why I'd never thought of mocha French toast. Every time I looked up, I found Josh's eyes on me—sometimes my face and sometimes my pokey nipples showing through the thin cotton. It should have made me self-conscious, but instead I felt desired, and chose to own it. I sat up straighter and kept my shoulders back to accentuate the effect.

"We need to talk about work," he said as he swirled his last bites through the syrup.

I didn't want people at Rossi's knowing I was bedding the boss. Even though I was the founder's granddaughter, I'd still be judged.

"Yeah, you being the boss makes this complicated."

"That's not what I meant."

"What then?"

"With Lara not coming in to work to uncover the real embezzler, we need to go at it a different way if we're ever going to clear her."

Stunned, I could only manage to nod. How had I lucked into a man like him?

He smiled. "You told me you promised to take care of Lara, and I intend to help you keep that promise."

"Thank you." I watched him chew and wondered how he'd come to have such a big heart. "You surprise me almost every time you open your mouth."

"Only because you refuse to have dinner and get to know me."

I pointed my fork at him. "That's not entirely my fault." Lara seemed to interrupt us every time.

"I have an idea," he said. "Bill Covington's sister and her husband started a forensic accounting firm in town. I'll see if I can get them involved."

"Good idea," I said. What I really meant was: *I can't thank you enough for being so kind-hearted.* Ernst or anybody else in his position would have moved on and let the legal system chew Lara up and spit her out twenty years from now, assuming she lasted that long in prison. I couldn't contain the smile that overtook me.

"What's so funny?"

"Nothing. I'm just happy we're having this conversation."

Actually, I was happy to be here this morning with this particular man; the conversation was a bonus. I got tingly remembering how Josh had made me feel last night. I could write a ten-page poem about it, about him, about his compassion. The tingle between my legs reminded me I'd need to add passion to that list.

My phone chose that moment to ring.

Josh reached for it before I could. After glancing at the screen, he answered with a wink at me. "Miss Rossi's line... Why, yes she is, Sandy." He handed me the phone. "It's for you."

"Hi," I answered.

"Are you okay? And Lara?" Sandy asked. "I saw the article on the *Times* website and was worried."

"I'm fine. We're both fine." Looking over at the man in my kitchen, I was a lot better than fine, and for now I chose to believe Lara was safe. "What article?"

"The one about the murder on your street last night. The one that implies Lara did it."

That made my blood boil. "She didn't do anything except be in the wrong place at the wrong time."

"I know that, girl. I was just worried is all. So...moving on, who's answering your phone this early in the morning?"

I wasn't touching that one. "I haven't read the article yet. I'll have to get back to you."

"I knew it. Tell me it's Barbados Josh. I knew he'd be good for you."

"I'll read it after we get off."

Josh chewed slowly and appraised me with a questioning look.

"I get it. You can't talk. Good for you, girl. Now don't start overthinking and fuck it all up. He sounds like he has potential."

"I'll do my best."

"Let's have lunch and you can give me all the juicy details. And I mean *all* the details."

"I'm not sure I can make that," I told her.

"I'm not taking no for an answer, and does he have any brothers? Tell me he has brothers. We could go double on a weekend in Hawaii."

"Yes."

"Can he set me up with one of them?"

Josh chewed and sent me another curious look.

I tilted my head at him and shrugged, trying to look bored. "I don't know the answer to that."

Josh sipped his juice, not taking his eyes off of me.

"Help a girl out and let me know," Sandy said.

"Here. You can ask him yourself." I offered the phone to Josh. "Sandy has a question for you."

He swallowed and took the phone. "What would you like to know?" His lips turned up in an expanding smile. "The Lakers? Sure, I think they have a chance this year… Uh-huh, even against Golden State… Nice talking to you too, Sandy." He hung up.

I lifted the last piece of my breakfast to my lips.

He put the phone down and stifled a laugh. "What did she really want to ask me?"

To give myself time to think, I pointed to my mouth as I chewed. It didn't help me come up with a witty response. "She wanted to know if you could set her up with one of your brothers."

"Sorry, they're all taken," he said, sipping some of his coffee.

I navigated on my phone to the *Times* website and located the article.

Anger heated me as I read. It mentioned the similarities to the case five years ago and included plenty of implications that the police considered Lara to be the prime suspect.

The details could only have come from that asswipe Beal. I vocalized the only thing that fit. "That asshole."

"Who?" Josh asked.

I handed him the phone. "Beal. He really has it in for Lara."

Josh swiped up and down the page. "It only happened last night. They didn't do any investigating. They only wrote what they were told, I'm sure."

"You're defending them?"

He put up his hands in surrender. "Not at all. But they're just merchants of misery out to make a buck. I'm on your side, remember?"

Josh's phone rang as I cleaned up the dishes. He declined the call. "Unknown number."

It rang again and again.

He answered it the third time. "Hello?"

He motioned me over a second later and put it on speaker.

CHAPTER 27

Nicole

"They think I did it," Lara's voice came over the phone. "All I did was stumble onto it."

I answered. "Hey. It's good to hear your voice. Are you all right?" I tried to sound happier than I felt. She probably needed it.

"I couldn't stay," she said, her voice still jittery.

"Are you okay?" I repeated.

Again she ignored my question. "I had to get out of there, and you do too," she said with real fear lacing her voice.

"Slow down," Josh urged her. "What happened? You know leaving looks bad."

"I know, but looking bad is better than being dead."

"Where are you?" I asked.

Josh put a hand on my arm. "No, Lara, don't tell us."

I looked over at him incredulously.

"Detective Beal is looking for you," Josh explained. "We told him we don't know where you are, and we should keep it that way. But tell us what happened."

"He should be looking for the guy," she complained.

"What guy?" I asked, though it sounded stupid as soon as I said it.

"The guy that stabbed Mr. Tanaka."

I noted that she said *stabbed* and not *killed*. Did she know he was dead?

Josh held up a finger to hold me back. "First, are you in a safe place?"

We heard her take in a big breath. "For now."

"Why didn't you call me?" I blurted. She'd called Josh instead of me when she was in danger?

She snorted. "Duh, the cops are probably already tapped into your phone."

Her logic seemed plausible.

"Let's get back to what happened," Josh said. "Start at the beginning."

"After dinner," she sniffled, "Echo came in with blood on his face, but he ran right back out the doggy door." She sniffed. "I thought he'd gotten into a fight with a coyote or something and went out after him."

Josh looked at me and mouthed, "Coyote?"

I shrugged. Coyotes weren't unknown in LA, but mostly they went after cats and small dogs, not one the size of Echo.

"But when I followed him, it was just like before." She started to sob. "It looked just like when Vern…" Her voice trailed off. She sniffed and continued. "I ran over to him. There was just so much blood, so much blood everywhere."

I wanted to ask if Maro was still alive when she found him, but was afraid to.

She sucked in a loud breath. "Maro said to run, to get away before he came back."

I forced out the question. "Who?"

"He didn't say. That was all he said, before…before he stopped breathing."

Her words made my knees go weak.

Josh's jaw clenched. "You should have called 9-1-1."

I wobbled as I imagined how terrible it was, how terrible it must have been for her.

Josh put the phone on the counter and rushed to pull me to him with a strong arm.

My legs went weak as my heart pounded in my head.

"I ran to the house," Lara continued. "And when I heard somebody on the back deck, I panicked and called you."

"Who was it? Did you recognize him?" Josh asked, as he added another arm to hold me up.

"I hid until I heard him go back down the steps. Then I dumped the phone and went out the front. I never looked out the window. I'm not stupid. If he'd known I was in the house, I'd probably be dead now."

Joshed lifted me up onto one of the barstools, but kept a protective arm around my back, steadying me.

"The cops think you did it," I told her weakly. She needed to know.

She was silent for a moment. "That figures. I bet it's that asshole detective from last time. He still thinks I killed Vern."

We didn't have to answer that one; she'd hit it on the nose.

She sighed. "I get it. I know how it looks—me skipping out and all—but I know how the system works. That detective has already decided to pin it on me."

I looked up to gauge Josh's reaction.

The straight arrow didn't look happy with the way this conversation was going.

"Staying away isn't going to help," he told her. "The longer it is before they hear your side of it, the longer it is before they look for the real killer."

Josh's phone rang with a train whistle sound as another call came in, drowning out Lara's words. The screen said Dad. He hit ignore. "I'll call him back later. Sorry, Lara. We had another call coming in. Go ahead."

"You haven't seen how the cops operate from my side of the street," she said. "I gotta go and figure out what to do next."

From my side of the street—she viewed herself as separate from me. She'd seen my desire to avoid a conflict with Ernst as taking his side over hers. I was really only trying to hang on until my thirtieth birthday when the dynamic would change.

Josh shook his head at her reply. "I'll see if I can get some help from this end. How do we get in touch with you?"

"You don't. Change the price of bananas in the discount flyer to end in a zero, and I'll call in."

That was an idea she'd pointed out years ago when we were watching a cop show on TV, and a slick one. Our prices always ended in an eight or a nine, and the flyers went out all over the area. "Gotta go," she added.

"Love you. Don't forget about the dog walker," I said.

"Let us help," Josh suggested.

"Bye," was all she said before she ended the call.

The conversation had drained me. "I don't know what to do to help her."

I'd wanted to hear from her, and I'd expected it to make me feel better, but all I felt inside was the cold emptiness of frustration.

I shivered. "I'm scared for her," I admitted.

She was out there, alone, hunted by the police, and the killer.

Josh squeezed my hand.

CHAPTER 28

NICOLE

WE WERE LATE GETTING READY FOR WORK AFTER LARA'S CALL.

Josh insisted on driving me in.

I resisted at first, but I'd almost been ready to leave Casa di Rossi with him last night when he'd given in to me. It seemed fitting this morning to not fight him on this.

He stopped the car at a light, and I brought up the obvious, the elephant in the room we hadn't talked about.

"About last night…" I couldn't bring myself to ask the hard questions.

"Yeah?" he asked without looking over. He wasn't making this easier.

I slapped his shoulder. "You know what I mean." Being the woman in this situation put the onus on me to clarify things.

The signal turned green, and he accelerated. "Being a dumb USC guy, I don't know what you mean if you won't spit it out."

"It's a small company, and people talk. I don't want them to know we're…" I wasn't sure how to finish that.

"We're what?" he asked.

"I don't know what we are."

We hadn't been on a real date. Were we fuck buddies just boinking, or had last night been a pity fuck because I'd had such an awful night? Or something else…

He pulled the car over and stopped before facing me. "Look, we haven't had time to talk this out." He took my hand. "I think you are amazing. If you don't understand how I feel about you, you're not as smart as I thought."

Warmth grew in my chest. He'd eliminated pity fuck and one-night stand as well. "But I don't know the first thing about your…uh…personal situation."

Was there a delicate way to ask if he was dating anybody? I'd heard him talking to a Serena on the phone once, and it hadn't sounded work-related.

"With Serena and all."

He took in a breath and nodded. "Okay, let's get that out of the way. You can expect that I won't see anyone else, and I absolutely won't share you with anybody either. Same as I told you before, you can expect full honesty from me, and I expect the same from you. I will treat you with utmost respect, and if you ever feel I'm not, you need to say so. If you don't like to be spoiled, that's tough shit. Learn to deal with it. Starting now, I'm dating you, and I don't do it half-assed. And by the way, Serena is my sister."

The torrent of clarity that had come from his mouth was something I'd never experienced before.

It took a second to process it all. "Don't I get a say in this?" In a few moments we'd gone from what-the-hell-happened-last-night to you're mine?

"Sure you do. You're in or you're out. Which is it?"

Subtlety was clearly not his strong suit.

"What if I'm not sure?"

He'd said it as if starting today I belonged to him, like he was setting rules for me, for us—caging me in.

He surprised me by leaning over and pulling my face to within an inch of his. His fierce eyes bored into mine as he spoke softly. "Then I spend every day of the next week convincing you to say yes."

I bit back a laugh. "What if a week isn't enough?"

His lips turned up. "Then I'm not doing it right."

In that moment, I couldn't imagine more romantic words. Being decisive had been his lesson for me, so I laid a soft kiss on him. "Then yes."

"The kisses are going to have to wait, Nickels." He released me and put the car back in gear. "We still need to get you to work before the day is over."

As we pulled back into traffic, I looked over at the protective hunk of a man next to me and decided there were a lot of worse things than being his woman. Daddy would have liked him. Daddy would have liked him a lot. Daddy would have married me off to him in an instant.

Giving myself a mental slap, I decided I couldn't think like that. We passed a billboard for a new movie. The larger-than-life actress oozed sex appeal.

The bazillionaire driving me to work this morning could be dating her, or some tennis star, or any fucking woman in this town, if he wanted, and yet here we were. How had I gotten so lucky?

Like an idiot, I verbalized my fear without thinking. "Why me?"

"It seemed like a good idea," he said brusquely.

"Oh." I slumped down in my seat. I'd hoped for something more than that.

He glanced my direction a few seconds later. "You should have more confidence, Nickels. It would take longer than we have this morning for me to tell you all the reasons." He offered a hand across the console. "Have confidence in yourself."

My insides warmed, but I still needed to address the office. "How are we going to handle this at work?"

He raised a cocky brow. "I'd be happy to handle you in my office. I was thinking the desk, or maybe a closet, if you like the dark better."

"Stop being a goofball. This is serious. I think I want to keep it between us for now, as far as work goes."

"Sure. It's your call."

A moment later, I felt self-conscious about assuming Serena was a girlfriend. "You didn't tell me you had a sister."

"Now whose fault is that? You're the one who refused to go out to dinner with me."

"I guess." I squirmed in my seat. He was right.

"I have two: Serena here in LA and Kelly in DC. And three brothers."

"See? That's what I mean. We don't know anything about each other."

"I've seen you at work for a while now. I know nothing about your history, but I know a lot more than you think about the kind of person you are."

I punched the temperature down a few degrees on my side of the car. Why did everything he said make me hot?

He changed lanes. "We've got a few minutes. Go ahead, ask me anything."

I'd slept with and now agreed to date a man I knew almost nothing about, and suddenly I didn't have any important questions. Looking over at him, I tallied up what I did know. He was smart, kind, protective, honest, and blunt, which was a refreshing change from the deceit I'd experienced with other guys. And I couldn't forget decisive too. But I snorted a laugh when I realized I didn't know if he could pass one of my mother's old tests.

"What?" he asked, looking over briefly.

"Have you ever been in prison?"

"That's the best you can come up with? I thought you'd want to know my sign or something. The answer is no, I haven't been in prison. Have you?"

"No. Lara handles that part for both of us."

"Nickels, there are probably a million things I haven't told you yet. Let's start to fix that over dinner tonight."

"I'd like that." It was a bit backwards to sleep with him and *then* go out on our first dinner date, but a lot of things with Josh had been upside down.

"I'm looking forward to learning everything about you, Nickels."

I smiled back at him. "Not much to learn."

"I doubt that, and on the subject of Serena, you'll get to meet her a week from Saturday. I think you'll like her."

A cringe crept over me. Meeting a guy's sister always felt like a test. "Next week?" The bigger question in my mind was *would she like me*?

"I'm going to Kelly's place. I'd like you to come along."

This had grown from meeting one sister to both of them at the same time.

I wrapped my arms around myself. "You want me to meet both your sisters?"

"No. Everybody. The whole family. It's Kelly's engagement party." That wasn't a number, and it sounded like the actual number might scare me.

"Including your parents?"

"The whole family. I'm dating the most beautiful girl in town. Why wouldn't I want to show you off?"

I couldn't decide between being overjoyed at the compliment or pissed off at the show-me-off comment, like I belonged to him.

"I'm not sure I can—"

"Decision time again, Nickels," he said, verbally cutting off my avenue of escape. "It's too dangerous to leave you alone, so either you're coming with me, or I'm staying home with you. Which will it be?"

"Demanding much?" I shot back.

"Indecisive much?" he answered.

"You don't have to stay with me. I'll be fine home alone."

"After what just happened in your backyard, I'm not leaving you alone, Nickels. Now make up your mind."

"Which do you want?" I asked.

"Either way, I get to spend the day with you, and that's all I care about. Now make a damned choice, Stanford."

The sweet words didn't help. Everything with him was about making snap decisions.

I wasn't getting a chance to put this off. As much as I dreaded being thrown in front of his family after less than a week together, I would feel terrible if he skipped his sister's party on my account.

"I'd love to meet your family."

I'd done it, jumped off the cliff into the deep water.

He offered his hand over the console. "Trust me, they'll love you."

I took his hand and received a warm squeeze in return.

A minute later, his phone rang with his father's train ringtone.

I pulled it from the cup holder, and the screen verified what I suspected. "Do you want to answer it?"

"No... He can wait. I'd rather spend the drive talking with you."

And so we did.

Josh

After dropping Nicole off at work, I headed home to change.

When my phone rang with Dad's ringtone for the third time, I answered it. "Hello?"

"Josh, you've been a hard man to reach this morning."

A mild rebuke by my father's standards.

"I've had a busy night and morning. One of my employees had a police emergency last night."

"The body at the Rossi place?"

"Yes." I shouldn't have been surprised. Dad was incredibly well connected with both the Sheriff's Office and the LAPD.

"I apologize for pushing you last night. I didn't realize the situation. We can put off this meeting about you going out to Camper Heaven for a little while if you need time to deal with that."

I'd take whatever time I could get right now to solidify my explanation.

"Sure, we can talk later."

"Also, if you need any protection for your *employee*, I've already called the Hanson firm, and they'll have top people available for you, if you wish."

I hadn't thought that far ahead yet. "Thanks, Dad. I'll consider that."

"They're professionals, the cream of the crop. Anyway, that's why I was calling."

We got off the line after a few platitudes, and I contemplated the conversation.

After hanging up on him last night, which should have royally pissed him off, he was offering help this morning *and* stepping back on pushing me to go to Nebraska for Camper Heaven. This was a surprise, to say the least, but then I'd never pushed back very hard against him.

At my place on Wilshire, I changed and also packed a bag for a few days. I hadn't been successful last night convincing Nicole to leave her house for the safety of my condo, and I couldn't be sure of success tonight either.

The drive back to the Rossi's office building was long enough for me to spend some time thinking about Dad's call. He'd said it was good to have professionals on the case, and that brought to mind my call for help on our embezzlement issue. It wasn't a problem that would age well.

Dee corralled me as I arrived. She had the *Times* story up on her screen. "It's terrible what happened."

"What?" I asked, feigning ignorance.

"You need to read this. I'll send it to you. Then I think you should check in on Nicky. She must be devastated." Her concern was touching, as was her looking out for my reputation as a caring boss by suggesting I check on Nicole.

"I'll look at it right away." I went into my office and powered up my computer. After rereading the horrid piece, I marched out of my office to see my girl. "I'll see if there's anything we can do for her," I told Dee on my way.

Nicole had a line of people outside her office offering support. It seemed the entire company had already read about last night.

I waited my turn and offered the company's support if she needed it.

"Thank you, Mr. B. But I'm fine. There is one other thing, though."

Avoiding the urge to suggest she join me in my office, I waited.

"Lara won't be able to come in for at least a few days." Her lips became positively pouty as she said it.

I backed toward the door. "I'll let Rosa know. Tell Lara to take whatever time she needs." Being here and not undressing Nicole with my eyes was difficult.

"Thank you, I will."

Operation Keep-It-Under-Wraps had started.

AT LUNCHTIME, I WALKED DOWN THE STREET TO TACO BANDITO. UNFORTUNATELY, today's lunch partner wasn't Nicole, but Gary. I'd asked him to meet me here and to come alone.

He waited for his food at a table outside and waved as I walked up.

"Thanks for meeting me. I'll join you as soon as I order," I told him.

"Sure thing." He looked nervous, like a kid called down to the principal's office.

After ordering, I returned with my tray of chips and salsa—including the red sauce I *wasn't* sampling today. I'd learned my lesson.

He lifted a chip with a shaky hand. "What did you want to talk about?"

The sound was unmistakable as a Harley thundered up the street.

"I want to get to the bottom of the missing money. With Lara out for a while, I've decided to call in some experts."

"Experts?"

The loud bike pulled into the parking lot and then went quiet.

"That's them," I told Gary.

The rider and his passenger dismounted, unzipping their leather jackets and walking our way.

"Let me do the talking if you want to keep your teeth," I warned Gary.

He went pale.

I got up to greet the two riders. "Hey, Beast, long time no see," I said as we shook. I wrapped Nick Knowlton into a one-armed hug.

"Not long enough, college boy," he said, slapping me on the back.

I untangled myself and gave his wife, Katie, a gentle hug. "Glad you brought Beauty with you."

"Stop it," Katie complained.

I kidded her pretty much every time we met. We'd dated a few times before she married Nick, but he'd been the right match for her, and we both knew it.

I let go and made the introductions to Gary.

Gary lifted a chip after they went inside to order. "And how are they going to help?"

"They're forensic accountants. They're here to help us find out who took our money."

His brows shot up. "You're kidding, right?"

"I don't kid about money. She's a CPA, and nobody beats their results."

Gary's perplexed look gave way to a nod. "If you say so." He bit into his chip. Mentioning that Katie had her CPA had clinched it for him.

When they returned, Nick ribbed me about missing our last construction weekend, and I got him back by pointing out how his bike made more noise than it had horsepower.

We got down to business after we all had food in front of us.

"What's the problem?" Nick asked.

I motioned to Gary to explain.

"Some money went missing," he said sheepishly.

"How much?" Katie asked.

Gary looked at me for confirmation before answering. "A little over three million."

The number had no effect on either of them, and I knew it was because this was small potatoes in their line of work.

Katie was the first to speak. "How long ago?"

"It was going on up until a few weeks ago," Gary answered.

"Do you have any idea who is or was involved?" Nick asked after finishing chewing.

I knew how I would answer that, but instead nodded for Gary to give them his opinion.

"They arrested Lara Martini," he started. "But she was the one who uncovered it, and I don't think it was her."

Nick nodded. "Why not?"

Gary used a finger to wipe condensation off the side of this drink. "She's not the type, I guess."

I didn't have anything to add to that.

Katie broke the silence. "Our usual fee is five percent of the amount traced, and an additional five on any amount recovered." She looked at Nick, who didn't add anything to that.

"What about the friends-and-family discount?" I asked.

"You're not family, college boy," Nick shot back. "And friend is stretching it."

"How about four and four?" Katie offered.

"Five and five if Beast here can finish the red sauce in less than a minute, and three and three if he can't." I held my hand across the table to shake on it with Nick.

He took my hand in a vise-like grip. "Like takin' candy from a baby with you college boys."

I lifted my wrist to look at my watch. "Go."

He scooped the red sauce on a chip and started chewing. He picked up the dish and brought it to his lips to drink it down, but stopped as his eyes bugged out. He put the dish down and grabbed for his drink.

Gary choked back a laugh.

"Fuck, that's hot," Nick gasped after finishing his drink and grabbing for his wife's. "We should have arm-wrestled for it."

Katie laughed and pointed at the writing on the paper lining the tray. "You should have read this first." It was the same warning I'd missed my first time here.

After finishing off Katie's drink and dabbing at the sweat on his forehead, Nick was back to business. "We'll need access to the system and the books."

"Gary here will arrange whatever you need."

Gary handed over his card.

They spent the rest of lunch asking Gary about our accounting and computer systems.

As I listened to the conversation, I came out of it with a new appreciation for my finance guy. He looked young, but he'd had detailed answers to everything they asked.

"And who do we give our results to?" Katie asked.

"Me," I told her.

"We'll get right on it," Nick said as he stood and grabbed his tray. Nodding toward me he added, "I'll get you for this, college boy."

Katie slapped his shoulder. "It was your damned fault."

"Good to see you too, Network Knight."

After bussing our trays and getting out of earshot, Gary asked. "Network Knight?"

"Don't let appearances fool you. That guy is a first-class hacker, and he teaches computer science on the side at UCLA. He presents papers on system vulnerabilities every year."

"Hmm," was all he said.

"The fact that we've hired them is strictly between the two of us, and Nicole. Nobody else is to be in the loop, and I mean *nobody*."

We still had no clue who the real culprit was, and I wasn't taking any chances with loose lips.

Gary nodded. "You can count on me, Mr. B."

Back at the Rossi's building I found Nicole in her office and closed the door behind me to give her the good news.

CHAPTER 29

Josh

For the second time, I guided Nicole through the front door of Aldolfo's with a hand at the small of her back. The feel of her under my touch was just as electric as before.

"Hopefully the third time is the charm," I told Nicole as the hostess showed us to a table.

Nicole held up crossed fingers as she walked in front of me.

All I could focus on was the sway of her ass and what I knew lay beneath the dress—a dress I planned to have on the floor the second we got behind closed doors.

Our waiter arrived shortly after we were seated.

"Could we start with an order of bruschetta, but without the shrimp?" I asked him.

"You remembered," Nicole said.

"Naturally." I turned to our waiter. "And a chardonnay for the lady. I'll have a…make that two chardonnays, please."

He hurried off.

"You don't have to change your wine order for me." She winked. "I think we've already bonded."

Bonded was too mild a word for how I felt.

The wink of her green eye meant it took me a few seconds to formulate a complete sentence. "I just wanted to pick up where we left off last time."

"Going well, was it?"

I nodded. "I thought so." I tapped my forehead. "I have a very vivid memory of sitting across from the most gorgeous girl in town when we were interrupted. And tonight is looking very much the same." *Gorgeous* seemed too mild a word for how she looked tonight. Knowing how soft her skin only amplified her allure.

Her cute insta-blush returned. "Woman. And, that's not how I remember it."

"It was definitely like that. We were about to order, and she was soon going to tell me all of her most intimate secrets."

"Intimate? Hardly. I think we were going to start with you. You're the enigma, after all. I'm pretty boring."

"Don't sell yourself short, Nickels." She and boring weren't in the same universe.

"The way I remember it, you had just tried your best pickup lines on me, and they weren't very good."

"They were pretty bad, weren't they?"

"Terrible."

Our waiter returned with our wine and appetizer.

After a quick recheck of the menu, she chose the penne siciliana, and I ordered the scaloppine al limone.

I raise my glass. "To no emergency calls tonight."

Nicole repeated the toast and clinked glasses with me before we drank, and I got to watch my beautiful date swallow as I remembered kissing that neck of hers.

"This is about where we got interrupted last time," I said.

She laughed. "I turned my phone off, just in case."

I pulled mine out of my pocket. "Good idea." I swiped it off.

She picked up a bruschetta. "If we're going to get to know each other, tell me something embarrassing about yourself."

That would take us a mile off the beaten path, polite-conversation-wise.

"Embarrassing, huh?" This was a detour I hadn't expected.

"So cringe-worthy you haven't admitted it to anyone."

"That's a pretty high bar." I thought for a moment. I couldn't remember anything noteworthy I hadn't told at least one of my siblings—until I remembered Mike and the Honda. "I didn't do very well the first time I rode a motorcycle because I was too cocky to admit I didn't know how." That day had taught me a lesson I still remembered.

She leaned forward, seeming eager for the gory details.

I took a bruschetta. "It was a Honda. I figured since I rode a bicycle, staying upright would be a cinch. All I had to do was wear shades, shift gears, and look studly, but it wasn't that simple."

"Doesn't sound very embarrassing so far."

I finished chewing. "It was my friend Mike's bike. So I got on. No helmet."

She smirked. "You were too cool for a helmet?"

I nodded. "Way too cool, and way too dumb, so no helmet. I lied and told Mike I'd ridden my brother's Harley. He believed me. Anyway, I got on, started it up, pressed the gear pedal down for first gear, and let out the clutch. But, like a dumb shit, I was holding the throttle wrong. When the acceleration threw me back, I twisted the throttle harder and went hurtling directly toward a tree on the far side of the road."

She listened in rapt silence, and then opened her hands when I didn't continue. "And?"

"I ended up only nicking my elbow on the tree, but one foot to the right and I would have face-planted into it at thirty miles an hour with no helmet—like, bye-bye, baby." I made a slashing gesture across my neck. "Then you wouldn't have had to endure any of my pickup lines."

Her mouth dropped. "That's scary. And you never told anybody about this?"

"Mike saw it, but not another soul, and you can't repeat that to any of my family. It would kill my mother."

She made a zipping motion across her lips. "Your secret is safe with me."

"Your turn," I said.

She touched her chin. "First, tell me how you got the scar."

I ran my finger over the scar on my chin and went back to that scary day. "I was just a kid. My cousin and I were out messing around in a dry creek bed. They warn you about flash floods in the desert, but you have no idea what it's like until the wall of water comes at you. We almost didn't get out in time, and I fell on the rocks scrambling up the side. That wasn't a good day." I took a swallow of wine. *Definitely not a good day.*

"That's scary."

"I had nightmares about it for years. Now your turn."

She stuffed a bruschetta in her mouth and pointed to her full cheeks to hold me off.

I let her chew for a moment.

"Instead of most embarrassing, something different…" I waited for her.

She tried to drag it out, but eventually had to swallow and come up for air. "Okay, what?"

"Tell me about your last boyfriend." For most girls, that would only be mildly embarrassing.

Her mouth dropped.

I'd figured it would be a slight embarrassment, but her face showed something much worse—in the direction of truly awful.

Nicole

I BIT MY LIP, UNSURE WHAT TO DO NEXT. HOW HAD I BEEN SO STUPID? ASKING HIM about embarrassing moments would so predictably lead to something about Mo. It was obvious as hell.

I sighed. "His name was Mo, short for Maurice." I paused to take down a big swallow of wine. "He… He was…"

He put up a hand to stop me. "You don't have to. I shouldn't have asked."

Our food arrived, and I stayed quiet until our waiter retreated.

I'd been given a reprieve, but it didn't seem fair that I'd asked him to bare his soul and I was off the hook after starting us down this uncomfortable path. "Are you sure? I mean, I started this."

His smile brightened. "How 'bout you tell me the history of Rossi's instead?"

Relieved, I began. "It all started with my grandfather."

Josh seemed genuinely interested as I explained the establishment of our first store and how my parents had grown it to be the chain it was today.

Josh posed only a few questions as I babbled on about our emphasis on working with the growers.

I'd agreed to dinner, and I did want us to get to know each other, but as I took in the man across from me, echoes of last night kept intruding. Now that I knew what I'd been missing, words could wait. We were on a happy topic, and one I could normally go on for hours about, but every question only delayed our departure. More than once, I lost my train of thought as his eyes roamed over me in an I-want-to eat-you-alive kind of way. My lady bits were so heated, I was squirming in my seat.

I'd been flapping my gums so long that more of my food was getting cold than getting eaten, while he'd slowly consumed most of his. "I'm not as hungry as I thought. Maybe we should call it a night."

"Not yet, Nickels. This is get-to-know-you night, remember?" He looked at me over his wine glass. "And when did your father pass the torch to your uncle?"

The wine I sipped turned sour in my mouth as I remembered the horror of that time.

Keep it together, girl. You can get past this.

I couldn't stomach calling him my uncle anymore. "Ernst took over after my parents died." I blinked back tears. "They…" I paused, refusing to let history repeat itself. I would not let their deaths destroy me another time.

Josh reached across the table, and the touch of his hand drew my wet eyes to his. The pale blue of his gaze was oddly calming, as if holding contact with his eyes drew out some of the hurt, the anger, the dread I held within.

"You don't need to go into that," he said softly, with a tone as compassionate as his look.

I put my fork down and dabbed under one eye with my napkin. "No. I'm okay about it now. It's not something I can hide from. They died in an accident." It was time to slay this demon again, and not let it control me.

His fingers wrapped gently around mine. "I'm sorry. I didn't know. You really don't need to…"

Grasping the emotional life vest he offered would be letting the demons of my past control me once again. Their control had to end.

I wouldn't let it rule my future. "I need to get this out."

My therapist's reminders came back to me. "*Grief is okay,*" she'd said. "*Let it out. It's a beast that needs to be let loose to be conquered. It only has power over you if it remains in the dark where it can torment you. Once out in the sunlight, you'll be able to see it for what it is—a memory of a dark time that has passed. You can understand it as a part of your past that will never go away and at the same time refuse to let it rule your future.*"

I sat up straighter. "They shouldn't have…" I took a deep breath. "Let me back up and start at the beginning. I was away at school. Uncle Ernst…"

Fuck, I let myself call him my stupid uncle again.

I continued without correcting myself. "…had to be the one to call and tell me what had happened." I allowed myself a sniff. "The hardest part was not being around, not being here for them."

The warmth of Josh's hand around mine drew out some of the hurt.

The beast was out in the open, and I could see it for what it was: a pathetic fear that lost strength in the light of day.

"I'm sorry," he said. "I can't imagine how hard it must have been for you." The wetness in his eyes conveyed his compassion.

I would make his strength my own. "They shouldn't have made the trip at night, I guess." With my free hand, I twisted my wine glass like it was a sword plunging into the ugly beast on the table. "Anyway, that's when Ernst took over. After graduation, I joined the company again." I pulled my hand away. "It was a hard time, but I'm past it now." I meant that. I had the strength to go on, the strength to live my future without being controlled by my past.

"Again?" he asked.

"Daddy had brought me into the company as a teenager, and I've never worked anywhere else." I watched the demon disappear, and I put on the smile I deserved for having won this round.

"What about you?" I asked. This battle was over and I'd beaten the beast.

~

Josh

Right now I could have cursed Dad for a full hour for rushing this acquisition and not giving me time to learn Rossi's history, Nicole's history. Instead, I'd stepped on the emotional landmine without preparation, and with all the finesse of a bull elephant.

She deserved better.

Still, she wrapped it up with a smile.

"What about you?" she asked as she took a bite of her food.

"Benson Corp. the whole way for me too."

She circled her fork over her plate. "Tell me about it, so I get a chance to catch up."

I lifted my glass and peered into it, looking for a way to summarize our complicated family dynamics. "I'm the only son left at the company, so the responsibility is on me to carry on the…" I searched for how Dad would put it.

"Legacy?" she offered.

"That works. Legacy."

"What about your brothers?"

"I'm the youngest, so I was the last to join the company, but now all my older brothers have moved off into their own ventures."

She finished chewing. "Why'd they leave?"

She wasn't pulling any punches.

I flagged down our waiter as he passed and held up my almost-empty wine glass. "Another, please."

He looked expectantly at Nicole and her empty glass. "And you?"

She nodded with a full mouth. "Yes, please," she mumbled.

"Working for Dad is a lot of pressure," I told her. "You know…the expectations."

She looked at me with a polite nod, but not the knowing smile. Judging by her response, she'd had a different experience with her parents.

"It started with Dennis. He's the oldest and felt enormous pressure to get married."

Nicole shook her head. "What does that have to do with anything?"

Only someone who'd never met the great Lloyd Benson could ask such a silly question.

"Dad has always been a heavy-on-the-family-values guy. Dennis got the message hot and heavy that in order to be considered stable enough to run the company, he had to stop sowing his wild oats and settle down with a wife."

"And instead he left?"

I tilted my head. "No, but I'm sure he wishes he had. He married in a hurry. To say she was a mistake is putting it mildly. The divorce was inevitable and difficult."

Our waiter interrupted us again, trading our empties for fresh glasses of wine.

She held up her finger as she finished chewing. A grin appeared. "Now I guess we all know you Bensons are stupid *and* gullible. Having to get married to run the business is so last century."

I shrugged. "That pretty much sums up Dad's thinking on the subject."

She pointed her glass at me. "So do you have to find a future ex-Mrs. Benson that will make Daddy happy?"

I struggled to not spit out the water I'd sipped. "God, no. The debacle with Dennis put an end to that kind of talk from Dad. In the end, it caused Dennis to leave the company, and for a while it drove quite a wedge between him and Dad. She was an actress, and the whole courtship was just a giant act he fell for."

"I imagine that would put a dent in your self-esteem."

"It hit him pretty hard—not because he thought he could make it work, but because he was ashamed at having been taken in."

Nicole forked up the last of her dinner.

I continued. "Dennis and my next brother, Zach, are here in LA. Vincent, the youngest other than me, got out of town and is in Boston, married to a bad-ass FBI agent, if you can believe that."

"And so the responsibility falls to you now?"

"I'm the only one left." Instead of sounding happy for the opportunity, my tone was closer to it being a responsibility, a sentence. And that's the way I felt at the moment—obligated rather than enthused.

"And you're not thrilled about it?"

She'd read my mood, not that I'd attempted to hide it.

"Don't get me wrong, I'm not complaining. It's just that the bar is set pretty high, and I hate failing." I didn't *allow* myself to fail would have been more accurate.

"I had the same issue," she lamented, surprising me. "It seemed like Daddy was harder on me than the other employees. But I learned to deal with it."

So she did understand the pressures of having to live up to the older generation's expectations in a family-run firm.

I ran a hand through my hair. "I get that he doesn't want to be accused of favoring me, but sometimes it seems like more than that."

"Maybe you're overthinking it and just being hard on yourself."

The lilt of her voice, the upward curl of her kind lips told me she meant it nicely. But damn if it wasn't easier to say it than do it.

"No, it's real." Dad had been rough the past few months, colder and more distant than before. The extra criticism wasn't my imagination. "And getting worse."

"Have you considered pulling the ripcord, like your brothers?"

I blew out a loud breath and shook my head. "Not in my family. That's not an option for me. It's like reverse musical chairs. I'm that last one, and if I leave, it's like turning off the lights and abandoning Dad."

"Then have a talk with him. If it doesn't change..." She didn't finish the sentence. Instead she offered her hand across to me.

I accepted the gesture, as well as the kind gaze and smile that came with it.

"You'll do fine. Sometimes we're more sensitive when the critiques come from family."

Somehow the tables had turned, and instead of me comforting her, Nicole was providing support I hadn't asked for—support I'd uncharacteristically accepted.

I smiled back. "Thank you."

Our waiter bussed the dishes and dropped off the dessert menu for us to peruse, even though I already knew my selection.

Nicole had been restless in her seat for a while. "Could we move dessert to another night. Please?"

"Getting out of sharing tiramisu with me again?"

She batted those luscious eyes. "This dress is itching me something awful. I just have to get out of it." Her tongue slowly swept her upper lip.

Dammit, I'd been too worried about my predicament to get the message. I stood quickly and threw two Benjamins on the table. A different dessert was going to be on tonight's menu as soon as I got her home. Guiding her out through the crowd, the feel of her body heat under my hand had me wishing I'd caught her cues earlier.

CHAPTER 30

Nicole

The next morning, I woke again to a cold bed.

The slow burn of sitting across from Josh at dinner last night as his eyes consumed me had been almost too much to bear. By the time we got back and reached my bedroom, I was all over him like a cat in heat. I'd wanted another night like our first, fast and furious.

But he'd promised our second night would be slow and sensual—and it was. The tingles between my thighs still hadn't abated. The dark circles under my eyes from lack of sleep would require serious makeup this morning. If that was the price for the night we'd had, I'd pay it willingly.

But, an empty bed in the morning didn't cut it.

Josh had gotten up without waking me, and this had to stop.

After using the bathroom and brushing my teeth, I grabbed my robe and headed downstairs. I found him in the kitchen at the toaster.

"What the hell is going on?" I demanded.

He spun around, brows creased.

"I went to bed with a man last night, and I woke up alone. Again."

He shrugged. "I didn't want to wake you."

"Nice thought, but your execution sucks."

"I was pretty sure I didn't wake you."

"That's the problem. If I can't wake up next to you, I don't want you in my bed."

He laughed. "Seriously? I was being nice."

I dropped the robe to the floor. "In the morning, I don't want nice. I want to wake up next to you."

His eyes narrowed, and the predator shone through. "Not nice can be arranged." He reached me in three strides and slung me over his shoulder.

I shrieked, but it didn't change anything.

He mounted the stairs like I was nothing. "You want not nice? That's what you're going to get."

I held back a giggle and slapped his back. "Leaving a woman alone in bed is rude."

He flung me down on the mattress, spread my legs, and had his face planted over my pussy in seconds.

As his hands fondled my breasts and his tongue worked its magic on my lady bits, the heat in my core grew quickly. Each pinch of my nipples, every swirl of his tongue over my clit sent me higher at a pace I'd never experienced. The king of the jungle was loose, and I was at his mercy.

I trembled at his every movement. I couldn't hear anything but the blood rushing in my ears. I arched into him for more pressure and tugged at his hair to hold on. His tongue flicked and circled and brushed over my clit with increasing pressure. It rubbed and teased in a dance that took my breath away.

An explosion wracked my core, and I couldn't help it. I pulled his hair, forcing him further into me as the tremors rattled through my body. As the spasms slowed, my legs and arms weakened from the exertion.

He pulled his mouth away as he climbed up for a kiss—our kiss, with a taste of me and taste of him, the kiss of us.

The aftershocks of my orgasm gently faded away, and my muscles began to gain function again. I pulled myself to him and moved to grab his cock, but he pulled my hands over my head instead.

I knew it was useless to object, and I didn't really have any objections.

"My God, you're gorgeous, Nickels." He moved in and kissed my neck.

The weight of his stiff thickness lay against my thigh. He moved higher, placing the tip just above my mound. He ground forward and back, his heavy cock rubbing against my clit.

Each of his movements forced a sharp inhale from me. I wanted him to move lower and bury himself in me, but I didn't get my wish.

His stubble scraped against me as he kissed from my ear to my neck and out along my collarbone. I could feel the pulse of my heartbeat in my groin as my tension ramped up again. My desire was almost an audible crackle within me.

"Stay there." The command wasn't harsh, but the meaning was clear.

A quick rip of foil, and I watched him sheath himself.

I was about to get what I'd been aching for when I woke up this morning.

He returned to the bed and settled between the legs I'd spread for him. The weight of his cock teased my abdomen. "Tell me what you want."

His naughty command aroused even more need within me.

He brought his face closer, pinning my wrists above my head with one hand. "Tell me," he demanded again. "This is your first not-nice lesson." His stubble scraped my cheek. The lion lay just below the surface.

"I want you," I answered.

He reached down between my legs and positioned the tip of his cock at my wet entrance. "You can't have what you don't ask for, Stanford, so make up your mind."

I held my breath as I anticipated the coming sensation. Each time, I was intimidated by the size of him before we started.

"I want you."

"Don't Stanford girls know the words?" he asked sternly. He pulled away when I didn't answer.

"I want you inside me," I said. I wanted the cock he was withholding. I needed it.

He gave me a little with a gentle push.

"More. I need more," I pleaded.

He stilled himself. "Say it."

"More."

He pulled back out. "Not-nice girls learn to talk dirty."

I wanted the animal; I wanted the predator. "Fuck me, Josh. Fuck me hard."

He thrust in rapidly, stretching me with his size. "That's better. I'm going to fuck your brains out," he said hoarsely.

I gasped, desire flooding over me. I'd found the key words, and I would remember them now. The pressure on my walls was intense as he pulled out a little and drove in farther. The pleasure built with each thrust.

He moved my legs up.

I grabbed my knees, and he went in deeper.

He pulled my ankles up over his shoulders and grasped my hips as he plunged into me, harder and harder. "You are so fucking good, so fucking wet," he said again and again as he kept up the punishing pace.

Each thrust sent me higher, higher than I'd ever been before. "Harder," I pleaded.

He pinched my nipple with his free hand, sending a shock through me. He leaned forward to kiss me, bending me with him at the hips. "I'm going to fuck you so hard you can't walk today." He altered his position, taking my legs off his shoulders.

I wrapped them around him and pulled him into me with my heels behind his legs. I arched my hips into him with each thrust, taking the full length of him, to his moans of pleasure. "Fuck me harder, Mr. Bossman," I begged.

He raised up and put his hand between us, his thumb finding my clit. He ground down on it with each stroke, and the combination of his hand and his cock sent me over the edge again.

Intense spasms rolled through me, draining every nerve ending. I clawed at his back to pull him closer. My pussy clenched around him, trying to milk him dry.

With a final push, he tensed and froze above me as he groaned.

He shifted my legs and collapsed against my chest. His cock pulsed inside me as his hot breath tickled my neck.

After a moment, he lifted up and kissed my nose. "Is this a better way to wake up?"

"This is more like it."

"That was your first not-nice lesson. More to come."

I'd definitely remember to ask for not nice again.

CHAPTER 31

Josh

Friday morning, Gary and I were going over the cash situation again—as we had most mornings—when Dee poked her head in. "Libby called from Benson. They need you over there for a meeting."

"When?"

"Now. And before you ask, she didn't know the topic, but it's 'not about Nebraska,' whatever that means. Harold Snyderman and your father are the other attendees."

Organized and thinking ahead, Dee was a keeper for sure.

"Thanks, Dee." I grabbed my car keys. "Gary, how about after lunch?"

He gathered up his papers. "Sure thing, Mr. B."

The drive over to Benson Corp. for the meeting should have given me time to compose my thoughts. Instead, it allowed apprehension to take root. At least Dad had seemed to have kept his word about putting off any discussion of Camper Heaven. That was a battle I didn't want to have today.

Upstairs in the monster building I used to enter every day, the marble and dark, polished wood looked foreign. Even pushing the button for the elevator felt odd. In only two weeks, I'd acclimated to the worn carpets and beige walls of the single-story Rossi's building. At Rossi's, the color came from the people instead of the furnishings.

Libby pointed me toward conference room two instead of Dad's office.

Harold sat on the other side of the table when I entered. "Hey, Josh, you should be up in Nebraska helping Tony with Camper Heaven."

I pulled out a chair across from him. "I'm not done at Rossi's yet." This wasn't an argument I wanted to have with him right now.

The curtains were open, and behind Harold the city sprawled out for miles through the floor-to-ceiling windows. The vista was a stark contrast to the view of the parking lot I had at my new office.

Harold always sat with his back to the window—avoiding distraction, he'd once said. He'd even suggested painting over the windows at one point to increase productivity. Fortunately, better judgment had prevailed.

After a moment, Dad strode in. "Good to see you, Josh." He settled into his seat and sipped the coffee he'd brought with him. "What are we here to talk about, Harold?"

I schooled my face. I'd thought Dad had called this meeting, not Harold.

Harold opened his folder. "There are two issues I think we shouldn't let the grass grow under our feet on. We have a window of opportunity here with both Rossi's and Smith's under the corporate umbrella."

"Such as?" Dad asked.

Harold shifted forward. "Since it seems likely that we will want to pull the plug eventually, with flexible inventory transfer pricing, we could effectively shift some of this quarter's expenses off of Smith's and on to Rossi's. Then, when we exit, we'll actually show a profit from the short-term holding."

I interrupted. "That's not right." What he was proposing was clearly unethical.

"I assure you, we can do it in a way that doesn't raise any flags with the auditors. It's perfectly legal."

I sat forward. "The issue is ethics, not legality. Pulling out of the purchase *and* saddling them with additional debt is just plain wrong."

Dad was quiet. He'd made it clear to me at the outset that pulling out of the purchase contract wasn't in the cards. He'd obviously not had the same conversation with Harold.

The CFO sneered in my direction. "My responsibility is to maximize the return for Benson Corp., not any other entity. And there's no downside. If we keep the company, the Rossi's losses will be offset by the Smith's gains, and it won't cost us a thing in the consolidation."

Once again, he showed no concern at all for right and wrong. Shifting costs around to artificially create losses on the Rossi's side and gains on the Benson side bordered on immoral.

I turned to Dad. "This is a bad idea." I watched for a sign of support. I didn't get one.

Dad's face remained impassive. "You two discuss it and bring me a resolution."

My mouth dropped more than I should have allowed it to.

Dad wasn't backing me here, and I had no idea why. Any idiot could see how unfair this was to the Rossi's people.

"You said you had a second item," Dad said.

Harold perked up. "If we *are* going to keep the company, we should start the planning right away for the integration with Smith's." He shot me a mechanical smile.

Somehow this had degenerated into something I wasn't prepared for. I had no idea why Harold had planned to ambush me today.

"Good idea," Dad replied.

"I haven't decided that's the way to go yet," I stated. This was my baby to shepherd, not Harold's.

"The synergies are too obvious to ignore," Harold said, as if it were fact. "The economies of scale will help the bottom line without a doubt."

Dad stood and picked up his coffee cup. "I'll let you two sort that out."

A few seconds later, Harold and I were alone in the conference room.

"Why didn't you bring this up with me first?" I demanded.

"Don't take that tone with me," he shot back. "I sent you a memo on it last Friday." The typical defense of the bureaucrat—he'd sent a memo.

"You should have called."

He stood and gathered his papers. "In the memo, I asked you to call if you had any questions or concerns."

"Rossi's is my company to run, not yours," I said as he approached the door. "I make the decisions."

"Funny. I thought it was owned by Benson Corp. And I'm the CFO here." He continued out the door without another word.

I headed for the garage to get back to the peace of the single-story Rossi's building.

CHAPTER 32

NICOLE

SUNDAY MORNING, JOSH GOT ME UP EARLY. ALTHOUGH I PREFERRED TO DAWDLE AT home, there was no slowing him down. And "lunch by the beach" was all I'd gotten out of him.

I checked my phone and found the text message from Mrs. Ringwold again asking if I needed her to walk Echo. I smiled—Lara was safe.

After a few morning hours at the office for both of us, Saturday had turned into a lazy day at the house. I'd worked a little in the trees while he hung out on the back porch with his laptop.

Today was not going to be a repeat. "Let's get a move on, Nickels," had echoed in these rooms a half dozen times already.

"Will Echo be okay out back all day?" he asked.

"Yes, but you said we were going to *lunch*."

He wrapped me up in a hug from behind. "I did, and we are, but it's not very close, and I want to enjoy as much of the day with you as possible."

I turned to putty in his arms. "Why don't we just go to Santa Monica? It's close."

"Everybody goes there. I have somewhere more special in mind for a special lady."

I wiggled loose and sat at the table. Another coin sat in the center. I'd found two on Friday and three Saturday. I picked it up. "Why are you leaving change everywhere?"

"The buffalo nickels?"

I turned it over in my hand. It was a coin from 1920.

"I leave them around as a reminder of how you are everywhere. You are always with me, always in my mind, my thoughts, Nickels. I even have one in my wallet."

I swooned at the words. "You are such a goofball." *What could be more romantic?* I got up and draped myself around him.

He spun me around and whispered in my ear. "We have to get going." His hands had a different agenda as they cupped my breasts.

His body heat against me always went straight to my core and melted my inhibitions. I wiggled my butt against the hardness behind me to tease him. "We haven't done the table in here yet."

"Careful there. We have to get on the road."

It seemed every time we embraced, I brought out that visceral reaction in him. It was intoxicating to excite him at such a primal level—all the time. It had never been like this with Mo. Hell, with any guy before. Sure, Mo got it up if I sucked him, but not just from holding me. The knowledge that I had this effect on Josh was...empowering. It was non-verbal validation that the relationship wasn't the thing I dreaded: one-sided. His physical reaction made it plain that I was desired, and his words recently had come to show I was appreciated.

After a kiss to my neck, he let me go with a pat to my ass. "The table will have to wait till we get back."

Trying to hold back my smirk, I put on a pouty face as I watched him adjust himself in his jeans. "We could be quick," I taunted.

His eyes went wide, and he sucked in a breath.

I'd waved the red flag at the bull, and anything could happen now.

He exhaled slowly. "Tonight," he said through gritted teeth. "You keep this up and I'm liable to jizz my pants."

"Okay." I turned and grabbed my purse. His words gave me an idea. I grabbed a fresh washcloth from the bathroom on the way out.

Each of the several times I asked where we were going, he gave me the same answer: "It's a surprise."

Reaching the 405, he got on going south.

"How far before we get off the freeway?" I asked.

"You'll see."

I opened my purse and pulled out my nail polish with a flourish. "I need to know if I have time to do my nails."

"Half hour or so if the traffic stays light. Is that enough time?"

I put my nail polish away. "I think so." I pulled out the washcloth and put it on the console before I leaned over and went for his belt.

"Hey," he exclaimed.

"You wouldn't give me what I wanted, so I'm taking it." I pulled his belt buckle loose.

He looked to the left. "They can see you."

The SUV to our left had a lady in the passenger seat looking my way.

I waved, and she averted her eyes. "They won't suspect a thing if you keep your face under control." I could already feel the monster growing in his pants.

He braced himself against the steering wheel.

"Move your seat back a few inches," I told him as I pulled down his zipper.

He inched the electric seat back.

I pulled out my big, thick prize and started stroking.

His breath hitched, and he scooted his pants down a few inches on one side, then the other.

Now I could reach his balls as well. His cock was warm and hard in my hand as I looked out the windshield and one-handed him. "How's this?"

"You have no idea." He gave a little jerk as I squeezed the tip.

"Oh, I think I do." I laid the washcloth over the top and continued my hand action, looking over at his expression every once in a while. The rest of the time, I kept my eyes forward, just like any other passenger in the cars in the other lanes. The height of his Escalade kept the others from looking down into his lap to see my hand bobbing under the cloth.

"Jesus, I can't take this."

"You threatened to jizz in your pants. I'm just helping the process along," I said with a smile. I stilled my hand. "You want me to stop?"

"Hell, no."

Before long, my arm grew tired, and I couldn't change hands without making it obvious what we were doing. I decided we had to speed this up. "You have no idea how wet I get when I hold your cock. It makes me want to beg you to pull over and do me in the backseat. I don't care if anybody sees us. I need you inside me, baby. I need this." I squeezed. "I don't know if I'm going to last until we get home. We're going to have to find a place behind a tree or, I don't care, anywhere I can bend over."

I looked over at his clenched jaw.

His leg started to shake.

"I want you to pound into me like there's no tomorrow. Pound me so hard I can't walk."

That last line got him over the edge, and he jerked under my hand. "Oh, fuck, fuck, fuck, fuck."

I reached over, held the washcloth in place, and milked his throbbing cock.

The magic of dirty talk had done its job.

His shallow, rapid breaths slowly returned to normal. "I have to take you on more road trips."

I cleaned him up and stowed the cloth on the floor of the backseat. "You know, if you had an old pickup with a bench seat, this could be reciprocal."

"Now there's an idea."

I got tingles just thinking about driving down the freeway next to Josh with his magic fingers down my pants, me with my head back, screaming, while the cars one lane over were oblivious—the danger of public mutual masturbation at freeway speeds. So long as we didn't pull up next to a semi, everything would be great.

I had Josh back together and buckled up by the time he turned south on the 710 toward Long Beach.

"Nickels, you can have the table tonight, or any other damned thing you want when we get back," he said with a contented smile.

"I'll let you know." Sandy had once told me I should try up against a door, and tonight might be my chance.

As we got closer to the water, we continued south toward the harbor, not the sand.

He turned left, and suddenly the Queen Mary loomed ahead.

"Sorry to break it to you, USC, but that ship doesn't qualify as a beach."

He nodded wordlessly and continued past it. The building he parked in front of scared me shitless: Catalina Express.

"We're taking the ferry to Santa Catalina."

Painful memories came flooding back, and my stomach lurched.

I unbuckled, threw open the door, and got out just in time.

With my hands on my knees, my breakfast splattered on the asphalt.

Josh

I RAN AROUND THE CAR AND HEARD IT HIT THE GROUND BEFORE I SAW IT.

Hunched over, with her hands on her knees, Nicole dry heaved. Her breakfast was already on her shoes and the ground.

I pulled open the car door and grabbed a box of tissues. "Here." I took out several and offered them. "Are you okay?"

The stock question came out without thought. Of course she wasn't okay. Tears streaked her cheeks as she straightened up.

I pulled her away from the mess and wiped her chin with some tissues. "What happened? What did I do?"

She blinked back the tears. "I'm sorry. It's nothing you did. I can't go out on the water." She straightened up and took a few more tissues from the box to clean off.

I guided her to the back of the car, away from the smell of the mess, and leaned her against the bumper. "Rest here."

"I'm really sorry."

"Hey, it's not your fault. I'm the one who cooked breakfast this morning. I fucked something up."

She took in a deep breath and slowly exhaled. "It's not the food. I just can't..." She looked toward the ferry terminal and back at me. "I can't."

Now it seemed it wasn't her nausea but the idea of being on the ferry that had brought this on.

"Stay here," I told her while I fetched a bottled water from the backseat. "Swish and spit."

She opened the water and did as I suggested, twice. "Thanks. It tastes a lot better going down than coming back up." She laughed—a good sign.

"I'm a good listener."

"Maybe somewhere else."

"Sure. Trade ya." I offered the tissue box and took the water from her. "Stay there." I wet some tissues and knelt to wipe off her shoes.

"Thank you."

I pointed back down the road we'd come in on. "Is a Starbucks okay?"

She nodded.

Ten minutes later, I ordered us grande mochas, and she eyed a breakfast sandwich but decided against it.

She snuggled up against me as I paid. "I'm sorry."

I hip-bumped her. "Say that one more time and I'm making you pay."

She giggled, which had been my desired outcome. "I'll get us a seat outside."

When the drinks were ready, I found her outside, staring in the direction of the ocean with a decidedly sad face. She looked back and her mood shifted several notches up the happy scale when I pulled out my chair.

I sipped a bit of my hot drink. "I added cinnamon for you."

"You're too nice."

"No such thing in the boyfriend handbook. I looked." It didn't get the giggle I'd hoped for, or even the smile.

"I'm sorry. I—"

"That'll be ten bucks," I said cutting her off. "That's today's rule."

She looked at me incredulously. "But I am sorry."

"Now it's twenty. Pay up and stop saying you're sorry. You've used your quota for today."

"I owe you an explanation about before."

I held out my hand. "You owe me twenty bucks. I won't listen to your explanation until I get it."

She laughed—finally the reaction I was fishing for. She reached for her purse, and I got my twenty.

I pocketed the money. "Now I'm all ears."

"You're a goofball."

"So I've been told."

She sighed. "You know Uncle Ernst took over because my parents died."

I nodded.

She blinked several times. The tears threatened again. "They died in an accident."

I nodded. "A nighttime accident on a trip is what you said." It had been so obviously painful for her to say even that much that I hadn't brought the subject up again.

"It was on the water." She started to sob. "They were…" Sniffles followed but no more words.

"You don't need to go into it. I understand."

She took the napkin and dabbed under each eye. "No. I need to. It's not something I can hide from. I have to face facts and move on. They died in a boating accident."

"I'm sorry." I wanted to hold her and soak up the hurt she was feeling. Losing your parents before their time wasn't something anyone should have to endure alone. I felt shitty that I'd triggered this by suggesting going out on a boat.

"They shouldn't have gone..." She took a deep breath. "Let me back up." She seemed to be getting stronger as she released the pent-up emotions.

She continued after another sip from her cup. "I was away at school. I told you that part. Ernst called and told me they went missing after taking the boat to Catalina for the weekend. They loved going to Avalon, but they never made it to the island that night." She sniffed. "We never found out what went wrong, and our boat was never found. The hardest part has been not knowing, not having closure."

I didn't know if I should ask any more about it—if that would help her or hurt her.

"They shouldn't have left at night, I guess." She twisted her mocha. "Anyway, they searched, and for days all I could do was cry and hope they'd ended up on one of the other Channel Islands."

I waited.

"After less than a week, the Coast Guard called off the search. I begged them to keep looking—you know, check everywhere again, but they said they'd done all they could. Uncle Ernst had the company pay some people to keep looking, but that didn't get us anywhere either. I couldn't function. I could hardly get out of bed."

As she spoke, it became apparent how hard it had been for her to face the loss.

"You're going to think I'm stupid."

I reached across to touch her hand. "Never."

"I paid a psychic." She looked down before twisting her cup. "Two actually, and the best I got was that they were not far away. News flash: Catalina is only thirty miles offshore. When Ernst heard I'd wasted twenty thousand on that, he threatened that if I didn't get some counseling, he was going to have me committed." She huffed. "Can you believe that?"

I silently waited for more.

"Well, long story short, I did start to see someone." She twisted her cup again. "She helped a lot. It took a while, but I got over it—all except the boat part. The idea of getting on a small boat is something I still can't deal with."

"I'm sorry. I wish I'd known."

She smiled and held out her hand. "Give me back ten."

"Is that the way we're going to play this?" I asked.

"Fair is fair," she said with a smile.

I happily pulled out a ten. It was worth it a hundred times over to lighten her mood and see that smile.

"When the Coast Guard said they had no explanation, all I could think of was a West Coast Bermuda Triangle, and I could be next. I haven't been on a boat since. My therapist said I need to focus on something else, something positive, so after graduation I started back at the company. It's what Daddy always wanted me to do, and here we are. Now you know my fucked-up past."

CHAPTER 33

NICOLE

THE WET LICK ON MY EAR WOKE ME TUESDAY MORNING. "NO, ECHO," I MUMBLED AS I pried open my eyes. The room was still dark.

"Is that any better?" Josh asked before he licked my ear again.

I cringed at the cold as he blew on my wet ear, and I rolled over to face him. "You're a goofball. You know you could just say good morning."

"Early morning is a time for nonverbal communication."

He was like a kid refusing to listen to reason.

I lowered my hand and grabbed the morning wood I found. "Is this nonverbal enough for you?"

"That's the idea." The hitch in his breath said more than the words about how he liked it.

With my hands on him, I had some of the control. "Let's go back to the boob squeeze if you can't handle words." I gave him a hard yank.

It didn't faze him.

He seemed to always wake before me, but I'd broken him of leaving me behind in bed after a few days. The first morning, he'd woken me by squeezing my breast. He'd nearly ended up with a broken nose when I jerked awake and head-butted him. The nipple-pinch mornings and tickling mornings hadn't gone much better, but this was like having a slobbery Echo wake me up.

Josh pulled away and rolled off the bed. "I've got to go into the Benson Newport Beach office early. Remember I told you I had to go in early today?"

"Yeah, I forgot."

He'd mentioned it, but I'd forgotten, and not enough of our time in bed had been spent sleeping. I rolled over to get more shut-eye.

A few hours later, when the sun was up, I got ready for work and headed downstairs.

Hot coffee was my first order of business. Once again, my phone held the reassuring text message.

RINGWOLD: Do you need me to walk Echo today?

Lara was safe, wherever she was. All I could do was wait for Josh's accountant sleuths to find the truth.

~

Josh

After several boring hours on the freeway, I walked up the stairs to the Benson offices before nine and asked for Ben Crenshaw, the CFO candidate Harold had suggested I interview for my opening at Rossi's.

An hour and a half later, I was back on the road north. It took a full fifteen minutes before I was calm enough to call Harold.

"What did you think of Crenshaw?" he asked when he answered.

"He's not a fit." That was more polite than I felt like being with him. He knew perfectly well that Crenshaw was too junior—no CPA, and only a year of experience since business school. What had Harold been smoking when he recommended him?

"Personally, I think the kid has a lot of potential."

I kept my cool. "I'd really like Sandman on this. Crenshaw is way too green for something the size of Rossi's."

"I told you, George isn't available right now."

At least *right now* held the promise of later.

"I'll let you know when I come up with another candidate for you to talk to," he assured me.

"Thanks, Harold," I managed with more enthusiasm than I felt.

At least we hung up without me venting my frustration at how he was sandbagging me. It seemed he had intentionally wasted my time today.

CHAPTER 34

Josh

Mid-afternoon on Thursday, Dee poked her head in my office. "There's a Mr. Bremmer here to see you, Mr. B."

It didn't ring a bell. "Bremmer?"

"He said Harold Snyderman sent him over."

The name came back to me. Wenzel Bremmer had been the controller at Smith's, the grocery chain Harold had been pushing to integrate Rossi's with, which now looked like a stupid idea. This must be Harold's latest brilliant thought, since he still refused to lend me George Sandman. If he'd called ahead, I could have objected, but now I had no choice in the matter. Either Dad or Harold had played me. But I couldn't take it out on Wenzel—he was the pawn in this. At least I knew Wenzel had more experience than Crenshaw had.

"Show him in. And ask Gary to join us."

A moment later, Wenzel Bremmer walked past her and offered his hand. "Reporting for duty, as ordered." He spoke in a jovial tone, but still made it clear that Harold hadn't given him a choice in the matter.

I shook with him. "Wenzel, I appreciate that you could spare the time to help me." We both knew he couldn't leave until I said it was okay.

"Harold isn't giving me much time to get this place straightened out."

Gary appeared at the door, breathless. His appearance didn't give me the opportunity to set Wenzel straight that I was running the show here, and he was only dotted-line to Harold.

Wenzel turned.

"Gary, come on in. Meet Wenzel Bremmer. He's here to help out as CFO for a while." I'd mentioned early on to Gary that I'd be looking to get an interim CFO, so he wouldn't be surprised.

Gary offered his hand and a genuine grin. "A pleasure. Gary Fontaine, controller."

"Wenzel Bremmer." Wenzel's countenance didn't match Gary's enthusiasm.

"Gary, why don't you show Wenzel around and get him situated."

Gary nodded.

"First, take him by Rosa to get him on the payroll," I added.

Wenzel didn't look thrilled. "What are your priorities for me, Josh?"

"Pay the bills and get a handle on our finances, to start with."

Gary and Wenzel left with Gary smiling, probably because he no longer had to deal with me asking endless questions.

Nicole

GARY SHOWED UP AT MY DOOR WITH A STRANGER IN TOW.

"Got a moment, Nicole?" he asked.

I stood. "Sure."

The stranger followed him in—a banker from the looks of his suit.

"Wenzel, this is Nicole Rossi, our VP of operations," Gary announced.

The stranger extended his hand. "A pleasure, Ms. Rossi. Wenzel Bremmer."

Gary shuffled his feet. "Wenzel is here for Mrs. Quantell's position."

The statement brightened my day. We couldn't go long without somebody as CFO. It was just odd that Rosa hadn't mentioned we had a candidate to interview today.

"Thanks, Gary. I'd be happy to squeeze in some time for an interview."

Wenzel's mouth twitched. "I believe I already have the job."

Gary grimaced. "I forgot to say, Mr. B already brought him in."

This was getting curiouser and curiouser. "Really?"

Wenzel nodded. "Gary's been nice enough to introduce me to the...uh, *players* here."

The way he called us *players* turned my stomach.

"You seem surprised, Ms. Rossi," he added.

"Nicole, please. It's just that Josh hadn't mentioned anything to me about you."

"Ah, I see..." Wenzel stroked his chin. "Need to know, I guess. He requested my services from the Benson organization, and I'm only here temporarily to help out. I'll let you know what I need from you after I get my bearings. I was pulled over from the controller position at Smith's, most recently."

I worked hard not to show my relief when he said *temporary*. Rossi's didn't need any more surprise changes at this point, like forcing another Benson person on us.

Josh had been pissed that the last candidate the Benson group had suggested had next to no experience, and if this guy had been the Smith's controller, he'd have some grocery knowledge.

An hour later my phone rang with an unknown number. I considered not answering, except the area code was 202, and I was expecting a call from the FDA.

"Hello?"

"Nicole? This is Kelly Benson calling, Josh's sister."

"Hi, Kelly."

"Nicole, you're coming Saturday, right?"

Josh had locked me into attending by telling me he'd already told his whole family I was coming.

"Sure am. I'm so excited for you."

"Me too. Wish I could say the same for Adam. He's a little nervous about the party, with the history and all."

Josh had given me the short version of the animosity between his family and Adam's.

"Meeting the other family can be a little overwhelming."

"Yeah, I guess that goes for you too."

"A little," I admitted. I shifted in my seat realizing it was actually more than a little.

"The reason I'm calling is... I don't want to be indelicate or anything, but I'm planning the menu, and are you vegan or anything I should be aware of?"

I laughed. "Put me down as omnivorous with one exception. No shellfish. I'm allergic."

"No problem. I can handle that," she said.

We talked for a few more minutes. From the sound of her, it seemed I was going to like this woman.

"I'm glad we got a chance to talk ahead of time," she added before we ended the call.

I thanked her and sat back in my chair. Saturday was looking less scary than it had yesterday.

CHAPTER 35

Nicole

Saturday afternoon, the pilot called back to us to buckle up for landing at Dulles International near DC. I was traveling with Josh and his family for his sister's engagement party—traveling in style in Lloyd's big corporate jet.

It had been an uneventful week at work, if you didn't count Wenzel Bremmer showing up from Smith's. Lara's safe messages had continued.

Every day, Josh assured me it was just a waiting game regarding the Knowltons investigation so we could find out who was behind our money problems, because it couldn't have been Lara.

Every day I tried to guess the connection between the broken door, the message on the carpet, and the note in the orchard, all of which had targeted Lara. What had Lara done to have all this shit come down on her?

Josh hadn't been much help. He thought I could be the target, and didn't agree that it was all aimed at Lara. But, Josh hadn't been here to live through what had happened to Lara with Vern and see the similarities that I saw.

On the Josh front, things were good. Because Josh's condo was closer to work, I'd agreed to spend weeknights at his place and the weekend at Casa di Rossi. Suggesting something like that for efficiency somehow fit Josh. He'd asked and given me all of ten seconds to decide. But it only took one morning waking up in his luxurious bed to confirm I'd made the right decision.

After we landed, Josh and I followed the group from the plane into the Signature Aviation private terminal. This family sure knew how to travel in style. No humiliating security check, no waiting in lines, and when we landed, only a few dozen yards separated us from the private terminal and waiting cars.

Josh held me back so we were apart from the group and spoke into my ear. "How was the flight?"

We'd been on the same plane, but I knew he meant how had I fared in the back with the other women.

The men had held court with his Dad up front, while I sat with Josh's sister, Serena, Zack's wife, Brittney, Dennis's Jennifer, and Josh's mother, who had insisted I call her Robin.

"They're very nice," I told him.

"And?" He was clearly fishing for what we'd talked about.

"I do like Serena," I added. "I like them all."

Meeting a guy's sister was always awkward, but Serena and I had hit it off just fine. She'd bucked the family tradition and attended Stanford, same as I had. She'd gone into management consulting after graduation. With Josh's mother in the group, I didn't think it polite to ask Serena why she hadn't joined her father in business the way I had.

Serena's job sounded interesting, and she was getting a wide breadth of experience, but I didn't envy the traveling she had to do.

"What did she have to say?" Josh asked before we reached the terminal.

"We just talked about girl stuff. Oh, and that she was trying for a transfer to the Paris or London office." I wasn't about to go into how worried Serena was about Dennis meeting Kelly's fiancé, Adam.

Apparently they had a history from college that wasn't pretty. It had been so bad that Kelly had kept her relationship with Adam secret from the family for a long time. The women were also worried about Josh's father Lloyd's reaction, given the long-standing feud between him and Adam's father. I didn't ask for a history lesson, and none was offered. But it had been clear that it would be best if there were no firearms or sharp objects in the vicinity when they met.

"Why?" I asked.

"I wondered if she asked you about staying over at our place."

"No."

"Duke wanted to know if they could crash with us for a few weeks while the bathrooms at their place were being redone. I didn't want to commit without talking to you."

Somehow the condo had gone from his place to our place, and I'd gone from insta-girlfriend to she-who-must-be-consulted. It felt good. "It's your place, but I'd say yes, if I were you. They're family, and she can probably cook better than you, so it's a net positive all the way around."

He put his hand over his heart. "Oh, that hurts. I thought you liked my cooking."

I hip-bumped him. "I love your cooking. It's the extra garlic I could do without." We followed the others into the terminal.

When Serena went to use the lavatory, I took the opportunity to get Jennifer's perspective on today. "Will Dennis be okay with this?"

She nodded. "He didn't sleep much last night, but I'll be damned if I let him ruin this for Kelly. He'll work through it. I'll make sure of that."

The lady at the desk had separate cars ready for us and each of the other couples. Josh's parents had a driver and were the first to leave.

Even though the plane had a bathroom in the back, I'd avoided using it, so I visited the one inside the building before we left. Out by the car, Josh put the address into his phone, but didn't open the door.

"Are we waiting for Zack and Brittney?" I asked.

"No, just giving Dad a head start."

"Are you worried about him and Adam?"

"Just trying to give them some alone time to start off. They don't need an audience."

Zack and Brittney were standing around outside their car, too, and Serena and her boyfriend, Duke, were still inside the building. The siblings had apparently cooked up this plan together. Dennis stood next to Jennifer, checking something on his phone.

"Somebody in this town has to have it," he told her.

"Are you worried about this afternoon?" I asked Josh.

"Dad has been very… How shall I put it?… Antagonistic toward the Cartwrights for as long as I can remember. But, between Kelly and Mom, I think they'll keep him under control. Kelly didn't give him any say in this, and she's already engaged, so what can he do now?"

"He seemed in good spirits this morning when we got on the plane," I noted.

"Yeah. I hope he and Adam's dad don't get into it and ruin it for Kelly." Josh checked his watch. "Okay, he's had enough of a head start." He opened his door, and I climbed in on my side.

Not having spent much time outside California, the greenery and the thickness of the trees off the side of the highway as we drove through the Virginia countryside surprised me after the brown of California's hills this time of year.

~

WHEN WE ARRIVED, THE WOMAN WHO OPENED THE DOOR HAD LIGHT BROWN HAIR and striking emerald eyes. "Josh," she almost screamed as she jumped forward to give my boyfriend a big hug.

When Josh got loose from her, he put a hand to the small of my back. "Kelly, I'd like you to meet Nicole Rossi."

I offered my hand, but Kelly wrapped me in a hug similar to the one she'd given her brother.

"Mom and Dad are in the kitchen interrogating Adam," she told us.

We followed her to the kitchen in back, where we were introduced to Adam Cartwright, Kelly's fiancé, along with Josh's brother Vincent and his wife, Ashley, who'd flown down earlier from Boston.

Not long after, Serena and Duke, and Zack and Brittney joined us, but still no Dennis and Jennifer.

I was surprised to learn that not only was Josh's sister-in-law Ashley an agent with the FBI, but Adam was as well, assigned to the field office here in DC.

The champagne flowed freely, and the discussions were amiable, but getting animated as the alcohol loosened everybody up.

Josh's father had Vincent in the corner. "Your Uncle Logan is leaving us, and I need someone I can trust over there. I need you," he said, poking Vincent in the chest.

I didn't catch Vincent's full response, but it had certainly included 'no way.' His father didn't look pleased.

I ducked into the other room where I found Serena and Ashley.

Vincent joined us a minute later, without his father in tow.

Serena made Ashley recount for me the story of how she and Vincent met. Ashley, it turns out, had been assigned to investigate Vincent, and had joined his company undercover, working as his PA and expecting to arrest him.

I laughed at the story, and judging by the looks they gave each other, it had worked out exceptionally well.

She'd expected to put cuffs on him, and I stifled a giggle as I wondered if eventually she had, in a more intimate setting. Sandy would have blurted that question out, but I kept it to myself.

I looked around. Dennis and Jennifer were still unaccounted for.

"You have to think outside the box," Josh's father told him loudly as I approached.

"I do," Josh responded.

"Mind if I borrow this young man for a minute?" Lloyd asked me.

"Sure thing." I left them alone for more father-son time. When I looked back, Lloyd had a blue folder in his hand and took Josh around the corner.

~

Josh

Dad pulled me around the corner for privacy and put a hand on my shoulder. "Something's come up, and we need to talk."

I shifted. "Okay."

"Your Uncle Logan has been diagnosed… The specific issue isn't for me to discuss, but the short of it is that he's stepping down."

Dad's cousin Logan had been running our European operations out of London forever, and I had been scheduled to replace him eventually, a move I'd been meaning to talk to Dad about pushing further out ever since I'd started at Rossi's.

Dad continued. "He wants to spend time with the family, which is understandable, and that means I need you over in London in three weeks." He opened the blue folder that held my future in it and placed it on the table.

"You brought that here?" I asked.

"I promised to always keep it up to date." He pulled out a pen and signed both copies before handing me the same pen.

Ambushed again. I had no play here, and he knew it. Refusing to sign and fighting with Dad on today of all days was out of the question.

I took the pen. "I don't think the timing will work for me."

"We can talk back home." He gestured to the paper. "Let's get back to the party before they finish all the champagne without us."

I signed my name to both copies. I'd have to find the right time to tell him I wasn't going to London, not without Nicole. But today was not that time.

Nicole

I joined Kelly, who had broken free to check what was simmering on the stove.

She looked back toward the main room for the third time.

That's when I noticed the wetness in her eyes. I guessed at her concern and gave her a side hug. "Dennis probably just got lost."

"I hope that's all. Something awful went down between him and Adam in college, and neither of them will deal with it."

I leaned close. "Jennifer and I talked. She'll make sure he shows."

She smiled. "Thanks. I hope so. They have to get past it sometime."

"Jennifer will come through for you. She seems like a strong woman."

"She has to be to put up with my dumbass brother."

We both laughed at her sister humor, which probably had more truth to it than anybody wanted to admit.

I put my hand over hers. "From what I see out there, everyone loves Adam. This is going great."

"You think so?"

"Absolutely," I assured her.

She gave me a hug. "Thank you."

"It'll be okay. You'll see."

She nodded.

When Josh reappeared, I pulled myself away from Kelly. "What did your dad want?"

His jaw twitched. "Dad never leaves without work. It was just a little corporate business."

I maneuvered him off to the side. "Do you think Dennis chickened out?"

"I doubt it. Maybe he has to psych himself up for this—either that or get liquored up first."

I nodded around. "He could do that here."

"Yeah, that's what has me worried. Maybe I should call him."

I reached for his forearm and nodded toward his father. "Your dad and Adam seem fine. Dennis has to work this out himself." I smirked. "Jennifer won't let him skip out."

Josh nodded. "Okay. I'll give him twenty more minutes. Then I'm going to kick his ass."

"What do you think of Adam?" I asked.

"I like him, but more importantly, I haven't ever seen Kelly this happy, and her vote is the one that counts."

His saying that made me proud to be with him.

If there was any bad blood between the two families, you couldn't tell it by the way they treated Adam. He circulated around the room with ease and got a universally warm reception.

A few minutes later, the girls and I took Kelly aside to admire her ring. It was stunning. But then, to me, almost every engagement ring looked magnificent, half because they made the wearers so happy. Mom had told me more than once that it was something I could look forward to someday, and I hoped she was right.

After enough time bothering Kelly, Serena guided the group of us over to her date to show off Duke and his tattoos. She made him give us explanations of the inspirations for them.

*Ooh*s and *aah*s spilled forth as he went from tat to tat. Serena made a point of running her fingers over each one, and the look it pulled out of the big man showed he was putty under her touch.

Kelly broke away to pass appetizers around to soak up some of the bubbly, and I helped with a tray of tiny wieners with barbecue sauce.

As I sipped my champagne and accepted another compliment from one of the women, I realized there hadn't been any reason to fear this family gathering. The Bensons and their significant others were a welcoming bunch, each one taking a moment to make me feel at ease as the new addition to the group. Despite the fact that they traveled in private jets, everyone here struck me as very down to earth, without any of the pretense I'd feared.

And actually, getting engaged to Kelly made Adam new to the family as well. After hearing stories of the previous rivalry with his family, the way the Bensons accepted him was surprising, and heartwarming.

I followed Kelly, and we joined Ashley and Adam who were talking shop with FBI acronyms and case names I couldn't understand.

"Did I interrupt something?" Kelly asked when they abruptly stopped speaking.

Ashley leaned in. "You didn't tell me Adam was getting the Medal of Valor."

Adam shook his head. "It's not official yet."

"I didn't know, myself," Kelly said with a raised eyebrow.

Ashley put a hand on Kelly's arm. "That's a really big deal. You should be enormously proud of him."

Kelly wrapped an arm around her fiancé. "I would be. But he hasn't told me anything." She elbowed him lightly.

Serena joined us. "What's the big deal?"

"Nothing," Adam said quickly.

Serena gave him a stern look, but Adam didn't relent. Modest, that one was.

His phone rang, and he answered—"Yeah, Rylie, what's up?"—as he moved to the other room to take it.

Ashley nodded toward Adam. "I mean it. They don't give those out easily."

Slowly, I was getting the drift. Adam had been hiding the importance of this award from everybody, including Kelly. So not only did the family have two FBI agents, but one of them was a certified hero. I'd only just met Adam, but already I thought Kelly was very lucky to have found a man like him.

I glanced around and caught Josh looking my way. As his gaze locked with mine, I knew Kelly wasn't the only lucky one in the room.

A moment later, Adam was back with a concerned look on his face. "Ashley," he said forcefully. "You and I need a moment with Lloyd. We have a problem."

Adam hadn't said the word *problem* like they had run out of champagne,more like a plane had crashed. He pulled Josh's father away from Vincent and Duke, and the group disappeared around the corner.

A shiver ran down my spine. Something was terribly wrong.

CHAPTER 36

Josh

My stupid older brother still hadn't made it to the house and was making us all look bad by not facing Adam like a man. Adam was marrying into the family, for Christ's sake. Dennis couldn't avoid him forever.

Nicole was talking with Ashley, Adam, and Serena when Adam got a call.

I started toward them. If that was my chickenshit brother saying he couldn't make it, I was going to wring his neck.

Adam hung up and disappeared around the corner with Ashley and Dad.

A moment later, Dad reappeared and gestured for me to join them.

The group looked conspiratorial as I walked up.

Dad put his hand on my shoulder. "I need to tell you something about your cousin Debbie."

I nodded. As soon as he said her name, I knew where this was going. "I already know she was spotted," I told him. "Dennis told me and Serena."

Although we'd always thought Debbie had died years ago after her kidnapper was shot, she'd actually survived. That was the good news. The bad news was that we only knew this because her DNA had shown up at a bank robbery in the DC area. The worse news was that a teller had been shot, which as far as the FBI was concerned, turned Debbie from a kidnapping victim to a robbery and attempted murder suspect.

Dad shook his head with a huff. "Can't any of you keep a secret around here?"

"I just got a call," Adam said. "Debbie called the tip line. She wants to talk to Josh."

I backed up. "Me?" It didn't make any sense. Why me?

Adam nodded. "She's going to call back tomorrow afternoon, and all I know is she'll only talk to you."

"And that's it?" Dad asked.

Adam put up his hands. "That's it until tomorrow."

"Okay," Dad said. "I guess we'll have to wait. Now, not a word of this to the others."

The group disbanded, and I knew the secret wouldn't last a day in this family.

Adam took me aside for a second to discuss strategy for tomorrow.

When we got back to the group, it only took a minute for Nicole to ask, "What's up?"

I tilted my head toward Dad. "Tell you later, but I think it's good news."

Nicole grabbed one of the Swedish meatballs from the counter with a toothpick and offered it to me—delicious.

The doorbell rang.

Serena followed me and Kelly to the front. "That better be the big lug."

Adam wasn't far behind.

When Kelly opened the door, it was Dennis and Jennifer, finally.

"Jennifer, this is my youngest sister, Kelly," Dennis said, making the introduction.

Kelly hugged Jennifer briefly.

Adam moved forward to offer his hand. "Adam Cartwright."

Jennifer took it with a gracious smile.

Adam and Dennis appraised each other.

Dennis made the first move and produced a bottle from behind his back. He offered it to Adam. "A peace offering."

Adam accepted it, and the two shook. "Welcome to our home."

Dennis lifted a brow at Adam's description of *our home,* but Adam had staked our Kelly as his now.

"Glad you invited us," Dennis added.

Adam examined the bottle. "Macallan 1926?" A hint of a smile crept across his face.

"Dennis thought you'd like it," Jennifer interjected.

Kelly urged the group to move from the entryway to the living room.

Serena grabbed Jennifer. "Let me introduce you to Vincent and his wife. They're down from Boston." After they left, it was just Kelly, me, and the two silent bulls eyeing each other.

"I have something to say," Dennis started.

Kelly stayed, but that was my cue to leave and let them settle it in private.

Before long, the three joined us in the back of the house, and everyone looked much more relaxed—no one was bloodied.

We opened the expensive bottle of scotch, and before long, everyone had a glass in hand.

"A toast to the couple," Dennis said loudly.

The group quieted.

Dennis held up his glass. "To a long, happy, and fruitful—"

"That means lots of babies," Serena added.

The giggles took a second to subside.

Dennis continued, "Marriage. To the future Mr. Cartwright and Mrs. Benson-Cartwright."

"Mr. and Mrs. Cartwright," Kelly corrected him.

The laughs continued.

Kelly, Adam, and Robin disappeared toward the front for a while.

All I heard when they returned was an "I guess they're not coming" from Adam.

Since the whole Benson clan was here, I could only guess he'd been referring to his parents. We wouldn't have to worry about his father and my father ruining this for Kelly and Adam after all.

I downed the remaining scotch in my glass and poured a little more.

Debbie was alive, and she wanted to talk to me, of all people.

~

NICOLE

AN HOUR LATER, AFTER TOASTS TO THE ENGAGED COUPLE AND SOME HASSLE WITH A ring Adam had wanted to take off, I couldn't wait any longer and corralled my boyfriend off to the side.

"You need to tell me what happened."

Josh took my hand and pulled me toward the front of the house. He didn't say a thing until we were out the front door. "I have to stay another day."

"Why?"

Even though we were away from everyone else, he still spoke softly. "I'm not supposed to tell you this. It's Debbie. She called in, and she wants to talk to me tomorrow." His cousin Debbie's name had only come up once before between us, but with her initials on his ankle, she was clearly important to him. She'd been kidnapped at a young age and recently found to be alive, out there somewhere, was all I knew.

I put my hand on his chest. "That's great. Do you know if she's okay? Where is she?"

His heart beat rapidly beneath my palm. "I don't know any more than that until I talk to her. I need to stay here for at least another day, and I want you to go home with the others."

I leaned closer. "I'll stay with you."

"No, you won't." His tone was the this-is-not-up-for-discussion one I'd heard before. "You're needed back at Rossi's on Monday, and I don't know how long I'll be."

"Why not?" His secretiveness scared me.

"Because Adam says the FBI wants me to push for a face-to-face meeting, and that could take some time."

"If the FBI wants to arrest her, is that a good idea?"

"All I can say is Kelly trusts Adam, and he's one of us now."

I nodded. It made sense, given the close bonds this family had.

I fisted his shirt. "You better come home to me soon."

He pulled me into one of his tight embraces. "As soon as I can, Nickels. You can count on it."

CHAPTER 37

Josh

At noon the next day, I waited in a conference room of the District of Columbia FBI Field Office. Nicole and the rest of my family were in the air on the way home. It was lunchtime, and a half-eaten Subway sandwich and a Coke sat in front of me. Nervousness had destroyed my appetite. Debbie had said she would call at two, but I'd been here all morning, just in case.

I typed out a text to my girl.

ME: Miss you

She wouldn't likely get it until she landed, but what the hell. I added another few.

ME: Waiting for the call

Not wanting to spend a minute of time away from Nicole, I hadn't brought my laptop on this trip, and now I had to settle for looking out the window to keep myself occupied.

Adam's partner on the case, Rylie Brolin, opened the door and poked her head in. "How you holding up?"

"Okay, I guess. The waiting sucks."

"Tell me about it. You should try an overnight stakeout. Talk about bored out of your mind."

The TV shows depicted the life of an FBI agent as packed with excitement, and she was clearly setting me straight.

The truth was, I was more nervous about this than anything in a while. Dad and the rest of the family were relying on me to keep Debbie safe, and the goals of the FBI might not align with that.

"Any idea why she insisted on you?" Rylie asked.

I gave the same answer I'd given each time before. "No. Not really."

I'd known Debbie when we were younger, but that was a long time ago, and if she wanted to talk to a family member, why hadn't she asked for her parents?

Did that mean she knew they were dead? If she knew, what did that tell us about who had taken her and how she'd been held captive? Merely thinking like that had me making dangerous assumptions.

Adam had warned me that we didn't know anything for sure. It was more important to draw out information than to provide it. The purpose of the call had to be either locating her or setting up a meeting. That had been drilled into me.

Adam's boss, Dempsey, wanted a meeting so the FBI could apprehend the bank-robbing crew she was working with.

My sister-in-law Ashley had told me before she left that although Debbie had been the victim of a kidnapping years ago, Dempsey viewed her as a suspect to be apprehended, and to be careful. When I learned the evidence tying her to the robbery was a video, I'd asked to see it, but was rebuffed by Dempsey.

~

At a quarter before two, the room filled up. Adam was joined by his boss, Dempsey, his partner, Rylie, and his previous partner, Neil Boxer, with whom he'd worked the original bank robbery where Debbie's DNA had been identified.

"We'll all be listening," Dempsey said as he pointed to the headsets attached to the phone in front of me. "You use the phone, not the speaker. We don't want to spook her."

He'd explained this to me twice before, like I was a kid or something. "As far as she's concerned, it's just the two of you on the phone."

I stated the obvious. "She's calling the FBI, so she has to know you're listening."

"Even so, we want her to be at ease. This is just two old friends talking." He said old friends as if it hadn't been almost twenty years. "Remember, we want to set up a meeting, just the two of you."

When I'd asked him what he recommended, he hadn't been definitive. "*Whatever she's comfortable with*," he'd said.

Dempsey repeated himself a few more times before the appointed hour, and finally added, "Remember, we want to stop this crew before anybody else gets hurt."

It was almost exactly two o'clock when the phone in front of me rang.

Dempsey checked around the room and gave me the thumbs up.

I picked up the handset nervously. "Hello?"

"Who is this?"

"Josh, Josh Benson," I replied.

There was silence on the line for a few seconds. "Josh?" Her voice sounded tentative.

"Yes. Is this Debbie?"

"You don't recognize me?"

I didn't lie. "No. It's been a really long time."

"I don't remember your voice either." That was a bad sign.

"We were both kids," I said.

Dempsey looked worried and wrote a word on the pad in front of him, which he held up. *Meeting*.

"How do I know it's you?" she asked, fear lacing her voice.

"I was told you asked for me by name, so I'm here, just like I was for you before."

Adam slid me a note—*convince her*.

She was silent as I wracked my brain for something that would make her trust me. "We're twinsies, remember?"

"Right," she answered. "Where is yours?"

"Back of my neck, just like you." We'd thought it was the coolest thing ever that we both had small birthmarks on the back of our necks.

She didn't say anything to that.

"What did you want to talk about?" I asked. "I hear you might be in a little trouble."

She snorted a laugh. "A little?"

Dempsey motioned for me to keep her talking.

"Isn't that why you're calling?" I asked.

"I guess. I want to help."

"How can you help?"

"But how do I know you're Josh?"

I had to get her past that. "Ask me a question I should know."

She sighed. "I don't know," she whined. "I thought I'd remember your voice."

This wasn't going well, and it was time for a decision. "You can reach out to me by email if that's easier. My email's listed on the Benson Corp. website."

Dempsey's face darkened, and he wrote out a quick note—*keep her talking*. Then he pointed to the other one again—*meeting*.

"Do you ever hear the roar at night?" she asked.

I shivered as that terrible day came back to me in a rush. "Not in a long time," I answered truthfully. The nightmares had stopped years ago.

She sighed loudly. "I still do." The sound of a motorcycle in the distance came over the line. "I have to go now."

Dempsey looked positively frantic, pointing at his two signs.

"I remember the water," I said.

"Me too."

"I still have the scar." That would be something nobody else would know.

"I have to go, Josh." She finally seemed to accept that I was her cousin. "Bye."

"Email me."

"Okay," she said before the line went dead.

Dempsey exploded. "What part of keep her on the line didn't you understand? We needed to set up a meeting."

I'd had enough of this bully. "You heard her. She's scared, and pushing her wasn't going to help."

Adam and the others stayed quiet while Dempsey vented. "We needed that meeting."

"That's not the priority," I shot back.

"It damned well is."

I stood. "She needs someone she can trust. She sure as shit isn't going to trust any of you."

He stood as well, seeming determined to stare me down. "You just blew our best chance."

"I just saved your only chance. She knows it's me now."

"She didn't say that."

I'd heard it, and if he hadn't, he was tone deaf. "Her voice did. I'll let you know when she gets in touch."

Boxer finally spoke up. "He opened up a second line of communication. That was smart."

Dempsey didn't look impressed.

Rylie added her two cents. "She was clearly scared to be on the phone. Maybe email will be easier for her."

Now it was three against one.

"Well, what's done is done. So we'll see," Dempsey said, backing down. He pointed at me. "If there's another injury or, God help us, a fatality, it's on you, Benson."

I knew his statement was nonsensical, but it *would* bother me if someone else got hurt in the meantime.

Dempsey left with a huff and an under-the-breath comment I didn't catch.

Adam stayed behind when the others filed out. "What was that about water?" he asked after the door closed behind the last of them.

It still brought a cold sweat to recall that day. "It was right before she was taken. I was visiting, and she and I went down by the creek. A flash flood came out of nowhere. I've never been so scared in my life. We heard the roar even before we saw anything. A literal wall of dirty, brown water came rushing down the creek bed, and we almost didn't get out in time. It was probably only five or six feet, but it looked a mile high to me."

I stayed and talked with Adam for a few minutes before calling an Uber to get to the airport.

Once in the car, I typed out another text to Nicole.

ME: Still missing you

ME: Have a surprise waiting for you when you land

As I suspected, she didn't respond.

~

Nicole

. . .

We went through an elaborate hugging session after walking off the plane in Santa Monica. Saying goodbye to everybody was emotional for me, as my thanks to them all was heartfelt. The entire family had been so welcoming to me —the newcomer they didn't know at all.

I heard more than once that if Josh said I was an "okay kid," they didn't need to know any more. Even though I was certain some or maybe all of them knew of Lara's travails, not once did I get so much as a sideways glance for having a troubled youth as my cousin.

Lloyd and Robin had been especially nice to express their condolences on the loss of my parents. I hadn't even known they'd been acquainted, but they had apparently been out on Daddy's boat with them twice, years ago, and Lloyd even remembered the boat's name—the *Stella Maria*. Daddy had named her after his mother, my Nonie, and he'd loved going out on her. The time I'd spent with Josh's father reminded me so much of Daddy it made me cry as we said goodbye. He was an M&M, just like my father had been—a soft, sweet center under the hard shell.

The group dispersed, and there were town cars waiting for each of the couples with the requisite drivers wearing black coats and slacks who helped them with their luggage.

I didn't seem to rate the same ride home.

A woman in a leather flight jacket and jeans who had been standing next to a black SUV walked my way. "Miss Rossi?"

Lloyd Benson watched from beside his car.

I waved and pulled my bag behind me. "That's me. Nicole."

"Constance Collier," the short woman said as she reached me and extended her hand.

I took it and was surprised by the strength of her grip.

"4312 Orangebranch," I told her.

"I know. Josh sent me." She handed me a card.

Hanson Security. "I don't understand."

"We've been contracted to provide security for you," she explained.

"But I don't need anything like that."

"Mr. Benson disagrees," she said.

Seeing my standoff with this lady, Lloyd walked our way. "Is there a problem?"

"The assignment will be more difficult if she doesn't want to cooperate," Constance told him.

Lloyd put on his grandfatherly face. "Nicole, I can assure you Constance here is first rate. You won't even know she's around half the time. Josh wanted you to have security while he was gone. I'd hate to have him mad at me for not keeping you safe. Please do me a favor and accept Constance's help."

When he put it that way, I had no choice. I couldn't turn him down. "Sure, if you think it's best."

"I do," he said. "And don't underestimate Constance. The Secret Service trained her well."

Constance might've been a hardened ex-Secret Service agent, but Lloyd had her blushing.

"Okay," I said, following her to the SUV. "How does this work?"

She opened the back. "First, we get you home."

I hefted my bag in, and a minute later we were on the way.

"So, Secret Service, huh?" I asked.

She was shorter than me, and I'd always pictured big men in suits with short hair wearing dark glasses as the Secret Service type, not her.

"Ex, now."

"Why'd you give it up?"

"It was getting old. This pays better, and the protectees are more appreciative…generally," she added with a sly smile.

Ouch. "Sorry," I said. "It's not you. I just don't think I need—"

"I get it, Miss Rossi."

"Let's make it Nicole, please."

"Okay, Nicole. Would you like my professional opinion?"

"Sure." The question was a loaded one, and it sounded like I was going to get the answer regardless of what I said.

"When someone dies in your backyard because lightning struck them, you don't need me. When you get threatening notes and someone is murdered on your property for a reason you don't understand, that's when you should be careful. A crazy ex is one thing. You can relax if you know he's not around. But an unknown assailant with an unknown motive? That smells like danger to me."

After that explanation, I'd sound crazy to not want her around. "Thanks. I'd love to have your help."

She turned off the freeway toward Casa di Rossi.

"After we get home, how does this work?" I asked.

"Most of the time I just hang around and try not to get in your way. When I'm not available my partner, Winston Evers, will be your detail. You'll meet him tomorrow."

"What about at work?"

"Mr. Benson didn't think you were in danger there. He specified the house and the neighborhood, but we can expand the assignment, if you'd like."

Bringing personal guards into Rossi's was the last thing I wanted to do. How would that look to the rest of the people in the building? "No. Let's not include work. That's better for me."

We stopped at a light, and she looked over. "Nicole, I'm only here to keep you safe, not to interfere in your life. I won't say much, but if I do, follow my instructions exactly."

I sucked in a breath, sensing her seriousness. "Thank you. Sorry I was…" I searched for a nicer word, but settled for the crass one. "Bitchy before."

"You were just being honest, and I appreciate that. Sometimes that can be in short supply in this town."

I smiled. "Have you worked for Josh before?"

Constance shook her head as we turned onto Orangebranch. "No. Met him a few times at Habitat weekends though. Nice guy, but then all the Bensons are, if you ask me."

"Habitat?"

She pulled to a stop. "Yeah. Habitat for Humanity, volunteers building houses for low-income families. My partner, Winston, goes regularly with the Bensons, and I've joined him twice. A hard day's work, but fulfilling, if you know what I mean."

I climbed down from the SUV with a new set of questions for Josh. What was a bazillionaire like him doing at a Habitat for Humanity construction site? And she'd said Bensons, which had to mean more than just Josh.

He didn't know it, but my man had surprised me once again. How big could his heart be?

I unlocked the door to Casa di Rossi.

Constance stopped me just inside and latched the deadbolt behind us. "Stay right here while I clear the house." She drew a gun.

I felt useless standing by the front door of my own house while my bodyguard scurried from room to room. When she went up the staircase, I'd had enough and walked to the kitchen. After pulling a bottled water from the fridge, I took a long swallow. Echo's food dish sat empty in the corner. I'd have to pick him up tomorrow from the kennel.

"Nicole?" Constance yelled.

"In the kitchen," I yelled back.

She rushed in, holstered her gun, and leveled me with a glare. "Don't scare me like that."

"Scare you? You're the one with the gun."

"I tell you to stay, you stay. Got it?"

"What's the big deal?"

"As I said, I won't give you many instructions, but when I do, follow them. They're for your own good… Maybe Josh was wrong about you."

That last bit confused me. "Huh?"

"He said you cared about the people who work for you."

Pride welled up in me. "I do."

"Then why do you care less about me? You get so much as a hangnail, and I get in trouble."

Guilt washed over me. "Sorry. I'll be better." At least this would only be for a day—a thought I didn't verbalize.

She unlocked the back door. "I'm going to check the property. Keep the door locked until I get back."

I considered a salute, but settled on, "Sure." I'd gotten us off on the wrong foot and needed to fix it. "Be careful."

She smiled appreciatively. "Always."

After locking the door, I took another swallow of water before realizing I hadn't remembered to turn on my phone after the flight. I dug it out of my purse and powered it up. It woke with a few text messages. The top ones were from Sandy.

SANDY: How was the trip with the hunk?

SANDY: Did any of his brothers show up in need of a date?

SANDY: How about lunch this week?

Then some from Josh.

JOSH: Miss you

JOSH: Waiting for the call

JOSH: Still missing you

JOSH: Have a surprise waiting for you when you land

Now he tells me. Constance was a surprise, all right.

Before bed, I checked my email to see if Lara had been in touch—so far only radio silence from her. Until Josh's forensic accounting crew got us something, there wasn't much else we could do to help her.

CHAPTER 38

Nicole

The Wednesday morning light streamed in the floor-length windows of Josh's palace in the sky. From my seat at the table, the city stretched out behind him.

He'd cooked waffles for us this morning—cinnamon mocha, of course.

Nothing beat breakfast across from my man with the city waking up outside our window.

I had to mentally check myself. I'd just thought of this as our place, and it hadn't freaked me out. It would be four weeks this Saturday since my almost-dinner with Josh in Barbados.

"You know what next Monday is?" I asked him.

He looked up and chewed. "Got me."

"Think hard, Mr. Caveman. You can get it if you try."

"If this is one of those Cosmo tests, I refuse."

"Come on, I'm sure a USC guy can figure it out."

He shook his head. "Pass." To emphasize the point, he filled his mouth with a huge piece of waffle.

I sighed. "Our one-month anniversary, dummy."

He nodded and finished chewing before he spoke. "A month and you still won't honor your promise, you mean?"

"What have I not done?" I shot back.

"Your turn to think hard, Miss Stanford grad."

Stanford had been replaced by *Miss Stanford grad*, which wasn't much of an improvement.

"Starts with a T."

I searched my brain. *Blowjob* and *swallow* didn't start with a T, and those hadn't been promised anyway.

"Think back to the first note I wrote you."

It came to me in a flash. "Tiramisu," I shouted.

"Dinner and dessert. You owe me the whole enchilada, Nickels. I keep my promises. You should learn to do the same."

The truth of his words shamed me. I'd been the one to refuse the dessert at our last dinner. "I've been judged and found wanting. Can I make up for it with Aldolfo's tonight, including dessert?"

He offered his hand across to me.

I took it and got that electric spark I felt every time I looked into those blue eyes of his and saw the connection I longed for.

"Nickels, I don't find anything about you wanting, and I'd be honored to escort my girl to dinner tonight."

"Woman," I corrected him.

"Lady," he countered.

I didn't deserve the designation, but I'd learned to not argue that one.

~

Josh

At the end of the day, I cornered Dad in the Benson building before I had to leave for dinner with my girl. "I have a question."

"Shoot," he said.

"What have I done wrong recently to get on your bad side?"

Oddly, he smiled. "You noticed, did you?"

"Hard not to."

"Don't tell him I told you so, but Harold thought you needed a little toughening up. He suggested we put a few speed bumps in your path."

I was fed up with the testing, and since when was it Harold's job to decide what I needed? "And you agreed?"

"We think you've done great." The *we* showed how the two of them had ganged up on me.

"So making things harder for me has just been a game for you two?"

"It's not at all like that. You need to be ready for London."

I turned and left. That's exactly what it had been for them; a game. He didn't realize these testing games of his had driven my brothers out of the company.

"Josh," he called after me just as the door closed.

I shook my head. I had a dinner to get to, and much better company than this.

Nicole

We returned from Aldolfo's, finally having had the complete dinner—including tiramisu for dessert—that we'd promised each other since getting back from the Caribbean.

Josh closed the condo door behind us and flicked off the light I'd turned on. "No need for that."

"Oh," I said breathlessly.

"Did I ever tell you what tiramisu does to me?"

In the moonlight, I found the first of his shirt buttons. "Pray tell."

He moved my hands away and slowly unbuttoned my blouse, without answering my question.

"Josh," I whispered as it slid to the floor. His finger came to my lips.

"Shh."

Evidently this wasn't a time for words. It was a time for touching, a time for hands and lips and tongues.

I went back to work on his shirt as his fingers traced the outline of my bra and teased the sensitive skin up to my collarbone, out to my shoulders, and back to my neck. Then he dipped inside my bra, coming teasingly close but not touching the hardened peaks of my nipples.

He slipped a hand behind me and with a quick pinch of practiced fingers, undid the hooks of my bra as I finished his buttons.

I unzipped my skirt and slid it past my hips, kicking it aside. I stood in front of him naked, save for a thong and my heels.

"My God, you're so fucking beautiful," he said in a voice raspy and coated in lust.

Without words, all I could do was show him. I circled a hand behind his neck, pulling myself up to him, my mouth to his. I kissed him like I had never kissed a man before.

I covered his mouth, and my tongue demanded entrance and began the dance with his. I tasted the wine on him as we exchanged breath, hunger for each other, and lust. I tried to give back to him as good as he gave me.

His hands found my back and my ass, pulling me against him, hard. I could barely breathe. I didn't care.

I broke the kiss and pushed away enough to reach his belt. In a mad dash of hands, we stripped each other bare, save the heels I still wore.

We fell back onto the bed, me on top of him, heels and all. My legs straddled his as I rubbed my soaked slit the length of his cock. I leaned over, my breasts scraping against his chest, my eyes conveying my wordless wishes.

He kneaded my breasts as I sat up. Then he tweaked my nipples, sending shocks through me.

I knelt and took him in my mouth for a moment, determined to finish the act the way I never had before for a man. I could do it tonight—I could swallow it. I wanted to, for him.

"Not tonight, Nickels," he said as he pulled me up, spun me around, and in a few steps pinned me against the bedroom door.

With the cold wood against my back, I clawed at his shoulders. I was his to take, to have as he wished. All I wanted was him inside me. "I'm yours."

"You are so fucking beautiful," he repeated, with hunger in his eyes. "And you are mine. You're my everything."

Tears threatened as I saw the truth of his emotions shining in his face.

I worked my hands over his torso, his arms, his neck, feeling the bunched muscles as he kissed along my neck and collarbone.

He released me and leaned over to reach for a condom in his pants.

I pulled his arm back. "Not tonight. Please. I'm on the pill, and I'm clean."

He came back to me and kissed my nose. "Me too," he whispered.

I jumped up and wrapped my legs around him.

He lifted me against the door.

The sensation as he entered me was pure bliss. We fit so perfectly, and he filled me so fully, it was as if his cock was made for me and me for him.

Then he was inside me, gliding in and out, thrusting, pounding—it didn't matter. The way he made me feel was nothing I had ever expected to find.

With every thrust, I clenched more tightly around him. He brought me closer and closer to the cliff, building pressure within me until I couldn't withstand it and the sensations crashed through me. The tension built, but I didn't want to come. I didn't want it to be over.

I held off my orgasm as long as I could. All I wanted was to stay like this, joined with Josh, banging against the door.

I gave him all I had, all I could. I was his completely. I needed to be his, to stay his.

With several more powerful thrusts, Josh reached the end of his rope and exploded inside me. He pushed harder and deeper, pounding me against the wood, pushing me over the cliff into my soul-blistering orgasm, and we screamed each other's names.

I kept my legs wrapped around him as he carried me to bed, my pulse banging in my ears. Our hearts beating together filled my thoughts.

I had given him all I had, for him to take—my body and my heart.

He collapsed backward onto the bed. I untangled my legs and laid on top of my man as my breathing slowly returned to normal.

Eventually, he rolled me off to the side and brought me a washcloth.

I shed my heels and nestled up against him, my arm over his chest, my head on his shoulder, still sensing the beat of his heart.

In less than four weeks, he owned my heart.

CHAPTER 39

Nicole

On Thursday, Wenzel knocked on the frame of my open door. "Got a minute?"

"Sure," I said, instead of telling him how I really felt about his visits. I kept wanting to call him Weasel instead of Wenzel.

He was followed in by an older, balding gentleman in a suit who offered his hand.

"Nicole, this is my boss, Harold Snyderman."

Hmmm…a Benson guy. They needed to learn to dress more casually over there.

I shook with Snyderman. "A pleasure. How can I help you, Mr. Snyderman?" I recognized the name as the CFO at Josh's family's company, and I guessed Wenzel had introduced him as his boss to smooth the way back into the big company later.

"Wenzel and I have a few suggestions on how to consolidate vendors between Rossi's and Smith's that I'd like to go over with you."

This sort of thing repeated like a broken record. Wenzel would bring me a difference between how we handled things and the way it had been done at Smith's, always with the implication that the Smith's way had to be better.

"Wenzel, we've been through this. The vendors don't overlap well."

The reception that response got from Snyderman took the temperature in the room down several degrees.

"You're not being very cooperative," he said.

I sat up straight. "Yes, I am. We looked at it. There isn't much overlap outside of canned goods."

"I disagree," Snyderman said. "Both divisions buy significant produce and dairy, for instance. Isn't that right, Wenzel?"

Wenzel nodded. "Yes, but using different suppliers in pretty much all cases, and paying more than Smith's for equivalent items. At least the ones I checked."

"That's where your misunderstanding is," I scolded. "The items are not equivalent."

Snyderman scoffed. "An egg is an egg; an apple is an apple."

"And the store space is significantly underutilized," Wenzel added. "Over at Smiths, Andy Neufelt has dramatically increased salable shelf space with optimized store layouts that would benefit Rossi's as well."

I couldn't believe how out of touch these two were with the Rossi's customer base and their expectations. "Spaciousness is a part of our customer experience."

"So, I take it you're not interested in Mr. Neufelt's help?" Snyderman asked.

I shook my head. "No, thank you. The concepts are different."

"What about taking advantage of Smith's buying clout to lower your produce and dairy costs?" Snyderman asked.

"Thank you again," I told him. "But, no."

He clapped his hands on his knees. "Then I guess that's it for today." He stood, and Wenzel followed his lead. "Thank you for your time, Miss Rossi."

"Nice meeting you," I told him as he walked to the door. I'd have to ask Josh later who had shoved the stick so far up Snyderman's ass.

Snyderman stopped at the door and turned. "This is not over." His tone conveyed more threat than prediction. "We'll revisit this in two weeks."

Wenzel followed him out.

I had only just met the man, and already I didn't like him.

Getting up, I strode toward Josh's office to get this fixed.

"He's in a meeting at the Benson building," Dee told me as I checked his office. "His father called." She waved me closer and whispered. "What's going on?"

I took the visitor's chair next to her desk. "What do you mean?"

"That Mr. Snyderman and Mr. Bremmer were in Mr. B's office, and when they came out, Mr. Bremmer told Mr. Snyderman he wanted to replace the furniture. Mr. Snyder agreed. What is that about?"

It sounded odd, but Dee didn't make many mistakes. "I'll check into it," I assured her.

First I checked with our receptionist, Cynthia, and yes, Snyderman had left the building. Then I found Wenzel in his office.

I closed the door behind me.

He looked up. "It's nothing personal about the supplier consolidation. I'm just trying to do my job on the cost-reduction front."

"I know." I didn't bother sitting. "What were you doing in Mr. B's office?" I hit him right between the eyes with it. No sense beating around the bush.

The blood drained from his face, and he slumped in his chair. He would have melted into the carpet if he could have. "I might have been jumping the gun a little," he squeaked out.

"On what?" I demanded.

"Well, Harold said he was going to recommend me for the job. Nothing personal against you, I just think he knows me better. He and I have worked together for a long time and all, you know." He was jabbering out a lot of words, but no facts—nothing that made any sense.

"What job?"

"The corner office," he said meekly.

I couldn't put together what he was saying. If Josh had been planning office shuffling of some sort, he would have told me.

"Mr. B is going off to London in two weeks to run Benson Europe."

My legs went weak, and I collapsed into the chair. This didn't make any sense.

Wenzel waved a hand in the air. "Something about the succession plan and replacing a sick uncle who's leaving. Now, don't get me wrong, I think Mr. B has been a great boss, but when opportunity knocks, I'm putting my hat in the ring."

Wenzel had gone from panicky at getting caught in Josh's office, to giddy at the prospect of taking over, the weasel.

Succession plan… The words rattled around in my head for a moment.

The blue folder Josh had mentioned—his father's plan for him.

I stood and left Wenzel's office without another word.

"I think you do good work," the brown-noser called after me.

From the first day I met him, I couldn't have cared less what he thought, and that feeling had only gotten stronger with time.

Douche-nozzle.

I barged past Dee's desk. "I need a minute." I closed Josh's office door behind me. I'd seen him put it away once, and tried to remember where.

Sitting in his chair, I found it in the first drawer I opened.

Josh Benson Advancement Plan, the folder was titled.

Steeling myself, I opened and began reading.

It got worse and worse the farther I went.

There were sections about getting experience in various departments, followed by acquisition rationalizations—now I understood where the word came from—and then the final two steps.

A transfer to run Benson Europe, followed five years later by ascension to the CEO position of Benson Corp.

This was a map of the yellow brick road Josh had been traveling toward his future, his duty—his unalterable destiny.

At the bottom, it was dated the day of Kelly's engagement party, and signed by both Josh and his father.

Above the signatures it said *Promised this day by Josh Benson and Lloyd Benson.*

With those words, it might as well have been signed in Josh's blood.

My vision blurred as the room threatened to go dark. I set my head down against the desk.

I felt faint because my heart had been replaced by a black hole of nothingness incapable of pumping blood, incapable of anything except tears and self recrimination for having been so stupid as to repeat my past mistakes.

Grabbing tissues from his desk, I dried my eyes. A Rossi couldn't be seen like this in the Rossi building by the Rossi employees. I would not degrade my family name by crying in this office. *I'm a Rossi, goddammit.* Maybe the last Rossi to work here, but I was still responsible for the family reputation, and I would not let Daddy down.

My hands felt wooden, but I managed to put the folder back where I found it. I knew what I had to do now. I would end things between us before he did.

My destiny was repeating like a broken record.

Josh was leaving me. He'd known it since that weekend in DC, and probably before.

Once again, I'd been used as a convenient bed-warmer, but no more.

At least this time I found out before he'd packed his suitcase. My victory would be getting to be the first one out the door.

I stood up straight, like Daddy had taught me, dried my eyes again, and marched out. I'd clear my things out of his condo and get back to where I belonged every night of the week.

The tears stayed at bay until I'd pulled the car door shut and started the engine.

Then the waterworks began.

Why me?

~

A SHORT DRIVE LATER, I STRODE INTO JOSH'S CASTLE IN THE SKY FOR THE LAST TIME.

"You're home early," Serena greeted me cheerfully. Duke was checking the fridge.

"Yeah." I proceeded to the room Josh and I had shared.

The bed that had been so wonderful this morning now reminded me of what a fool I'd been to fall for the wrong guy *again*.

I sure could pick 'em.

Have me think he's the one for me—check.

Convince me he thinks I'm the one for him—check.

Not be honest about his plans for the future—check.

Ready to leave me here and move on—check.

Not willing to tell me until he's on the way out—check.

I pulled my two suitcases from the closet and started filling them. Folding was a luxury I didn't bother with. This would be quick, because I hadn't brought much over. I only spent weeknights here.

After throwing my bathroom items into a plastic trash bag, I clicked the suitcases closed and hefted them off the bed to the floor.

Serena caught me before I made it ten feet out of the bedroom. "Where are you going?"

I didn't deny the obvious. "I'm done. Josh and I are done. I'm going home where I belong."

She looked at me like I'd grown a second head. "Say what?"

"We're done." Those two words pretty well summed it up. Our relationship had been a roman candle that burned hot and bright, but quickly went out.

"Did you two fight?" Duke asked, coming up behind Serena.

That didn't describe it. "No. But it won't work for me."

"Did you try to talk it out?" Serena asked.

The slope was slippery, and I was losing my footing in this conversation. "There's nothing to talk through. It won't work between us."

Duke put his arm around Serena. "Did you tell him?"

I looked down at my feet. That was the hardest question of all. "Not yet. I will when he gets home. I didn't want to do it over the phone." I started for the door.

"Echo, come here," Serena called.

My dog bounded up to her, tail wagging as always.

She bent down to hold his collar. "You have to stay and talk to Josh before you leave. I'm not letting your dog go otherwise."

"Leaving without talking is a chickenshit move," Duke agreed.

Holding my dog hostage was mean, but effective. "I said I would. I'm just taking my bags down."

Duke let go of Serena and snatched one of my bags. "Let's go, cupcake. I'll help."

I hissed a breath out, but didn't have anything to say, so I followed him to the door.

I turned. "Serena, you've been great. It just won't work between Josh and me. I can't explain it right now."

"I'll call you later," she said.

I sniffed and nodded. I'd give her the best goodbye hug ever when I came back up.

Josh

I'D SPENT THE LAST TWO HOURS AT DENNIS'S OFFICE, ASKING FOR ADVICE ON DEALING with my Dad and the London situation. In the end, neither of us had a good solution. Selling off the European operations was the best we could come up with, and neither of us felt certain that would fly.

Dee greeted me as I walked back into my Rossi's office. "That Mr. Snyderman was by, and whatever he said didn't make Nicky very happy. She left without a word, and she always says goodnight."

I put my bag down. "Thanks for the heads up."

I'd warned Harold to leave this place alone, and if he was stirring up shit, I'd be the one calling a meeting with Dad next time.

After a quick tour of the offices, I didn't find Nicole, although her office door was open. My final check was with Cynthia up front.

She confirmed that my girl had left the building in a hurry.

Closing up her office and my own, I packed up and headed home myself. It was Tuesday, so she'd be at the condo tonight. After my altercation with Dad, I could use a stiff drink and some cuddle time with Nicole. I texted her before starting the car.

ME: On the way home. Should I get some takeout?

I figured she might not feel like cooking; I certainly didn't.

No return text arrived before I parked at home.

Oliver greeted me in the lobby. "You just caught her, sir."

I gave him a quizzical look.

He approached with his hand out. "She gave me this to give to you." He handed me a key—the condo key I'd given Nicole. "She just went up again."

"I don't understand."

"Nor do I, sir. I shall miss her, and that nice dog of hers."

This did not sound good. "She had Echo with her?"

"No, sir. Not yet. She brought bags to her car."

Taking things to her car and dropping the key with Oliver? My stomach turned. This was all wrong.

The ride up to my floor took an unbearably long time. The door was closed but unlocked.

I tried a cheery greeting. "Nickels, I'm home."

Serena and Duke appeared.

"We'll let you two talk," Serena said as they passed.

The door closed behind them, and the room was eerily quiet.

I spied Nicole sitting in the chair that faced the window. "Nickels?"

She didn't answer or even look my way.

I came up behind her. "What's wrong, honey?" I put my hands on her shoulders to rub them.

She jerked away and stood. "Don't you dare. I'm not your honey. I'm not your Nickels. I'm not anything to you, and you're not anything to me. Got it?"

My heart climbed into my throat as I moved around to the end of the couch. "What's wrong?"

"Stop right there and answer one question honestly. When did you plan on telling me?"

I didn't dare hazard an answer that could get me in more trouble. "Tell you what?"

"About going to London?"

Fucking Harold. This had to be his doing.

"I'm not going," I said.

She stared daggers at me. "Your father thinks you are."

"And I think I'm not. I'll work it out with him."

She seethed with anger. "I saw it. The stupid blue folder."

"That's old history."

"I saw the date on it. Last fucking week isn't old. You told me weeks ago you were going to talk to him, and you obviously didn't."

Her accusation cut me to the bone, because it was the horrible truth. "The timing wasn't right," I explained.

It was all I had. Dad had pulled me aside at Kelly's engagement party to sign an amended plan, but with the whole family around, that hadn't been the time to start an argument. It would have blown up Kelly's big day.

Nicole walked around me. "I'm going back to Casa di Rossi." She picked up Echo's leash. "Here, boy, we're going for a walk."

"It's not safe there."

She ignored me. "And you're not welcome. I don't want you to come over. I don't want to hear from you. Not ever."

I walked toward her. "Don't go. You don't understand…"

She backed away with fire in her eyes. "Stay back. I understand perfectly." She leashed up her dog before continuing to the door where she turned. "I can't afford to quit, but I've got vacation time coming, so I won't be in for the next two weeks."

"I told you I'm not going," I objected.

Sooner or later the truth had to win out.

"Enjoy London," she said as she shut the door behind her.

The truth hadn't won today.

I slumped into the leather chair, and my eyes welled up. This was all fucked up, and I didn't understand why.

Her words had pierced my heart and broken me.

I'd ruined things with her. The one thing in my life I had to get right, and I'd screwed it all up.

Benson men didn't cry, not ever, Dad had drilled that into us. We persevered, we overcame, we conquered, and we won. I was failing at that part of being a Benson as well.

CHAPTER 40

Josh

After I had my wits about me again, a quick call to Bob Hansen took care of my first concern: Nicole's safety.

He agreed to task Constance and Winston with watching over her until I figured out how to get her back, how to convince her I was staying—staying for her, staying because of her.

But I couldn't answer Bob's question about how long the assignment would be. Without a plan, I had no clue.

I paced the long windows in my apartment and searched the vista for a plan. Looking over the city spread out into the distance usually gave me inspiration. Today, not so much. I didn't see order in the layout; I saw a jumble, just like my thoughts.

Concentrate, dammit.

Analyze the problem, deduce options, be decisive, pick the optimal solution. That system had always worked for me. There had to be a way. Treat this like any textbook problem—that had to work. The system, *my* system worked. I knew it. First make a plan, then execute, and don't dawdle.

I went to the liquor cabinet and pulled out my best bottle of scotch. After tasting the Macallan 1926 that Dennis had brought as a peace offering for Adam, I'd added that to my cabinet. It was surely the drink for today. I poured two fingers and took a sip.

Dumb fucking move.

I spit it back in the glass. Some landed on the floor and some on my shirt.

Another dumb fucking move.

I fetched a paper towel, cleaned up the floor, capped the bottle, and put it away.

I needed clarity, not a buzz.

Verbalize the problem, verbalize the solution. Execute.

"Think," I said out loud.

The problem came first. *What is the problem?* The problem was that my girl—*scratch that; she hates it when I call her that*—my woman thought I was leaving her to go to London. She believed the paper she'd read, the damned folder Dad had made to keep me tethered to the company. The *succession plan,* he called it. The *probation document* was more like it.

It had been a low blow to bring it to Kelly's party. Dad knew I wouldn't dare create a scene in front of the entire family. If I'd refused, he'd have made sure it exploded in my face in front of everyone. That day, I'd had only one objective: to make the party a great welcome for the two newcomers. Adam, because Kelly deserved it, and Nicole, because she was the best thing to ever happen to me. Signing his stupid folder was the price to pay at the time to ensure a smooth event, and I'd do it again if I had to.

Why didn't Nicole believe me when I said I'd fix this? She didn't understand how much I loved her. This had all happened so fast. We hadn't had enough time together for her to comprehend it all.

Women were supposed to get that stuff, though. Why hadn't she understood? Wasn't *that* the problem? She couldn't sense it clearly enough. I hadn't done enough for her. Maybe I should have sent Wenzel packing to tamp down the Smith's anxiety? Maybe I should have said out loud that I didn't think a merger with Smith's would work as soon as I'd seen how flawed Harold's suggestion was? Maybe I should have suggested converting the Smith's stores to the Rossi's format? That would have shown her how much I cared.

Should I have sent more flowers? Well, that's pretty much always a yes. More flowers, check.

That, I could solve right now. After a little begging and an extra fee, I convinced the flower shop near her to deliver two dozen red roses this evening.

If flowers was the first step, what was the second?

I played back our exchange in my mind.

She thought I was going to London.

I'd told her I wasn't, not without her.

She hadn't believed me. She said I hadn't told her about London.

That part she had right, but she didn't give me the chance to explain.

She still thought I was committed to going.

Dad was under the same impression—another fucking problem.

Telling her again I wasn't going to London hadn't changed her mind. Why not? I'd never lied to her.

I turned at the sound of a key in the door, and the door opened.

It was Serena, followed by Duke.

My face must have fallen a yard at the disappointment. I'd hoped it would be Nicole coming back for something, giving me another chance to explain.

"Don't look so glad to see us," Serena said. "We went out to get dinner fixings." She lugged a grocery bag to the counter.

"Filet, man," Duke added, bringing another bag to the kitchen.

"Or," Serena said, opening the fridge. "We could have what you're having. A big bowl of pity-party soup, is it?"

I shook my head and sat in the chair. "Very funny."

"So…how did your talk with Nicole go?" she asked.

"Not good."

Duke pulled a beer from the fridge and came my way. "She didn't look happy. What'd you do?" He took a seat on the couch across from me.

"Nothing," I complained. "It's what she thinks I'm going to do that has her bothered."

Serena joined Duke on the couch. "Why'd you let her leave, then?"

I rolled my eyes. "What am I supposed to do? Tie her up and make her stay?"

"It worked for me," Duke quipped.

Serena punched his shoulder. "Like you're the poster boy for good behavior."

"Well, it did," he said, rubbing his shoulder.

"And what are you doing here, exactly?" Serena asked.

"Figuring out a plan," I said.

Duke huffed. "Wuss move, man."

"Huh?"

"No. I get it. You don't care enough to want to keep her, so what's the problem?" Serena asked.

"Bullshit. I fucking love her," I shot back at my bratty sister.

Duke shrugged. "All I see in front of me is a puddle of mush too sorry for himself to fight for his woman and make her understand how he feels. But, fuck, what do I know? I'm not the poster child for shit."

I stood. "Big help you are."

Serena leaned back. "He's right, you know. Every minute you stay here says you don't care enough. Stop overthinking it and go talk to her. Explain how you feel. That doesn't take a plan. Tell her again how much you love her."

Now I was the one overthinking a problem?

Duke chimed in. "Yeah, chicks dig that shit. Make her listen."

Serena elbowed him. "She's not a chick, and it's not shit."

Duke nodded. "I stand corrected. Women appreciate it when you connect with them at a deep emotional level by baring your soul and expressing your innermost feelings in meaningful and heartfelt dialog of sufficient sincerity and duration." He glanced at Serena. "Is that better?"

Serena coughed. "Wiseass."

I headed for the door. I'd gotten the message: get my ass in gear and over to Nicole's house before it was too late.

New plan: talk to my woman whether she wants to listen or not.

I heard Nicole's words in my head. *"And you're not welcome. I don't want you to come over."*

Screw that. Going over was the only way to solve this.

~

Nicole

I OPENED THE DOOR TO CASA DI ROSSI. IT LOOKED FAMILIAR AND DIFFERENT AT THE same time. This was the place I'd always called home, and yet it felt a little off, a little foreign.

Echo bounded in toward the kitchen when I let him off his leash. He started by checking his food bowl. That part was as it always had been.

Closing the solid front door behind me, I surveyed the front room. The rug was missing—the one that had been defaced when we came back from Barbados. It still sat rolled up behind the couch.

Then it hit me. I'd just used *we* instead of *I* when thinking back to that night. That was the real difference here—there was no more *we*. Casa di Rossi had become Casa Vuota, the empty house.

Echo padded back to me.

"I know, boy. Let's fix you dinner."

My dog would never leave me. Lara was gone, Josh was gone, but the house wasn't truly empty, not as empty as my heart.

I walked to the kitchen, and my furry friend followed. "I think you deserve wet food tonight. None of that dry crap. Whaddaya think?"

His tail wagged even more vigorously than normal—a yes for sure.

A glass of wine later, Echo had been out, and I sat on the couch wrapped in a blanket. I scrolled through the TV listings for something to take my mind off my fucked-up life, off Josh and how I'd fallen for it once again. Color me gullible. I chose a *Friends* episode because I couldn't take anything with substance to it.

The laughter coming from the screen felt fake because it conflicted so dramatically with how I felt. I'd done what was right, what I had to do to protect myself from the bad news headed my way. Hadn't I?

If I'd stayed for the day I knew was coming—the day he left—it would only be worse. Ten times worse.

Mo hadn't been one-tenth the man Josh was, and his leaving had almost broken me. If I was being honest, he had broken me for a time. This way the heartbreak was on my terms, with my timing. That was better, wasn't it?

I put my feet up on the coffee table, and there it was—another of those damned nickels Josh left lying around.

The tears started, and I couldn't hold back the flood. Even the comedy on the screen couldn't break through.

His words echoed in my brain as clearly as if he were here. *"The nickels? I leave them around as a reminder to myself of how you are everywhere. You are always with me, always in my mind and my thoughts, Nickels."* He'd even had one in his wallet.

Later I'd asked why he picked old Buffalo nickels.

"Because they don't make them anymore," he'd said. *"And, like you, they are unique. Another one as special will never be minted."*

I'd swooned at those words and wanted to jump his bones right there.

I had to mentally slap myself. Josh was now a part of my past, not my future. He had to be. It was the only way I'd survive.

CHAPTER 41

Nicole

THE *FRIENDS* EPISODE HAD ALMOST FINISHED WHEN THE DOORBELL RANG.

Echo barked once.

"I hear it," I told my lazy alarm dog.

I checked through the curtain. Josh's car was parked outside.

Asshole.

He knocked loudly. "Nicole, we need to talk."

I ignored him.

"I know you're home, Nickels. You wouldn't leave Echo. I'm not going away."

My nails dug into my palms as I clenched my fists. I had to stay strong. "I'll call the cops." I wasn't giving anything away by talking. He knew I was here.

"They won't arrest me. I have a key."

Fuck.

I'd forgotten to ask for it back when we were at the condo. A real dumbshit move on my part. "I'll ask them to take it from you."

"Then I'll wait by the street until you come out. I've got groceries for a week in my car."

"You do not."

"Come out and check," he challenged.

"No."

He was silent for a few seconds.

I listened for him to go down the stairs, but didn't hear anything.

"Then you can listen while I talk," he said.

"I'm going upstairs. You can talk all you want."

"If you do, I'll have to yell. How will that look to the neighbors?"

I knew how it would look, and it wouldn't be pretty. "Okay, talk." I slumped to the floor, my back against the door.

"By the way, I brought your favorite: chicken tacos from Taco Bandito."

My traitorous mouth started to water. "No thanks."

"You're welcome to have some when you change your mind. I think I'll eat mine while we talk."

"Get it over with so I can get back to my television."

"What are you watching?"

I knew this game, and I wasn't playing. "I'm not answering any of your questions." *Shit*. I'd already been talking when I should have refused.

"Fair enough. Let me tell you a story that starts a few weeks ago. I once went on a work trip to Barbados. I say a work trip, because all I'd planned on doing was studying boring books for my job—things that would please Dad. But a funny thing happened while I was there. Want to know what it was?"

"No," I answered before realizing I shouldn't even be saying that.

"I'll tell you anyway. I noticed the most alluring girl watching me from a row back on the beach. This girl pretended not to be watching me, so I pretended not to notice. She was with this friend of hers, also a looker, by the way."

If I told Sandy that, she'd go nuts.

"But," he continued. "I only had eyes for the green-eyed goddess. And as luck would have it, she sent me a drink at dinner. That was an invitation I couldn't resist."

I had to correct him. "Sandy sent you the drink."

"That's not what Diego told me, but regardless, I invited her to join me for dessert."

I interrupted him. "This is pretty boring. I don't have all night."

"What are you going to do instead? Waste the night away watching *Bachelor* episodes?"

"I have better taste than that." I had to at least stick up for myself.

"As I was saying, I thought the night would end well, but then she clumsily fell in the pool."

"I was pushed," I countered.

"And there I was without a date for dessert, so we set a date for the next evening."

"You actually said another time," I reminded him.

"But the next day, I learned she'd lied."

"Misspoke is more like it," I said.

"But even so, the next day turned out to be the best of my life."

I waited for the explanation of how a near plane crash was a good day.

"At the end, I got to hold the woman of my dreams in my arms all night long."

My eyes watered with his words. This was going entirely the wrong direction. "This isn't changing anything. We're done, over, *finito*."

He ignored me. "It also started the most frustrating twenty-four hours of my life. First, I got to hold this special woman in my arms—so special that I didn't dare screw it up by pushing her into even so much as a kiss."

I sniffled, remembering how he'd been so much more gentlemanly than I'd wanted him to be.

"I was so scared I'd ruin it if I pushed. And then the next morning, she declared she hated me."

My gut tightened.

"She wouldn't believe me when I told her I had only the best intentions regarding her family's company. I told her once that she only had to look back to Sioux City to determine my character. And she told me then that she believed me. But now she doesn't."

He was twisting everything up, trying to confuse me. "That's not true."

"Then tell me what's changed. Tell me why I'm not that person anymore. Tell me why you can't trust me. Tell me why we're not a team."

His words tore me apart. I should have gone upstairs and refused to listen. "You haven't changed. That's the problem."

"Want your tacos now?"

"What?" His change of subject caught me off guard.

"It's a simple question. Do you want your tacos now?"

"Good, so we're done talking about us?" I shot back. "That works for me."

"Not at all. I want to hear why I'm such a terrible person."

"You're not a terrible person. We're just not right for each other."

"We're perfect together. Want your tacos?"

He did it again, trying to distract me.

"I'm done talking if you're not going to listen."

"I'm listening, Nickels."

There was that name again—my special name. I wiped a tear and listened as the sound of paper being unwrapped came through the wood of the door.

I wiped my cheek with my sleeve. "I know how you think there's this law passed down on a stone tablet that you have to honor your promises, or kill yourself or something."

"You're being a little dramatic," he said.

"You remember the night we got back here and found my door broken?"

"Vividly. That's the night I got to hold you all night long and keep the drunk Nicole safe from the dark. You felt so good up against me because we are good together."

I could do without the reminder that I'd imbibed way too much. "Stop it. You said I had to come home with you because you promised to keep me safe, right?"

"I did promise to keep you safe. I did, and I always will."

"When I refused, you said you'd never forgive me if I didn't let you keep your promise. That's what you told me, and that's the problem. You said you'd never forgive me."

His silence showed I'd hit a nerve. He didn't have a comeback.

I continued. "You promised your father you'd go to London, and you even signed it."

"That's off now," he objected.

"How can it be? I saw the blue folder in your desk. The one with the paper you and he signed barely two weeks ago that said you'd go to London."

"I told you I changed my mind. I'm staying here with you. I love you, Nicole."

Love?

I gasped. It was the one thing I'd wished to hear for weeks. But not now, not today, not after what I'd read.

"How dare you do that?"

"Do what?"

"Say you love me. That's a high school trick. You can't get what you want, so you say you love her to get into her pants. It's not fair. You can't say that now."

"But it's true," he yelled.

I blinked, trying to hold back tears. "Look, Josh, you're a great guy, but you have to go to London, and I can't leave Rossi's. I have to stay here."

"I know that. That's why I'm staying in LA. For you."

I began to cry. "I am not going to wake up a month from now, or a year from now, and see in your eyes that you hate me because I made you choose between me and your dad, between me and your promise. Your dream."

"You won't. It won't be like that."

"Don't you see? You have to go to London or let him down, let your family down, and renege on your promise—the very same thing you said you'd never forgive me for. I won't let you do that. It's not fair to you, and in the end, it's not fair to me when you end up hating me for it."

"I can't hate you; I love you."

"Stop saying that. You're probably the most principled man I've ever met. And I won't let you destroy that about yourself on my account. You have to keep your promise to your dad and to your family. Family comes first, remember? Isn't that the Benson way?"

"You don't get it. You're more important to me than that."

I banged my head back against the door and tried again. "I've grown up in a family company. I know how it is, which is why I have to stay at Rossi's. It's my duty, my destiny—my family's legacy is at stake. The same is true for you, but that destiny runs through London. You told me so yourself. You've had your heart set on running that operation. I can't do long distance. Maybe some people can, but I can't."

"I'll quit the company and stay here with you, at Rossi's."

"It would break your father's heart for you to quit. Just as there's no Rossi's without a Rossi at the helm, you have to stay at Benson. You're the last brother standing. You told me so yourself. You'd still end up hating me later. I won't let you quit the company over me."

"You're still not listening to me, Nickels. I love you, and love conquers all. We can make this work. You have to know that in your heart. I can leave the company if I have to."

Talking about my aching heart was a place I couldn't go. "It's been a long day. I'm going upstairs."

"Tell me you don't feel the same way about me that I feel about you."

"I'm going upstairs now, Josh."

"Are you lying to me again?"

I blew out a breath. "I am not lying to you."

"Then tell me you don't love me, and I'll go away."

I couldn't utter those words. They'd be a lie. He'd know it, and worst of all, I'd know it. "Josh, we're done."

"Okay. We'll talk another time."

I let out a relieved breath. "Another time," I repeated.

"This isn't like dessert in Barbados. This time it's the truth, right?"

"Josh," I said, shaking my head.

"Is it?"

I felt tricked again by his logic. "It's the truth. Another time."

"I'll leave your tacos here by the door, in case you're hungry. Or you can feed them to Echo—your choice."

I snorted. "He doesn't eat Mexican."

"How do you know if you haven't tried?"

"Goodbye, Josh."

"Later gator."

"Later," I replied.

"Love you, Nickels."

I pushed up off the floor and trudged up the stairs without responding to that. When I reached my room, I peeked out the window. His car pulled away from the curb. Exhausted, I flopped back onto my bed.

When I closed my eyes, I saw it all. Josh, my rescuer, demanding money from Bad Dad for my phone. Josh, my rock, keeping me sane during those terrifying minutes on the plane. Josh, my savior, getting me back from Iowa in time to bail out Lara. Josh, my protector, taking me to his palace in the sky when my door had been broken down. Josh, my knight, holding me all night long, protecting me from the demons in my sleep. Josh, Rossi's savior, who'd written a personal check to keep the company afloat. Josh, Rossi's protector, who'd fended off the push to merge us with Smith's. Josh, my everything.

It had all started for me that weekend too, just the way he'd described. I'd never met a man like him, and probably never would again.

I forced my eyes open. "Stop fantasizing about what can't be, Rossi," I yelled at the empty room. "It was good while it lasted, and now it's over. Get over it, woman." I huffed at my lack of self-control. I had to be stronger than this. I came from better stock. I was a Rossi.

Tacos.

I rushed downstairs and pulled open the door. The bag was there, just as he'd said. I picked up the food, slipped back inside, and locked the door behind me.

My mouth watered all the way to the kitchen where I pulled out the first taco. Even cold and wilted, these were still the best in town.

I couldn't prevent my smile when I saw the note scribbled on the bag.

> A tasty treat
> For my girl who can't be beat
> Love,
> Josh

"Goofball," I said to the empty room.

CHAPTER 42

Nicole

A glass of wine later, the tacos were digesting, Echo had been out, and I sat on the couch again, wrapped in my blanket. I had *Friends* back on to keep my brain occupied.

The doorbell rang. Really? Again?

Asshole Benson.

Echo barked once—my backup doorbell.

I'd told Josh I didn't want to see him. He wasn't supposed to be back again today.

I put a hand against the door, took a breath, and prepared to crank up the volume. "I told you—" I yelled.

"Told me what?" came from outside. It was Constance's voice.

I opened the door.

Constance stood on the porch in her usual leather bomber jacket, jeans, and a smile.

Echo forced his way past me to sniff her.

She leaned over to rub his head. "Hi, boy."

"Sorry. I thought you were… Forget it."

"Josh sent me."

I'd figured that part out. "Why?"

"The same as before. Can I come in?"

"No, thanks. No offense, but I want to be alone. You can go back home or to the office or wherever."

Her eyes showed a hint of recognition or understanding, I couldn't tell which. "I'll be out in the car then. If you want to talk, let me know."

I sniffed. I couldn't keep myself together and talk about any of this, even with her. "You can go. I don't need protection, and I don't want any."

Constance backed up a step. "Like I said, I'll be in the car."

"But—"

She cut me off before I could object further. "It's the job. I'll be right out here." She turned and descended the steps.

I closed the door after wrangling Echo back inside. Constance was the one insisting on staying, but somehow I felt like the schmuck.

Constance was a nice girl. She wasn't the problem; he was.

"Fuck me," I said to the room. I'd done it again. I'd called her *girl* like Josh would have instead of *woman* as I would have before he'd corrupted me. *Dammit,* I needed to get him out of my system.

Returning to the TV, I restarted my *Friends* reruns. "Fuck you, Josh Benson," I yelled at the screen. It helped, but another drink of wine helped more.

Two episodes and another glass of wine later, I checked through the front curtains.

Constance was still parked outside.

I made a cup of the coffee she'd liked when she'd been here before and poured it into a travel mug. Marching outside, I took it to her SUV.

She rolled down the window. "Want to talk?"

I offered the mug. "I made you some coffee."

She didn't take it. "No thanks. Peeing in a cup once a night is gross enough."

I winced at the thought.

"I don't need more liquids."

I pulled the coffee back. "You really don't need to stay." I wrapped an arm around myself in the chill.

"Yes, I do, and it's not up to you."

I sighed. "Then I'll call the cops. I don't want you out here." I didn't need any extra reasons to be down, and her being out here made me feel worse.

"Don't bother. It's a public street."

"Who's your boss, then? I'll call him."

"Won't do you any good. Until the client calls off the assignment, this is where I'll be."

Josh was fucking with me again. "So I have to get Josh to tell you to leave?"

She nodded. "That's the score."

She brought the choice into sharp relief: talk to Josh or force her to stay out here.

"Want me to call him for you?"

"No," I said quickly. I was stuck in a no-win situation and had to choose the least-bad option. I nodded toward the house. "Come on inside." I wasn't going to make her suffer out here all night.

She opened the car door and climbed down. "Then I'd love that coffee."

I handed it to her, and we walked up to the house. "I'm not going in to work tomorrow. How are you going to handle that?"

She followed me up the steps. "My partner, Winston, and I will split shifts."

"Oh." I'd met Winston one evening when he'd come by to sub for Constance. He was a nice-enough guy, it seemed—a giant bear of a man. I opened the door. "What do you know…" I wasn't sure how to finish the question. "About the situation?"

She latched the deadbolt behind her and went to check the window. "Only that you two aren't together right now."

"Not now or ever again," I corrected her.

She moved to the next window. "And that he'll skin me alive if anything happens to you."

"How long are you going to keep this up?"

She stopped and turned. "Nicole, I've seen the police and autopsy reports. I've talked to Detective Beal and the first cops on the scene. I don't think this is a threat you laugh off."

I asked again, "How much longer?"

"You have to ask Josh. Or, until Beal catches the guy."

I slumped down into the couch again.

A text arrived.

JOSH: How were the tacos?

Constance looked over.

I didn't say anything as I turned off my phone. I wasn't falling into the conversation trap again.

Josh

When I got home, Serena and Duke were gone, which kept me from having to explain my failure to anyone.

The condo didn't feel right, since I knew Nicole wouldn't be arriving with her dog.

The liquor cabinet called to me. I surveyed the contents, and none of it looked appropriate. If I was going to get Nicole back, I had to start again the way we had in the islands—not the falling in the pool part, but the drink that had started it all, a green monkey.

Looking the name up on the internet netted me a host of different recipes, all of which were completely different. Some even used vodka, and I knew it had been a rum drink.

It took a few minutes to get connected, but I finally convinced them to get Diego on the line in Barbados. He remembered me—one perk of being a good tipper—and five minutes later I had the recipe they used at the bar there.

I assured him I'd send another tip his way soon and had him transfer my call to the front desk.

The clerk on duty thought it was an unusual request, but he took my credit card number and assured me the hundred dollars would make its way to Diego.

Forty-five minutes later, I was back from the store with the ingredient I hadn't had: passionfruit juice.

I made up a tall glass with the directions Diego had relayed and sat by the window, where I could look out in the direction of Nicole's house. A brain freeze was the awful result of sucking down the frozen concoction too rapidly.

I jumped up and drank a little lukewarm water out of the tap to relieve the pain. I was such a dork. Lesson learned: don't rush this. Going back to the window, I sat, closed my eyes, and with a small sip of the drink, transported myself back to where it had all started. That night, and the following day and night, played back in my mind and brought an overwhelming warmth with them.

I'd felt it. I'd known Nicole was different, special, a woman to be wooed more than pursued.

I sat by the window, trying to remember everything.

She'd won over my family at Kelly's engagement party, as I'd known she would. She was that special, and it showed in the way she interacted with them. Kelly had been incredibly nervous Dennis wouldn't show or that the interaction between him and Adam would blow up. She'd confided in me that Nicole's comforting words had helped when she'd been ready to break down that afternoon.

I finished the drink and made myself another.

Getting Nicole back was what I had to do. There was no plan B.

Halfway through that second glass, my phone sounded from the coffee table with Dad's ringtone.

I ignored it. He could wait. Everything could wait.

Only Nicole mattered. I'd texted her a bit ago to ask about the tacos. My phone showed no response, so I sent another message.

ME: Missing you

Again, nothing came back.

~

Nicole

The doorbell rang.

Constance jumped up to get it. "Expecting anybody?"

"No. I didn't even expect you." I ran to the kitchen in case it was Josh. "And I don't want to talk to Josh."

I heard the front door unlatch.

"Can I help you?" Constance said.

"I'm here to see my niece, Nicole." It was Ernst's voice.

I went around the corner. "Step-niece," I corrected him. "You can let him in."

Constance backed away.

Ernst walked in and held out his arms to me. "Nicole, I was worried and wanted to see how you were doing."

That set off my bullshit detector. "I'm fine." I stepped back.

Getting the clue, he put his arms down and turned to Constance with an extended hand. "Ernst Berg."

She took it. "Constance."

I answered the query his face conveyed. "Security."

He nodded. "Good idea. You two must be frightened after what happened."

"A little," I answered.

Ernst looked past me in the direction of the kitchen. "I'm worried about Lara. I'd like to talk to her."

I tried not to laugh at him pretending he actually cared. "She's not here."

He stepped toward the mantle. "Any idea where I might find her?"

"Maybe Idaho. Her friend from school moved there. I really don't know."

His squint said he didn't believe me.

"You know," he said as he searched the walls for something. "You wouldn't be in this position if you'd accepted my offer and moved out of this old...place." His eyes landed on a family photo on the mantle.

I stiffened. "This is my family's home and always will be. It's not a *place*," I spat.

Ernst's brows wrinkled. "Of course it is. I feel I owe it to you to keep the offer open, with the demise of the company and all—"

Constance's face showed she'd caught his deceit.

"The company is not in the least bit dead." I recited Josh's words. "I'm working... We're working to revitalize it."

"Yes. That's what I meant," he said. The man needed English lessons if he thought *demise* was a synonym for *revitalize*. "The money would give you a chance to get back on your feet."

"Not interested," I shot back.

"It really would be in your best interest, I think." He wandered to the mantle and picked up the photograph. "I know your parents wanted you to be able to afford a nice life."

I moved forward and put my hand out for the picture. "My life is fine, thank you," I lied. The last thing I would ever do is discuss my issues with him. "And they wouldn't have wanted me to give up Casa di Rossi, that's for sure."

He ignored me and placed the photo on the mantle before turning back. "I wouldn't be so sure of that. Your father and I had some very serious discussions about selling this place, and the land, to finance the company's expansion."

I shook my head at the obvious lie. "He never felt that way."

"I understand you wouldn't have known, because you were off at school. And being in college has a way of insulating one from the realities of life."

This had gone on long enough. "Thanks for stopping by, Ernst."

He looked startled that I'd just suggested he leave. "Very well. Keep my offer in mind. You'll let me know if you hear from Lara." He said this as a command rather than a question.

"Sure," I responded.

In a pig's eye, I would.

The gall he had to suggest Daddy had ever entertained the idea of selling Casa di Rossi. That was insane, seven ways from Sunday. Daddy would never have agreed to that.

That was the last straw for me. "Ernst."

He turned at the door. "Yes?"

"I don't want you back here anymore. I'll take care of the almonds from now on." I no longer had to work with him, or even see him.

"You can't do that," he protested.

"She just did," Constance said, moving toward him. "And I'll call the police if I see you here again."

He spun and slammed the door on his way out.

"Real charmer," Constance said with a roll of her eyes. "Who's he?"

"Lara's stepfather," I explained.

She nodded. "You think he's really trying to help you, or does he have some other play?"

"He's only ever out for himself," was the nicest thing I could think of to say.

"So you don't think Lara's in Idaho?"

I smiled. "Not a chance. Thanks for backing me up."

"Part of the service."

I picked up the photo Ernst had handled. I was in high school in that picture, about to start my senior year. That had been a good time, a happy time—Mom, Daddy, and me, with Nonie, a wonderful day at a restaurant in Avalon on Santa Catalina Island, back when I felt safe traveling there. This photo was the last one we had of Nonie before she died. Daddy had his sailing hat on, the one with Stella Maria embroidered on it. I put the picture back on the mantle where it belonged. Ernst had put it back haphazardly.

Except it hadn't been haphazard; he'd left the photo of him, Aunt Rossella, and Lara near the center and put our family picture on the end. What a turd move.

He'd pretended his visit was because he wanted to check on Lara. What a joke. She despised him, and he didn't care about her. His visit had been to remind me again that he wanted to take Casa di Rossi away from me and nothing else.

He probably already had the subdivision plans drawn up and machines at the ready to rip out the last standing bit of orchard in this part of town. He'd turn our little patch of history into some stupid condo development of lookalike stucco boxes and asphalt parking spaces. Yuck.

I looked out the window in time to see the jerk drive off.

We were only halfway into the next *Friends* episode when the doorbell rang once more.

Constance got up. "You're popular this evening."

I moved out of sight again, not wanting to talk to Josh.

"Can I help you?" Constance asked.

"I need to talk to Nicole Rossi." The man's voice was familiar, but I couldn't place it.

"Can I give her a message?"

"I need to come in and talk with her," he said.

"Stand back," Constance shouted.

"Or what?" the man shouted back.

I finally placed the voice. It was Bad Boy Billy. I raced around the corner.

Constance had backed away from the door. "Don't try it. I guarantee I'm faster than you." She had her hand on her gun.

The big man's eyes bulged out, clearly surprised that he couldn't push the little woman around. One hand was behind his back, the other held a folder.

"It's okay," I yelled to Constance. "I know him."

Constance wasn't backing down. "Show me your hands, slowly."

"He's from the bail bond company," I explained.

Billy brought out his hand from behind his back—empty.

"Turn around slowly," Constance commanded.

He did, and she pulled out the gun that had been at the small of his back. "You can have it when you leave."

He relaxed and turned to me. "Nicole Rossi?" He didn't recognize me, probably a result of dealing with a hundred people a day that he'd rather not remember.

"Yes," I answered.

"Is Lara Martini here?"

"No."

"Do you know where she is?"

"No," I repeated.

He threw the folder at my feet. "She didn't show this morning for her prelim. You can pay the one-ninety-five at the office tomorrow. If you don't, we file a Notice of Default on this house at the end of the day. Additional fees accumulate daily per the bail agreement. It's all in there. Any questions?"

I shook my head. Where was Lara, and how the hell could I keep from losing Casa di Rossi now?

He held his hand out toward Constance. "We're done."

In a few moves, she had the gun unloaded and handed to him in pieces.

"You really know how to use that?" Billy asked.

She shrugged. "At the range every week."

He looked my direction again. "There's a reward if you help me find her."

"No idea where she is," I said truthfully.

He opened the door. "Keep it in mind if you hear from her."

The door closed behind him.

"I assume that's not one hundred and ninety-five dollars," Constance said after securing the deadbolt.

I picked up the dreaded file. "Thousand."

"Bad day all around," she said.

"You could say that." I grabbed the wine bottle and poured myself another glass. The day had become a twenty on the ten-point shitty scale.

We both sat back on the couch.

I pulled my knees up to my chest, freezing cold suddenly at the prospect of losing the property. It was all that remained of my grandfather's legacy.

Constance looked over. "I'll bet your step-uncle's house was that bail guy's first stop."

The implication was clear. Ernst wanted the reward *and* my home.

Asswipe.

CHAPTER 43

Nicole

Friday morning, I looked at my coffeemaker and decided I deserved better. After finding my daily text from Mrs. Ringwold, I texted Sandy.

ME: Starbucks????

SANDY: Sure see ya in 30

I passed by the flowers that had arrived from Josh just after Bad Boy Billy had left—yet another trip for Constance to the front door. They were lovely, but wasted on me.

Constance hadn't allowed me to throw them out. She'd said it would be mean, and that's all it took. Mean was something I wouldn't be.

"I'm walking to Starbucks to meet a friend. Want anything?" I called to her.

"We're going together," she said, walking into the kitchen.

"You don't have to follow me everywhere," I complained.

"Job parameters," she told me. "Except at work."

That meant pretty much everywhere. "I'm not going in for two weeks."

"Is seeing him that bad?"

Nothing got past this woman.

"It's just until he leaves for London. It's easier this way." Really, it wouldn't be possible any other way.

On the walk over, Constance kept me busy by asking about the history of the Casa di Rossi property and what the orchard was all about.

We got to the coffee shop before Sandy. This one had both indoor and outdoor seating.

Only when we were in line to order did I realize what Constance had done.

"Thank you for the diversion," I told her.

She nodded. "Don't want you to get an ulcer over him." She'd provided me a few minutes of peace without Josh rattling around in my head, trying to convince me I was making a mistake.

I knew Sandy's drink of choice, so I ordered for both her and me.

Constance chose dark roast. She pulled out a credit card. "Make him pay?"

I nodded. "Absolutely."

It was a nice morning, and I chose a table outside.

Constance took up residence two tables over, facing me. When she put on her sunglasses, she looked the part of a Secret Service agent, except for the leather jacket.

The ball of energy that was my best friend arrived five minutes later and wrapped me in a hug. "Hey, girl."

"Hey."

She let go of me and turned to salute my bodyguard.

Constance raised her cup to us.

Sandy eyed me as we sat down. "Does she ever smile?"

"Sure," I replied. *Off duty.*

It only took Sandy one sip of the cup to get to it. "So what's the problem?"

"I just wanted to see my best friend, that's all," I answered.

"Right." She pulled out her phone and tapped on it before showing it to me. "It says here it's a workday."

"I decided to take two weeks off."

She nodded. "How long have we known each other?"

I didn't answer the obviously rhetorical question.

She lifted a single finger. "Once. That's the number of times you've wanted to meet for coffee during work hours." She waved the finger at me. "So what's wrong?"

I took a deep breath before diving into the deep end of the conversation that scared me. "We broke up." There. I'd said it. I waited for the storm of obscenities.

It didn't come. Sandy squinted over her cup and opened her mouth before closing it again. We were at a stalemate for some reason.

I didn't have anything else to say.

She merely watched me.

"What?" I asked.

"Is that all?"

Fuck me. I'd expected a reaction out of her, not a question. "Like what?"

"What did he do?"

My eyes misted up. The question didn't have an answer. "Nothing. He didn't do anything."

"Nothing?" she repeated.

I shook my head and hid behind my cup, taking another sip.

A smirk grew on her face. "When did you fall, exactly?"

"What?" I shook my head. "I don't know. I guess I fell for him that night we flew back from Iowa." A conversation with Sandy never did seem to go in a straight line. She'd verbally zig when I expected a zag.

"No, silly." She tapped her temple. "When did you hit your head and lose your damn mind?" She laughed. "This is hilarious."

I didn't appreciate the Sandy humor. "It's not funny."

"Of course not, girl. You hook the biggest fish in the sea, and you want to throw him back. Are you out of your ever-fucking mind?"

"I didn't *hook* him," I shot back. That was an insulting way to put it.

The serious Sandy came out of hiding as she leaned forward. "I know that. You fell for him hard. Do you love him?"

I sniffed and nodded. "I think so."

"Think or know?" she asked.

I looked at the table. "I do." I'd known for a while now. He was the best man I'd ever been with, and an impossible man not to love. That's what made this so hard.

"Now, will you tell me what's really going on in that screwed-up head of yours?"

I sniffed. "You're not going to believe me."

"Hey, I'm looking at the bright side. After you and I are done here, I'm adding him to my dance card."

I laughed at her joke. *It was a joke, right?* "If you do, I'll have to kill you."

"You love him that much, huh?"

It took me an hour to explain how wonderful things had been, and how they'd gotten so screwed up now.

Sandi nodded and listened and empathized the way I knew she would. She had always been my best friend—the one I could talk to, the one who understood, the one who had my back no matter what.

"So," she summarized. "Either you dishonor your father by leaving Rossi's, or he disappoints his father and loses his dream by not going to London. That's the choice?"

I sighed. "Pretty much."

"I still don't get why dumping the guy is the right thing to do."

"I wouldn't be able to take it, knowing what I'd cost him, and sooner or later, he'd realize what I'd done to him and hate me for it."

"Why not at least try the long-distance thing? He can afford the flights. You guys can do video-sex in between."

I scrunched my nose. "Eww."

"Don't knock it till you've tried it, girl."

"You?"

A broad smile ate her face. "You just close your eyes and imagine it's him. Hell, sex is all in your head, anyway. And, they make these really realistic—"

I held up a hand. "I don't want to know." I wasn't venturing into the gross zone with Sandy.

She checked the time. "I have a shoot I have to get to. It's guys this time, for Calvin Klein." She fanned herself. "Some of the models are real studs, and hung like you wouldn't believe. You and—" She nodded toward Constance. "—the assassin can come along. You'd like it."

I laughed "No. I think we'll head back."

She whispered. "Why? Is she gay?"

"Cut it out. You're too much."

She didn't give up. "It's an idea, now that you're back on the market and all."

I stood. "No, I don't think so. This has been great." It had truly helped to unburden myself. Being able to talk it out was cathartic, even if my decision hadn't changed.

Sandy rounded the table.

I stood to get my goodbye hug.

Instead she took my hands in hers. "I love you, girl, but I still think what you're doing is dumber than fuck."

I pulled my hands back. "I thought you were on my side."

"I am. That's why I'm giving it to you straight. This is the absolute worst decision you have ever made. Throwing away the kind of man you'll never find again over fear of what might happen is stupid shit."

My shoulders slumped as her mean words hit home. I'd thought she understood.

"If I found a guy like that, I'd fight for him. Circumstances change. This could all work out tomorrow. And if it doesn't, at least I gave it my best shot." Then she took me in for the long hug I needed. "But that's just me," she added.

"Thanks for listening," I told her as we released each other.

"Girl, you know I love you no matter what."

I nodded through the tears that had started again. "I know."

Sandy waved after crossing the street, and I waved back.

As Constance and I started back, she asked, "Good talk?"

"Yep. She thinks I'm a dumbshit."

I expected Constance to say something to that, but she didn't.

"She's a really good friend," I added.

Constance nodded knowingly. Or maybe her nod was agreeing with Sandy.

I wasn't brave enough to ask.

~

By mid afternoon, my arms were sore from all the weeding I'd been doing in the orchard. All I had left was filling in my damned dog's holes before going in.

Echo was a retriever, and wasn't supposed to be a digger by nature, but nobody told him that. He'd dig at a ground squirrel burrow for an hour after one disappeared down a hole. If he'd ever caught one, that was news to me. But he kept at it, and I had to shovel dirt every week and clean up the mess he made. It was hard, dirty work.

Maro had offered once to help, but since Echo was my dog, it was my responsibility—another thing Daddy had taught me. We were responsible for our animals' messes as well as our own.

Once finished with that, I cleaned up inside and roused Echo from his nap. "Time for a walk."

Walk, a magic word, turned a sleepy lump of fur into a prancing, tail-wagging, tongue-lolling monster that was hard to get leashed up.

I pocketed poop bags on my way to the door.

Constance followed and locked the door after us. After stepping in one of Echo's messes early on, she'd taken to following at a distance when I walked him.

A white Escalade drove by. It wasn't Josh, but it drew my mind back to him, back to us.

As we walked, my emotions spiraled in directions I couldn't control. I'd desperately wanted Josh and me to work, but the only scenario I could see was future heartache for both of us. No matter what Sandy said, if I felt bad now, I'd only feel ten times worse later when the inevitable end came.

Echo tugged on the leash, bringing my daydream to an end. He squatted to do his business.

I pulled out a poop bag and leaned over to pick up the smelly mess that resembled what my life had become.

Sandy had told me to persevere. She was wrong—dead wrong.

I couldn't launch us into the nightmare I'd foreseen. Josh didn't deserve it. He deserved a woman who could support him in his duty to his family, not one who altered his destiny toward unhappiness.

CHAPTER 44

Nicole

"Lover boy is here," Constance called from the front door Tuesday afternoon.

"Tell him to go away," I yelled back. It had been four days of this—Josh coming over every day.

"Not my job. You talk to him," she said, walking back to meet me. "Now go. You know it would be easier if you talked to him face to face."

"No, it wouldn't." I was certain of that. I didn't trust myself. If I had to look into those blue eyes, how could I tell him to go away?

If he touched me, wouldn't it be just like before? His magnetic appeal would weld us together, and all my effort to make this a sane situation would go down the drain.

I walked to the door. "She's not here."

"Hi, Nickels. I've missed you."

I didn't dare tell him I missed him too. "No Nickels here. Whatever you're selling, we've already got one. Try the next house."

"How's Lara?"

His question warmed my heart. "Still getting the safe messages."

"Good to hear. Guess what I have out here?"

I didn't need to guess. He'd brought a Taco Bandito bag each day.

And, each day after he'd left, I'd grabbed it from the porch and devoured it.

"Tacos. And as a special treat, I have containers of both salsas. So if Constance gives you any trouble, you can feed her a little of the red."

I laughed. "She's been good. No need for that."

"Well, I'll start eating while I read your mail here."

I pounded on the door. "You can't do that."

"Come out and stop me."

I took a deep breath to calm myself. "You don't have my mail, do you?"

"Sure I do. I've got one letter addressed to Nicole Rossi. Do you want to know who sent it?"

I took a long breath. "No. Just don't open it, whatever it is."

"It looks personal. It even has a kiss on it—in hot sauce no less. The red kind. Ouch. That had to be painful."

"You're making that up."

"No, I'm not. I wrote it."

Now I really didn't want him to read it. "I have to go."

"Sure you do. I'll leave the tacos here, but before you go, do you want to tell me about the Notice of Default that's nailed beside the door here?"

My heart stopped. "No."

"Okay. You know I could help if you'd let me, Nickels."

"That's taken care of. It's a mistake. They meant it for the house a few doors north."

My stomach lurched at the memory of Bad Boy Billy's visit. I was going to lose Casa di Rossi in two months. "I've got to go."

Rustling sounds came from the other side of the door. "Later, gator."

"Later," I said before I went upstairs to watch him leave.

~

Josh

I DOWNED THE LAST OF MY GLASS. "I'LL TAKE ANOTHER," I TOLD REGGIE BEHIND the bar.

Reggie and I had become good friends in the last few days.

Once I'd told him his place was close enough for me to walk home, he'd stopped cutting me off and was happy trading money for scotch. And, he stocked the good stuff.

He poured me another round.

"What do you think I should do?" I asked him again.

"Keep talking to her and wear her down." It was one of his four stock answers. He seemed to rotate them around randomly. It was *his* way of wearing me down, I guessed.

I peered into my glass, but nothing of help revealed itself. "I've been doing that, and it's not working."

I'd go over every afternoon and stand outside Nicole's front door to talk to her.

She'd listen for a few minutes and then say the same words: "It can't work between us, Josh. Go away and live your life."

I'd tell her again that she didn't understand, and then she'd go upstairs.

Eventually Constance or Winston would tell me to leave because Nicole was done listening.

I'd go home.

I'd given up calling, so I'd text her.

She wouldn't respond.

Dad would call again to harangue me.

I'd tell him no again.

He'd repeat that my answer wasn't acceptable, but that was tough shit.

I wasn't going to London. It didn't matter if Uncle Logan was leaving. My answer wasn't changing. Life would have to go on in London without me.

Serena would nag me about getting my act together. Duke wasn't much better.

So I'd turn off my phone and come here to avoid them all.

When it got late enough, I'd stumble home and drink more to finally get to sleep.

The next day I'd repeat the cycle. So far wearing Nicole down wasn't working for shit.

"I'd send her flowers," Reggie suggested. That was another of his four canned responses.

"I've been doing that too, every day."

Reggie didn't offer another of his answers right away.

"Did I tell you she has the most beautiful green eyes?" I asked him.

"Only a few thousand times." He left me, called down to the other end of the bar by another customer.

A hand pulled my glass away.

"Hey." I turned.

The hand belonged to Duke. "You're done for tonight."

"Bullshit." I grabbed for my glass, but he slid it farther away.

"Hey, Reggie, I need another," I called.

"No, he doesn't," Duke said.

"Yes, I do. And you can throw this guy out. He's bothering me." I indicated my annoyer.

Duke went into mean biker mode. "Try it," he snarled at Reggie.

Reggie eyed Duke and seemed to decide he feared him more than he wanted me as a repeat customer.

I didn't get my drink.

"What is your problem?" I asked Duke.

"I was told to get you back to the condo." He nodded toward the door. "Don't make this difficult."

I might hold my own against Duke on a good day, but today wasn't one of those days. I got up off my stool. "Sure."

Reggie waved goodbye. He had my card number for the tab.

The walk back went better than most evenings because I hadn't finished enough of a bottle yet tonight.

I followed Duke into the elevator. "What's the big deal?"

"You have a meeting tomorrow is all I know."

"No, I don't."

I hadn't been going into work since my life fell apart, and I didn't plan to until I got Nicole back. None of it mattered.

Once inside my unit, I heard Serena and another woman talking around the corner.

"She's really adamant about it," the other woman said.

"Thanks for all that. I think I understand now," Serena responded.

I rounded the corner.

The other woman was Nicole's friend from Barbados, Sandy. Her eyes narrowed when she saw me.

Serena and Sandy hugged before Sandy left, without a word to me.

"What did I miss?" I asked my sister.

"Nothing. We were just chatting.

"And?" I asked.

"This has all got to end," Serena said. "Mom has called a family meeting for tomorrow, and you're going to be there, and sober."

"Mom?"

"She sees you and Dad fighting, and it's making everybody miserable, including her. Especially her."

I thought I was the miserable one here. "I'm still not going to London."

"Both of you are talking, but neither of you is listening. That stops tomorrow," she said.

I went to my liquor cabinet. "Sure." I opened it, but it was empty. "Hey, what's going on?"

"Don't worry," Duke said. "It's safe, but like the boss said, you're cut off for tonight."

I stormed to my bedroom. "Fuck you too." Inside, I opened my drawer.

It was empty. Serena had taken my backup bottle as well.

CHAPTER 45

Josh

Wednesday morning I rolled out of bed, exhausted after a mostly sleepless night. My mouth felt like I'd chewed a squirrel and his tail was still in my mouth. I wandered out to the kitchen.

Serena was cooking breakfast. She handed me some tablets and a glass of orange juice. "Take these."

I held out the glass. "Only if you make it a screwdriver." I needed the hair of the dog this morning in a bad way.

"It already is."

I threw the tablets back with a gulp from the glass. "This is just orange juice," I complained.

"Yeah, and those were Tylenol you just swallowed. No alcohol. You remember what happened to Vasili."

Ever since Vasili at work had been diagnosed with liver failure and needed a transplant, I'd been religious about not mixing any Tylenol with alcohol. He'd thought washing down the pills with vodka would double the pain relief. Lesson learned: read the label. We had two eyes, two ears, and two kidneys, but only one liver. He swore he'd never violated the label, but I wasn't taking any chances with my liver.

"You're mean, you know that?"

Serena shook her head. "Somebody has to beat some sense into you. Now go take a shower. You stink."

After a good rinsing of the squirrel fur out of my mouth, I steadied myself under the hot stream of the shower. The scalding water pulled my focus away from the creature trying to claw its way out of my skull.

Slowly, the pills won out, and the pain subsided to a dull ache.

Before returning to the hell creature who claimed to be my loving sister, I checked my email on my phone the way I did every morning. The answer was disappointing again—still nothing from Debbie. We had no way to contact her. I'd been sure that giving her the email would let her get comfortable with the idea one of these days, and she'd reach out, but today wasn't going to be that day.

When I returned to the kitchen, Serena had breakfast on the table.

"I'm not hungry," I told her. What I really needed was a drink, except she'd fed me those awful pills.

"You need to eat."

"When did you get so bossy?" I sat down, in spite of my complaint. I didn't need the yelling of an argument this morning.

She finished chewing. "When did you get so stupid?"

My phone rang. It was sitting by Serena, and she answered it. "Yeah, he's here, and he's sober for a change... Winston," she said as she handed me the phone.

"I've got information on those items you asked me to look into," he said.

Finally some news.

"Shoot." I scooped up some scrambled eggs.

"First, what I hear is that Detective Beal is a straight shooter, nothing weird about his cases. That Tanaka murder is still being worked, but nothing has popped yet. Our girl's cousin is still top of the suspect list because she found the body and split, but they don't have a motive for her, or anyone else, so it could go on a while."

That wasn't good news.

I finished a bite of toast. "What about the Rossi case?"

"Now, that one looks odd to me. The Coast Guard ruled it an accident pretty quickly, and it was closed."

"What's odd about that?"

"Nothing at that point, but looking into it, the dinghy was the only thing from the boat ever found, and that was two weeks later."

I kept eating while he talked.

"Here's the odd part: it was found back inside Marina del Rey."

"So?" I asked.

"So, you leave Marina Del Rey harbor and your boat sinks out past the breakwater, and the dinghy breaks loose. How does the dinghy end up back in Marina del Rey, when the current would carry it up along the coast?"

I gulped down some more OJ. "I don't get it. What does that mean?"

"Let's say you want to disappear. You take your boat out, sink it, run the dinghy back to shore, and skip town. It's been done a bunch of times."

"That's nuts. Why would they do that?" I asked.

"I didn't think they had until I checked the banking records." His voice grew animated. "Their main account had most of its money wired to a Cayman Islands account three months after they disappeared. By that time, after the search ended, they were presumed dead. The sinking had been ruled an accident, and nobody was watching anything anymore."

"I don't know that I can believe that."

"I get it. Nicole is nice, and even though you never met her parents, you want to give them the benefit of the doubt."

"From what I hear, they were devoted to her, and to their business. Why would they just cut and run, and leave their only daughter?"

"We can't know the motivations at this point. But it's a classic scheme. The Coast Guard has jurisdiction, and the Coasties default to seeing it as a boating accident. It's just the way they work."

"And you think the Rossis took the money to disappear and never see her again?"

"That's what the facts tell me. Here's what cinches it: over the two years before the accident, almost another two million plus was wired to the same Cayman account at American Atlantic Bank. One hundred K a month like clockwork."

I asked what he expected me to ask. "Where did it come from?"

"A Tuscan Foods account. They'd planned this for two years and stashed money away for life after leaving."

"Are you sure of all this?"

"It's solid." He paused. "Are you going to tell her?"

"Tell her that we think her parents abandoned her? I don't know."

"It beats being dead," he pointed out. "Maybe they were being threatened by organized crime or something. It's happened before—the parents leave to save the children."

That changed the whole dynamic. "I don't know. I'll have to think about it." What could have made Nicole's parents fake their deaths? Could it have been to protect her?

Nicole

In the morning, I found Winston in the kitchen when I came down for breakfast. "Where's Constance?"

"Off on another job, so you're stuck with me," the big man said.

I pulled a bottle of orange juice from the fridge. "I'm glad you're here. I had something I wanted to ask, actually."

"Shoot."

I held up the bottle. "Juice?"

"Sure." He brought his glass over.

I poured for both of us. "Constance mentioned something about Habitat weekends."

He brought the plate of waffles over to the table. "If you want to come along, you're welcome. We can always use more hands."

I joined him at the table. "And the Bensons go?"

He pulled two waffles onto his plate. "Yeah, the whole family, even Lloyd. Why?"

"It surprised me a little, I guess."

"Why's that?"

I stabbed a waffle. "It just did."

He shot me an annoyed look. "Then you're not as smart as Josh said you were."

I cut off a bite of waffle, wondering if I should feel insulted.

"Look," he said. "If the idea that Josh, or me, or the rest of his family spends a Sunday building houses for people who really need them surprises you, you're not a very good judge of character." He got up. "I'm going to check outside."

"I'm sorry. I didn't mean—"

His eyes darkened. "Let me just say this: there are things you think you know that are wrong." He strode to the back door and opened it. "And not understanding how generous Josh is, is only one of them."

The door closed behind him. His waffles sat on the plate, uneaten.

An hour later, I found Winston on his laptop in the dining room, tapping away.

Gathering up my courage, I leaned against the doorframe. "I'm sorry for this morning. I didn't mean to insult you."

He turned and looked up. "No worries. We're good."

I nodded. "Or Josh."

He didn't say anything to that, but slid a nickel toward me. "You left this by the candlestick. You know what they say about a penny saved."

I pocketed it. "Thanks."

I thought I'd gotten them all, but apparently not. Josh's reason for picking buffalo nickels came back to me in a rush and brought an unintended smile to my face. I quickly wiped it away and changed the subject. "What are you working on?"

"Work stuff."

"What kind of work? I'm curious." I was also bored to tears being stuck in this house.

"Well," he started. "I'm following a financial trail related to a missing persons case."

"Can I help somehow?"

"No," he said firmly.

Josh

I chose to drive my Lamborghini to Dad's house for this meeting, just to emphasize that I could do what I wanted.

Duke rode his Harley, but Serena insisted on driving with me, to make sure I made it without turning around and heading for Reggie's bar.

Mom and Dad were out front when we pulled into the circular drive.

Dad turned with a distinct scowl and retreated into the house as I exited the bright yellow car. Driving the Lambo had produced my desired effect.

Serena, Duke, and I all got hugs from Mom before entering.

We were the last to arrive. Dennis, Jennifer, Zack, and Brittney were already here, and we all exchanged greetings.

Dennis whispered, "Do you have any idea what this is about?"

I guessed, even though Serena hadn't been specific. "My execution, most likely."

My answer startled him. "What did you do?"

"I think it has to do with me telling Dad to shove it."

He chuckled under his breath. "Good luck with that."

Mom offered coffee all around before inviting us into the dining room, which had enough chairs for everyone.

I took a seat midway down one side.

Serena sat next to me, with Dennis on the other side.

Mom conspicuously chose the head of the table where Dad usually sat. "Thank you all for coming. Unfortunately, we are one short, but she can be filled in later." Mom directed her gaze to me.

Everyone was here. Even Vincent and Ashley had been summoned from Boston.

"Who's missing?" Brittney asked.

"Nicole," Mom answered.

It seemed like all their eyes moved instantly to me for confirmation.

Serena knee-bumped me under the table.

Mom looked at me and tapped the table. "And that is, in a way, the reason for this meeting."

"I don't think she's the problem," Dad offered.

Mom shut him down instantly. "That's right, Lloyd. You are."

The room hushed.

"You and each of our children. Today it happens to be Joshua," she continued.

I was in for it if Mom was using my full name.

My shoulders slumped as I felt the heat of everyone's gazes.

"You two are tearing this family apart with your refusal to compromise," Mom added.

"I don't understand," Zack said.

Mom turned to Dad. "Yes, Lloyd, why don't we start with you explaining your position to everyone."

Dad brightened. He seemed to have been waiting for his opportunity to tell everyone how insubordinate I was. "Benson Corp. wouldn't be the same without a Benson at the helm, and Josh is slated to replace me after he finishes his advancement plan, which involves several years running the London office."

The group seemed to be going to sleep listening to this.

Dad lifted his coffee cup in my direction. "However, Josh has decided to renege on his written promise to me, and won't go to London."

Zack's eyes widened. He understood the line I'd crossed.

I sat up. "Nicole can't go, and I'm not leaving her. It's as simple as that." That was my stake in the ground.

Dennis spoke up. "Dad, just have him skip the London assignment."

"It's not that simple," Dad replied as he stared at me. "Logan has developed… a medical condition, and I need somebody I can trust to replace him. It has to be a family member. Anybody else would be too risky at this point."

Logan Benson was Dad's only cousin. As a family member, he was the only one Dad trusted to run such a large part of the company without direct supervision.

Dennis had a smug look as he leaned toward me and whispered, "You could fly back and forth."

"What was that?" Mom asked.

Dennis shook his head. "Nothing."

Mom wasn't settling for that. "You forget, young man, that all you boys share responsibility in this. And you too, Lloyd."

Dad looked offended.

"Not me," Zack complained.

"Yes," Mom said. "All of you abandoned the company earlier and left Josh as the last one to carry it on."

Dennis shrunk in his chair. He'd originally been the one tapped to take Dad's place.

"Your mother and I have discussed this," Dad said. "Much of this is my fault. We wouldn't be in this mess if I hadn't been so difficult to work for. And Josh wouldn't be in this position if I hadn't run each of you off until he was the only one left, but that's where we are today."

I could see where this was going if I didn't put a stake in the ground. They'd all decide that the easiest route was for me to stay working for Dad, and punt the problem down the road.

"There's more to it," I said. "I originally agreed to go to London because I'd be running my own operation within Benson, just as each of you have been able to run his own company. It's not fair that because I'm the youngest, I have to stay a VP working for Dad and bear all of the family responsibility."

The looks around the table showed I'd transferred some of the guilt for this situation to them.

"Well put," Dad said, surprising me. "This is a problem for the whole family to pitch in and solve, not just Josh and me. You've placed too much of a burden on him. And yes, I had a hand in that as well. Maybe I shouldn't have been so hard to work with."

Everyone exchanged looks around the table, trying to figure out where this was going.

"Thank you, Lloyd," Mom said. "Now it's time for us to discuss alternatives that don't put us right back where we were yesterday."

CHAPTER 46

Nicole

Thursday morning, I walked the orchard rows.

Ernst was such a terrible caretaker of the trees. He would have starved a century ago if they had been his livelihood.

I'd given the almonds the water they needed, and then run some extra at the bases of the two sickly ones he'd never replaced. Any good farmer knew the sick trees had to be weeded out and replaced with strong ones to make proper use of the land.

Things always seemed to go better for me after I put in time in the orchard. Daddy had always said staying close to the land was the best medicine.

After throwing a chain in the bucket, I climbed up onto the tractor's seat. The old Ford belched a little black smoke and settled into its normal fast idle. That was the good thing about a diesel tractor—if the battery turned it over, it would start, and this one had served our family faithfully. The small backhoe on the back made digging holes for new trees a breeze.

I rumbled down between the almonds and lowered the bucket when I got to the first of the two sickly trees. A good shove as I floored the tractor, and the tree bent over a little in the moist ground. After wrapping the chain around the trunk and attaching it to the bucket, I lifted, and the tractor squatted down in its tussle with the tree's roots. It took several tries, but the tractor's hydraulics won, and the tree came out.

The second wasn't any easier than the first, but machine eventually won out against nature there as well. The chainsaw would make short work of all the branches now that they were down, but my parched lips demanded something to drink first.

On the walk back to the house after parking the tractor in its shed on the corner of the property, I tried to be casual as I looked next door.

Lara had been right. For a second, I caught a glimpse of our creepy neighbor Hugo Lenz in a window, looking my way.

I changed my path toward the center of the orchard, away from prying eyes.

Before I made it past the first row, what seemed like a dozen police cars roared down the street. Their lights were flashing, but there weren't any sirens. They passed my house and converged down the street somewhere. I couldn't tell where from back here.

A half minute later, Winston appeared on the back porch.

I waved.

"You should come in," he called, waving me toward the house.

"In a minute."

"Now," he yelled emphatically.

I'd tried arguing with Winston once. It hadn't gone well. It was like having a discussion with a hunk of granite. Nothing budged him if he'd made up his mind.

I reached the stairs. "What's the problem?"

"There are too many people on the street for you to be outside right now."

I waited at the bottom just to tick him off. It was fun sometimes. "I don't understand."

"Come inside, or I carry you in. Clear enough?"

This wasn't going to be one of the fun times if I persisted, so I climbed the stairs.

Once inside, I went to the front and peeked out the window. From here it was clear what Winston had been talking about.

The cops were in front of Lenz's house next door, and a crowd had already converged to watch as they carted boxes out.

"What's going on?" I asked.

"Executing a search warrant, it looks like," he said.

He should know, seeing as he was ex-FBI.

"What do you think they're looking for?"

"I've learned not to guess."

Eventually, the cops left and Winston let me go back out to do chainsaw battle with the downed trees.

~

I'D JUST CUT THE ENGINE ON THE CHAINSAW WHEN MY PHONE RANG. ROSA'S NAME appeared on the screen.

"Hi, Rosa," I answered.

"How's the time off going?" she asked.

"Bored out of my mind." She wouldn't understand if I told her I enjoyed uprooting trees.

"I have something that needs your signature, if you could come by."

I couldn't chance running into Josh at the office—avoiding him meant not a minute in the building. "I can't come in. Have Mr. B take care of it, or just give it to Dee and she'll figure out who to give it to."

"This needs to be signed by you. It's a modification to your retention agreement."

"What? I'm not agreeing to any more conditions."

Rosa was positively giddy. "I think you'll like this change. It's all being accelerated."

Accelerated sounded like ending sooner, getting paid sooner. Possibilities raced through my mind. The two hundred thousand bonus would save Casa di Rossi if it came soon enough.

"Accelerated means what?"

"Paying off your loans and getting the bonus payment. Mr. B came by this morning and asked me to redo the paperwork. I think it's awfully nice of him."

"Yeah." I couldn't dispute that he was nice. This was a godsend, and though my first inclination the last few days had been to argue with anything Josh wanted, I wasn't stupid enough to turn this down. Later I'd make it clear that I wasn't giving in. I couldn't be bought.

"He couldn't say enough good things about your work," Rosa said bringing me back to the present. "I'm going to miss him."

What was I supposed to say to that? Josh was abandoning us, and me, and leaving Rossi's in the hands of that know-nothing, Wenzel. I couldn't tell her or anyone how much I would miss him when he was gone. Not being able to be honest with the people I'd worked with for years was a horrible side effect of all this.

"Oops," she said. "I wasn't supposed to say that. It's all very hush-hush."

Good thing nobody knew. They'd probably have people walking out today once they heard Wenzel would be in charge.

"When can I get the money?"

"That's why I wanted you to come in to sign."

For this amount, I'd walk there if I had to. "I'll be right in."

"Great."

As soon as we hung up, I ran to the house and found Winston. "I have to go into work for a few minutes."

He promptly informed me that he would be driving me.

After brushing the wood chips off my jeans, I gathered up my purse and waited for him. Arguing would have slowed us down and not changed the outcome. I wasn't wasting another minute cleaning up if it delayed getting the money to save Casa di Rossi. Brushing my hair could be done in the car.

~

AFTER WINSTON LET ME OUT, I WALKED THE BACK WAY TO GET TO ROSA TO AVOID coming anywhere near Josh's office. I found her behind her desk and closed the door behind me.

"Working in the yard," I said to excuse my appearance.

"People have been missing you, you know," she said as I sat.

"Thanks. I'm only taking a few days off." *Just until Josh leaves.* "So, what do I need to sign?"

"Mr. B. took the papers and asked you to join him for lunch to go over them."

I stood. "Then call me when you have them back in your hands. Or better yet, could you do me a favor and drop them by my house later?"

Rosa shifted in her chair, and instead of a nod, I got what looked like a shake of her head. "I can't do that."

I leaned on the back of the chair. "Come again?"

She bit her lip. "He didn't exactly *ask* you to join him for lunch. He said you two had to talk, and if you balked to tell you it was a condition of him signing off."

"Sounds like him," I huffed.

"I don't know what the problem is, Nicky, but I drafted the change myself. It's all good for you. I can guarantee that."

I loosened my clenched jaw and sighed. "Okay, I give. Where is this lunch?"

"Do you want to talk about it?" she asked. "You know that's part of my job."

Her position did entail dealing with issues between employees, but not like mine. The last thing I needed was for people to know about me and Josh.

"No, Rosa. It's nothing."

She cocked her head. "Whatever you say. Mr. B said he'd meet you at your favorite lunch spot."

"Which one?"

"He said you'd know."

I thanked her and left.

Winston was outside with the car door opened when I exited the building. "Sorry. I have to make a stop for lunch first."

"Sure." He held the door open and closed it after me, which I'd learned was part of the safety protocol I wasn't allowed to complain about.

"Where to?" he asked after starting the engine.

"Taco Bandito, three blocks down," I said.

When we pulled up to the Mexican restaurant, my stomach was doing cartwheels. But all I had to do was get through one simple lunch to get to my better life on the other side.

Shit.

The neon sign in the window said *closed*. They'd never been closed before.

He stopped the engine. "He's waiting inside."

I shook my head. "Don't tell me you're in on this too."

A smirk crossed his face. "It's my job to keep abreast of your itinerary."

After clambering down from the SUV, I slammed the door. Everybody was conspiring against me today.

Approaching the door, I caught the handwritten sign.

Private Party today
Reopening at 2:30

I checked the time: 12:30. I had to endure this for two hours.

Josh

My phone buzzed with a text message.

WINSTON: Here

I cleared the message.

Nicole knocked on the glass door, and Maria, the owner, looked at me.

I nodded, and she went to open it.

Nicole slipped inside. "Thank you." She looked stunning, backlit by the sunshine outside.

Maria indicated my table at the back. "He's waiting."

She walked up in dusty jeans, with a cute wood chip caught in her hair.

I rose as she approached and plucked a piece of wood from her shoulder.

She didn't pull away. "Sorry. I was working in the orchard when I got the call."

"You always look beautiful."

She sighed and tried unsuccessfully to turn the grin that appeared on her face into a grimace.

"Thank you for coming," I said.

Not expecting a hug or kiss to get a good reception, I settled for pulling out a chair for her.

"I didn't have much choice." The words came out hard and biting.

I took my seat. "Thank you all the same."

She nodded toward the third place-setting at the table. "Is someone else joining us?"

"A bit later."

"Who?"

"Like I said, later. All that matters right now is that you're here."

Her gaze was stern. "I'm only here because you ordered me."

I locked eyes with her. "No, that's not true. I invited you."

"You're holding something over me. That's why I came."

We had to get past the concept that she was being coerced.

Maria approached with the usual basket of chips and dishes of salsa, including the red that rarely got eaten.

Yolanda, who often worked the register, brought the Cokes I'd already asked for. She set them down.

"What would you like to eat?" Maria asked Nicole.

I had to concentrate to still my knee, I was so jittery. Everything rode on this meeting.

We both ended up ordering Nicole's regular choice of chicken tacos, and I added a bowl of guacamole to the order.

Maria and Yolanda retreated to the kitchen.

Nicole took a chip and gestured to the room. "Why this?"

"I wanted to talk to you privately, so you could feel free to yell if you wished."

I also didn't want anyone to see me cry if this didn't pan out.

She finished chewing her chip and took another. "We've talked every day, and nothing has changed. Nothing is going to change."

I hoped to change her mind about that. More than that, I was counting on changing her mind and getting her back. "Do you consider yourself a fair and honorable person?"

She cocked her head. "Yes, I guess so." Her voice seemed wary of a trap.

In a way, it was. "You're not sure?"

Her brows drew together. "I'm sure."

I opened the folder next to me, took out my pen, and signed the back page before turning it and sliding it to her. "I'm giving you your freedom. As soon as you sign, that is. It says we will pay you the retention bonus immediately, as well as assume your educational debt and COBRA payments if you decide to terminate your employment."

She eyed me warily. "Just like that?"

"Just like that. I'm offering you something of value without demanding anything in return." I gestured to the folder. "It's yours for the taking."

Her eyes narrowed. "And?"

"And nothing. You can sign it and walk out of here right now."

She picked up the pen. "What's the catch?"

"No catch. I know what that property means to you, and I'd like you to be able to save it from foreclosure."

This was the test of that old saying: If you love something, set it free.

She put pen to paper and signed. A smile grew across her face as she folded the papers and put them in her purse. "Thank you." Her eyes had gone from confrontational to warm.

"You're welcome, Nickels."

She stood and turned for the door.

My heart stopped.

I'd made a mistake. I should have waited until after our talk to sign the papers.

No. I'd done the right thing, the honorable thing. I'd been honest. I'd done this for her, so she could keep the house that meant everything to her. Her happiness had been my goal. It had always been foremost in my thoughts.

Now I knew I'd truly lost her. She'd refused to say whether she felt the same way about me as I did her. But she was answering with her departure.

No, she didn't love me.

She carried my heart with her as she walked to the door—a heart in a thousand pieces.

Maria rushed over to unlock it for her.

Maybe Nicole had never been my girl.

CHAPTER 47

Nicole

Maria unlocked the glass door and opened it for me.

The bright sunlight hit me, and with it came the realization that Josh had tricked me after all.

If I left, my answer to his off-the-wall question would have been a lie. A fair and honorable person wouldn't take from him and not offer something back, or even ask what he wanted. Leaving now would brand me as despicable. My parents raised me better than that. Rossis were better than that.

I might regret it, but I had to be the better person here. I turned and marched back to his table. I heard the owner re-lock the door behind me.

"What do you want?"

Relief flooded his face as he took a breath. "Nothing."

"Bullshit." I patted my purse. "What do you want for this?"

He gestured to the chair I'd vacated. "I invited you to an extended lunch. I thought we might have an opportunity to talk."

"And what does extended entail?"

He waved Maria over. "I thought we'd start with this."

A moment later, Maria and Yolanda returned.

They set out cloth napkins, real silverware instead of the plastic they used here, and a fine ceramic plate for each of us with a familiar multilayered dessert topped with cocoa powder.

"Tiramisu? Really?" I sat in the chair I'd vacated.

"Only the best for you. This is from Cardinelli's. Ever been there?"

"I've heard of it, but no, never been."

"I'll take you some time."

I didn't start the argument that would ensue if I pointed out this was our last meal together. Pointing at the plate, I asked, "Is this what extended means?"

"Part of it."

Lunch no longer seemed to be a big ask from him. What he'd freely given me —the means to keep Casa di Rossi—was certainly worth more. Every minute in his presence made him harder to resist, but if it was a temptation I had to endure to keep my property and feel good about the way I'd conducted myself, so be it.

I laid the napkin in my lap. "I accept your invitation."

"Thank you, Nickels. Will you stay for the entire meal?"

A smile overcame me. Even now, that name gave me a tingle when he said it.

I could only answer one way. "Yes."

He slid the basket of chips to the side, revealing a buffalo nickel underneath. "I still carry these everywhere."

"And it still proves you're a goofball."

He cocked his head. "An appellation I carry proudly."

Who said *appellation* these days?

I kept his new designation as *super goofball* to myself and pointed my fork toward the empty seat. "Shouldn't we wait for the mystery guest?"

"Tiramisu was always supposed to be me and you." He smiled.

I joined him, recognizing the rhyme. "You're a poet and don't know it."

"I'm afraid that's as far as my talent goes."

"Don't sell yourself short."

"What part of me are you calling short?"

I bit back the giggle. I wasn't going down to the gutter with him. "Drop the innuendos and eat your damned dessert." I cut into the square in front of me.

After a minute of silence we had each finished off half.

He sipped his Coke. "I'm leaving Rossi's."

"Not a newsflash, remember?"

His grimace at my words made me regret my tone. Instead of digging a deeper verbal hole, I sipped my drink.

He lifted a forkful to his mouth, with a grin that grew. After swallowing he said, "I think we have an excellent replacement planned."

I half spit out my Coke. Wenzel didn't come close to being an excellent anything.

"You okay?" Josh offered his napkin.

Feeling foolish, I dabbed at the mess in front of me. "I've got it. Thanks."

"And it still doesn't involve Smith's."

That brought me hope. "Thank you."

That was a good piece of news. Now all we had to survive was incompetent management. And Ernst had proven that could be done. I could breathe now—at least on that front.

Josh twisted his Coke cup and held my eyes. "It's the sensible choice, and you know I've felt that way for a while now."

"I thought Snyderman had a different opinion."

"He doesn't know a kumquat from a cucumber."

His assurance made me smile.

Our tacos arrived, and I bit into mine—delicious as always. "I wanted to thank you for bringing me food every day, but it really should stop after this."

"Okay," he said after finishing chewing.

Okay? Did that mean he'd finally accepted that we couldn't be together and would soon be across the pond where he belonged? Where he could fulfill his destiny?

"Is this goodbye?" I asked.

I'd been the one to bring this about, but even so, the reality of it hit me hard. Still, I knew it was the right thing and the only way forward for him, because there was no way forward for us.

He looked up, unaware of the turmoil running rampant in my mind. "Yes and no. I told you I'm leaving Rossi's. Today is my last day, actually."

My stomach rebelled. I put down the taco I held lest I choke on it. If this was his last day, I wouldn't even be there for everybody when they announced Wenzel would be taking the reins. They'd need someone to console them, to assure them things would work out. I'd do my damnedest to see that they worked out. But they'd face the announcement alone because I wouldn't be there, not today.

I pushed the plate away.

"Something wrong with the tacos?"

"No." I decided to be as honest as he'd always demanded. "The conversation."

"Yeah, I get it. Let's talk about something happier—at least I think it's happier."

I drank my Coke and waited for the inevitable.

"I got everything straightened out. It's all going to be fine."

And there it was, the latest feeble attempt to tell me everything would be okay when I knew it wouldn't. It couldn't.

"I don't believe you. It can't work."

One plus one could never equal three. The constraints could never be met.

"I thought you might say that…again."

I had been a bit of a broken record. "Yes, that's because I'm being logical. I won't start down a road that only leads to heartbreak."

Josh placed his phone on the empty place setting. "Then let's hear it from the horse's mouth." He tapped the screen a few times.

"Hello, Nicole." Lloyd's voice came out of the phone. "This is Lloyd Benson, and I wish I could speak to you in person, but I'm on my way to Europe—London, actually—today, and so this recording will have to suffice."

"What is this?" I asked, speaking over the recording.

He stopped the audio. "You promised to stay for the entire meal, and this is the rest of it. If you'll listen, I think you'll understand."

I crossed my arms and huffed.

He backed it up and started it again. "…have to suffice. Josh thinks you'll object." *He got that part right*. "But please indulge an old man and listen to what I have to say before you make up your mind."

I guess Josh hadn't told him I'd already made up my mind.

The message continued. "As you know, I have been after Josh to take over our London office for a little while now, and he used to be looking forward to that. But after meeting you, that changed for him. Now that we've had the pleasure of meeting you, ourselves, his mother and I agree with his choice to stay here with you. Robin, by the way, sends her regards. Now, back to the subject at hand. Josh has explained to me your trepidation that his not taking the London assignment will cause friction between him and me. Well, I've solved that particular issue. Josh's sister Serena—who is quite the accomplished management consultant, I might add—has requested that she be considered for the London posting. And—"

I put my hand up.

Josh stopped the playback.

"He's letting your sister into the company?" I'd thought it was a men's club of sorts.

"Of course. Mom and Serena put their heads together and suggested it. Dad never would have thought of it by himself."

"The patriarchy raises its ugly head?"

"I think you're ascribing the wrong motivation. Dad has never been able to control Serena. With us boys, he's always laid down the law, but the girls have had him wrapped around their proverbial little fingers. Kelly was never interested, but with Serena, as Mom tells it, Dad was afraid he wouldn't be able to control her, and he's all about control."

I nodded. This wasn't at all what I'd expected, if Josh was right. "So where does this leave you?"

"I get exactly what I want—well, almost."

"But you wanted to run your own thing."

"Listen to the next section."

"Okay."

He started the message again. "I think Serena will do a wonderful job over there, so she's taking on that responsibility immediately. She and Duke have been looking for a way to move to Europe anyway, so it's a good fit for both her and the company. But that leaves us with Josh's situation. He told me he was happy to stay with you at Rossi's, but we both know he aspires to a larger responsibility. And the situation is my fault. Over the years, I've been too—how do I put this?—demanding of my sons, and I've driven them all out of the company, leaving Josh as the last man standing. So it's time that the baton gets passed. With Robin's blessing, I've decided to step back to the chairman role only. I'll let Serena handle Europe and Josh handle the US. This will take some getting used to for me, but I'm going to do my darnedest to give them the latitude they need in their new roles."

My eyes started to water as I took this in. Maybe I hadn't seen all the possibilities.

Josh placed his hand over mine as the recording continued.

"Having met you at Kelly's party, and hearing even more about you from Josh..."

I squeezed Josh's fingers at that statement and got a squeeze back.

"The entire family and I... Let me back up here and thank you, Nicole, for being the force for good that you are. Your insistence that these problems be worked out has forced me to reevaluate my part in all this and made me find a solution that works for everybody, including my dear wife, who has been after me for years to take some time off so we might enjoy a little traveling before we're both pushing walkers." Lloyd laughed. "So, Robin and I and the entire family thank you, and we hope that you and Josh can find a happy way forward."

I couldn't stop my happy tears.

"I do hope you'll grant an old man one request. Please stand, take Josh's hands, and dance one dance for me to the song Josh chose. After that, it's up to you two kids to talk it out. And once again, thank you for coming into our lives."

Josh stood.

I joined him.

He took me into a light embrace as the music started: "My Girl" by the Temptations.

We swayed to the music as he sang the lyrics in my ear.

I cried into his shoulder with happiness I couldn't contain. And not once did I ask him to change girl to woman. When the song ended, I refused to let go of my man.

Lloyd's voice came back on again. "Josh has a question he'd like to ask you. And with that, I'll sign off. I hope you can join us at the next gathering."

The recording stopped.

I looked up into Josh's eyes with my watery ones. "What did you want to ask?"

He kept me swaying to the imaginary beat of the music. "It's more than one question, actually."

"Well, I don't know. Your father said one question, so you better make it a good one."

"I'm torn then, because they're both important."

I could wait. The warmth of being in my man's arms was all I needed right now.

"Okay, here goes. Will you please be my girlfriend? But before you answer, know that there are some conditions."

I laughed. "Conditions?"

"Yes. No more sneaking around denying it. We're out of the closet."

"But we haven't even tried the closet yet."

"Be serious for one second, Nickels."

I pulled myself up for the kiss that would provide the answer, and his lips met mine with the determination I wanted, that I needed. I'd needed him in my life.

His hands roamed my body and pulled at my ass.

I jumped up and wrapped my legs around him as I tugged his hair and clawed his back. The kiss was like that first one against the refrigerator. As we traded breath and moans and our tongues danced, the room fell away. I was wrapped around my man, transported to cloud nine, where the blood rushing in my ears drowned out the world, and the energy from our contact was all I craved.

He repositioned his grip to hold me up and broke the kiss. "I love you, Nickels."

This time I could say it back. "I love you too."

"Is that a yes?"

I did my best leg clamp on him. "Yes."

"Second question," Josh began. "Would you take over Rossi's for me?"

I yelped for joy. "Do you even have to ask? I thought you were going to put Wenzel—"

"Stop jumping to conclusions, Nickels."

"Wait a minute. We haven't discussed compensation yet."

He gently let me down, after I released my leg death grip.

Now I had to look up to him. I'd been at face level before—a better negotiating position.

He took my hand and led me back to the table. "I'm sure we can come to something mutually agreeable later. But first we have to go introduce the new boss."

I looked at the dirty jeans and work boots I had on. "I have to go home and change."

"They won't care."

"But I will."

"Okay, but hurry back. I'll be looking for a closet."

~

Nicole

I climbed into Winston's SUV. "Home, James."

"Yes, ma'am." He pulled into traffic.

I still tingled from the excitement. Being able to run Rossi's *and* have Josh was a double win. I couldn't have asked for a better day.

"How much did you know about this?"

Winston smirked. "Not the particulars. Just that I had to get you there. I take it lunch went well?"

I couldn't contain my glee. "Swimmingly." I'd always wanted to use that word but had never found the right time. Fondling my phone, I considered calling Josh to tell him again that I loved him, but I felt awkward in front of Winston.

Josh had said it so many times since I'd broken things off. With each utterance, I'd wanted to return the words, but couldn't bring myself to. Now I was eager to even the score.

A few minutes later, my phone rang. I was disappointed to find it wasn't Josh calling. The screen showed Detective Beal's name, the detective trying to pin poor Maro's murder on Lara.

"Hello, this is Nicole." I answered.

"Miss Rossi, I have some news related to the case."

"Yes?"

"We've made an arrest."

I gasped, afraid they'd found Lara.

"We searched your neighbor Mr. Lenz's property and located a bloody glove. The blood is from your…tenant, Mr. Tanaka, and Lenz has been arrested."

I breathed a huge sigh. "So it's over?"

"The DNA was a match, so yes, I would say so."

For Lara's peace of mind, I had to ask. "Do you think it was him six years ago?"

Winston sent a questioning glance my way.

Beal hesitated before answering. "We don't have any evidence to tie him to that case, but it's the most likely scenario, given the similarities."

A heavy weight lifted off my chest. First Josh, and now not needing to be scared of every shadow on my property? All the stars just might be aligning.

"Thank you for the update. Could you please explain this to my security?"

"Security?" he asked.

I handed the phone to Winston. "Detective Beal, LAPD."

He took it. "Winston Evers here… Yes, Hanson Security… And how solid is it?… What's he being charged with?… And the previous case?… Thank you, detective." He hung up the phone and handed it back to me.

"Does that mean you're done?" I asked.

"I'll talk to Josh. With what they're charging him with, he won't get bail, so I'd say you're safe now."

Relief flooded through me. I'd felt good hearing the detective's words, but getting the all-clear from a professionally overprotective ex-FBI agent made it official. I dialed Dee's number for my next task.

"I hear we have some good news to announce," she answered before I could get a word in.

"Well, that's true, but first, I need you to get a hold of Jenny and have all the stores change the banana price to a dollar a pound right now, and in the flyers."

I wanted Lara back.

"Are you sure?"

"Yes. And I mean right now. Nothing is more important."

She sighed audibly. "I'll take care of it. Now about that other thing."

"I have to change clothes first," I explained.

"Whatever you say, Ms. R."

After we hung up, I realized I'd inherited both my father's job and Dee's title for him.

It felt right.

CHAPTER 48

Josh

SATURDAY MORNING, MY MOUTH WATERED AS I TURNED THE BACON.

It had been two days since Nicole had taken over at her family's company and Dad had announced the changes at Benson Corp.

Constance and Winston were off protection since they'd verified that the neighbor, Lenz, was being held without bail for Tanaka's murder.

Things between Nickels and me had gone back to where they'd been—even better now that we didn't have to hide the relationship and could catch lunch together.

"Where's Echo?" I asked when Nicole bounced into the kitchen.

"Same place as he is a lot of mornings—out digging a hole, trying to catch a ground squirrel."

I turned and got a nice view of her ass as she opened the fridge. "Does he ever get one?"

"Nope, but not for lack of trying. Hey, we're out of eggs again," she complained, turning toward me.

My cock twitched at the sight of her nipples giving me a double-barreled salute through her T-shirt. "Want me to run out and get some?"

She bounced on her toes a few times. "Would you?"

She knew exactly what seeing her pokey nipples bounce under the thin shirt did to me. It was her trick to get me to say yes to anything she asked in the morning.

"Sure." I turned off the gas. I kissed her and copped a feel through the cotton on the way to the door. "Anything else?"

"Grapefruit juice, bananas, celery, and peanut butter."

On the way to my car, I recited the list to myself.

The Rossi's was a little farther than another market, but the better quality was always worth it, I'd learned.

Once there, I made quick work of the short list and decided to add ladyfingers and mascarpone to my basket. Nicole had expressed an interest in trying to make homemade tiramisu last night, but we'd been short these ingredients.

My phone rang with Nick Knowlton's name on it while I was in the checkout line.

"I have some results for ya, college boy."

I held the phone with my shoulder while unloading my haul onto the conveyor belt. "Go ahead."

"The thief was a Stephanie Quantell. Gary told us she was the previous CFO, and she's left the company."

"That's right," I told him as the cashier started ringing up my items. "You're sure?"

"Why does everybody always ask that? I wouldn't fucking give you a name if we weren't positive."

"Okay, I get it," I said defensively. "How was it done?"

I pulled out my wallet and inserted my card into the reader while the cashier bagged my items.

"It's complicated and technical. Katie would need to explain it, if you want to know."

The machine beeped at me, and I removed my card. "Maybe later." The cashier added my receipt to the bag.

"The money's where we can't get to it today, but I can set up a tripwire and we might catch it on the way out."

I hefted the bag. "Where is it?"

"Right now it's in the American Atlantic Bank in the Cayman Islands, and that puts it out of reach."

The bank name rang a bell, and brought up an awful thought. "Thanks, Nick."

"You can thank me by paying us. An invoice is already in your email."

I walked out the exit. "I'll get on it."

Now my mood didn't match the bright sunniness of the morning.

The bank was the same one Nicole's parents seemed to have hidden money in before their disappearance. I hadn't told Nicole about Winston's findings, and now it was possible they'd enlisted the old CFO to siphon more money out of the family company to finance their life on the run.

That would have to be a discussion for later. Things were too good today to mess up with this news. I shifted the bag to my other hand while I fished the key-fob out of my pocket and unlocked the car.

I should have written down Nicole's grocery list. Looking in the bag before setting it down, I got the feeling I'd forgotten something. Better now while I was here than make another trip.

I dialed Nicole's number. It went to voicemail, so I redialed.

Nicole

The doorbell rang.

It wasn't the first time Josh had forgotten his house keys, so I rushed to the door.

Ernst stood there when I opened it. He moved to come in.

I didn't object or block his way. Although I'd told him I didn't want him here anymore, it just didn't seem right.

He walked past me. "I got a call from that detective…"

I shut the door behind him. "Beal," I filled in.

"Yeah, Beal. He said they got the guy that killed poor Mr. Tanaka. Did he call you?"

"He did."

He walked toward the kitchen. "Could I trouble you for a cup of coffee?"

I followed him. "Sure."

Mom wouldn't approve if I didn't maintain the manners she'd instilled in me. "Is Aunt Rossella back yet?" I started the coffee machine.

"Heavens no. She's still in Florence with her cousin Francesca."

Aunt Francesca had been diagnosed with cancer, and Aunt Rossella had gone to help out about three months ago. It wasn't a good sign that she didn't have a return date yet.

I felt awkward not knowing, but I had to ask. "How is Aunt Francesca doing?"

"Not well, I hear. I'm scheduled to join them in a few weeks."

His answer made me feel worse. With all my travails, I hadn't thought to ask until now. The coffeemaker finished, and I handed him the cup.

"What happened to that lady, Constance, who was here last time?"

"Now that Lenz is locked up, she's gone."

He blew on the steaming cup. "Have you heard from Lara?"

"She called, and she should be by today."

"When she gets here, please ask her to call me."

"I will." Though I didn't expect Lara to follow through.

Echo pushed in through the doggy door that I'd unlocked now that we were off high defensive alert. He had something dirty in his mouth, and his paws were filthy from having dug again.

Ernst looked out the back window. "What did you do?" He opened the door and stepped onto the back porch.

I ignored him as Echo dropped his prize in front of me. I picked up the old cap. I took it to the sink and started to rinse the dirt off.

Ernst came back in and slammed the door. "What did you do to my trees?"

I turned to him. This had to stop. "I told you I'd take care of them from now on." I went back to the cap and held it under the water. "I pulled those two sickly ones that you should have replaced years ago."

"You can't."

"I did." I worked the dirt out of the fabric, and the lettering became clear—Stella Maria. I froze for a moment. "This is Daddy's sailing cap." It didn't make any sense that it would have been out back.

Ernst came over. "No, it isn't."

As the water and my fingers did their work, it was even more obviously Daddy's. "Where did you get this?" I asked Echo, as if he could understand the question.

He went to the door.

I followed. "Show me where you got this."

"Stop right there," Ernst yelled.

I turned back to him and screamed.

He held a knife.

Echo barked and lunged.

Ernst caught him with the knife.

"No," I yelled.

My dog yelped and fell to the floor.

"What the fuck?" I screamed.

Ernst pulled a gun. "Shut the fuck up, right now."

My heart raced as I scurried to Echo. What would I do if he died?

Echo whimpered as I placed pressure on his bleeding wound.

"Stay. Stay there, boy," I got out through my sobs. He had to stay down.

Ernst closed the Swiss army knife he always carried and pocketed it with his free hand. "Fucking dog." He paced back and forth, waving the gun wildly. "Why did he have to go and dig that up?"

Ernst wasn't making any sense.

My phone rang, and I pulled it from my pocket. My hands were so jittery from the adrenaline that I almost dropped it.

"Don't answer that. Put it down," he commanded.

I set it on the floor. "It's my boyfriend. I have to answer."

"No."

The ringing stopped and then started again.

"If I don't, he'll call the security people to come check on me." It was all I could think of.

Ernst nodded. "Okay. But put it on speaker. Get rid of him. One wrong word and I shoot the dog, then you."

I answered it on speaker.

"I got the eggs," Josh started. "Grapefruit juice, celery, and the tiramisu stuff, but I forgot what else you wanted."

Ernst pointed the gun at Echo's head.

"Shrimp was the other thing on the list," I said. "And you can bring it all over at six, gotta go." I hung up before he could respond.

Ernst moved back. "Smart girl."

"What do you want from me?"

"I wanted you to not mess with my trees, and I want to talk to Lara." He'd calmed a little now.

I stood slowly. "Shoot me if you must, but I have to bandage my dog if we're waiting for her. The first aid supplies are in the pantry."

He slid sideways and waved me in that direction with the gun.

I moved slowly and pulled the first aid kit from the bottom shelf of the pantry. I returned to Echo and wrapped my wounded dog's neck to stop the bleeding. If Echo died, I'd fucking kill Ernst if it was the last thing I did.

Ernst paced again. "When will she be here?"

I trembled every time he waved the gun. I hoped Josh had understood the warning. I almost threw up realizing Josh could get shot if he walked in on this.

"I asked you a question."

"I don't know."

"When?"

"I don't fucking know," I screamed.

I kept petting Echo and trying to remember my first aid. Was I supposed to get him some water or was that bad? At least thinking about that kept my mind off what my crazy step-uncle wanted with Lara. I had to keep her safe, but I had no way to warn her.

"What is wrong with you?" I asked.

Hyperventilating, he paced back and forth. "Everything would have been fine if you hadn't pulled the tree."

I added another bandage on top of the one already turning red from Echo's blood.

"Lara shouldn't have been poking around." He was getting more agitated with every lap of the kitchen.

Talking. I had to get him talking to calm him down. "Why was Daddy's hat out back?"

"Because that's where I put him," he yelled as the gun waved back and forth.

I couldn't breathe as the realization hit me, and I didn't dare ask the truly awful question.

Daddy didn't ever go sailing without that hat, and Ernst had just said that's where he put him, not put *it*.

"Why did damned Lara have to go poking around?" he ranted. Spittle flew from his lips.

I couldn't hold it in any longer. "Why?" I sobbed. "He welcomed you into the family and gave you everything."

Ernst's face went even redder. "A fucking job in purchasing? You call that everything?"

"I know he was training you for more," I lied. There had to be a way to calm him down.

He came close enough that I could smell his awful breath. "Bull-fucking-shit.

He was going to put you in charge. He was going to have *me* work for *you*, a fucking snot-nose kid with no experience."

A car alarm blared from the front of the house.

Ernst backed away and turned his attention to the noise.

The closest weapon I could see was the block of knives on the counter.

The alarm stopped and then started again.

Ernst paced to the hall and waved the gun toward the street. "Shut the fuck up," he yelled.

He was about to lose it.

The back door flew open, and Josh launched himself at Ernst's back.

The gun skittered across the floor as Ernst face-planted on the wood, Josh on top of him.

Ernst reached for the gun.

Josh pummeled Ernst's head, still not uttering a word.

I scrambled for the gun and reached it before Ernst did.

Josh grabbed his hair and pounded his face into the wood a few times.

Getting to my feet, I pointed the gun at Ernst's head through teary eyes. "He killed my parents."

Josh stayed straddling the man I wanted to kill. "Don't." The single word was a command. He motioned for me to lower the gun. "Nickels, you're better than him. Please put it down. I've got him."

My finger tightened on the trigger with all the hatred I felt. "Don't you understand? He killed them." I couldn't keep the gun steady.

The sound of the front door flying open came from behind me.

Ernst struggled, and Josh pounded his head against the floor again.

I wanted Josh to do it a hundred times more. I couldn't see straight through the tears.

"Put it down," Constance said over my shoulder. "You don't want to do this." She slowly walked around me with her gun pointed at Ernst. "You don't want Josh to have to visit you in prison. He's the one who deserves to be locked up, not you."

Josh's eyes pleaded with me. "I know you're hurting, but this isn't the way."

I lowered the gun, and Constance took it from me.

"I couldn't wait for you," Josh told her.

"Still stupid on your part," she said. She produced a set of handcuffs, and in a few seconds she and Josh traded places.

"He has a knife in his pocket," I said.

She located it and slid it across the floor.

My man took me into his arms, and the torrent of tears sped up.

I sobbed out all the hurt I felt now that I understood what Ernst had done.

~

Josh

Two hours later, redness still showed in Nicole's eyes from the crying as we sat on the couch across from Detective Beal.

Winston had arrived and taken Echo to the vet hospital where the prognosis for her dog was good.

The detective had confirmed that there were bones from at least one person out back, and a team was digging as we sat here.

"You should have told me what you uncovered on the financial front, and I would have figured this out," Beal said to me.

I doubted the arrogant prick would have put the pieces together. "Maybe."

He looked to Constance. "And him I get, but you should have known to call 9-1-1 before racing over here."

She answered calmly. "The situation didn't warrant it, given the information I had at the time."

He huffed and shook his head.

"What about the neighbor?" Constance asked.

"We still have him for Tanaka's murder," Beal answered.

"I'd rethink that given the site of the crime," she said. "I'd check DNA from inside the glove against Berg."

"Any other professional insights?" Beal asked.

"He had a folding Swiss Army knife. The blade length fits with the reports of both murders. I'd be disassembling it and looking for trace DNA in the hinges."

Beal sneered. "We'll get right on that."

I zoned out as Constance continued to lecture Beal. All that mattered to me was the shivering woman I had in my arms—my woman.

She'd been through hell and hadn't said anything since explaining how Ernst's visit had turned into the armed confrontation.

Why hadn't I seen it earlier, when Winston had suggested her parents had faked their deaths? Knowing Nicole and what she'd told me about them, it made infinitely more sense that someone else had faked their boat sinking to cover up their deaths. If only I'd put the pieces together earlier.

Nicole looked up at me. "You came for me."

I kissed her forehead. "Of course. Why would a woman allergic to shellfish ask me to get shrimp?"

She giggled. "You just called me woman."

I squeezed her tighter. "Because I'm the luckiest man alive that I have you as my woman, and I love you."

"Love you too," she said, with eyes that told me it was true.

CHAPTER 49

Nicole

(Nine days later)

This was Monday morning, the start of my second full week in charge of the family company, and I was still moving files around in my new—Daddy's old—office when I had time.

"You won't regret this," Gary said cheerily.

"See that I don't." I shook hands with him before he left my office as our new CFO.

Wenzel had requested the opportunity to go back to Smith's, and I wasn't stopping that.

Dee poked her head in the doorway. "Your cousin is here."

"Send her in." I checked the time.

Lara slid through the doorway.

"Close the door and have a seat," I told her.

I decided to stand and lean against the desk. The height differential was a tactic I'd seen Josh use to good effect with Wenzel.

"Yeah?" she said after sitting.

"You're late." My stomach knotted up.

"I'm here, aren't I?"

I crossed my arms. "You can lose the attitude, young lady. You agreed yesterday that you'd follow the rules and be on your best behavior. Being late doesn't cut it anymore."

She looked taken aback. "But I'm barely being paid."

I nodded. "You can collect your full paycheck after you finish paying me back the thirty-two thousand of bail I've posted for you over the years."

After the whole Ernst thing, the embezzlement charges had been dropped. Removing the other charges had required a phone call from Josh's dad, who seemed to know the right people. With the bail canceled, the notice of default on my house had been cleared, but I was still out the latest bail bond fee.

She slumped in her chair. "But you're taking half my paycheck. What am I supposed to live on?"

"Well, I'm providing you a place to live. It won't take long to pay it off—or you can get a second job. It's not my problem. It's yours."

"But he killed Vern." With her it always came back to being a victim.

I raised my hand. "And he murdered my parents. I have to live with that knowledge every day, but what I don't have to live with is listening to your excuses. Sure, you've had it tough, but it's not all about you. Get over it and get on with your life. I'm done babying you. Life is tough. Life is unfair. Get used to it."

Lara sat silently for a few moments. "Is that all?"

I rounded the desk back to my chair. "For now."

She made for the door.

"And," I said.

She turned.

"Gary said you did good work last week on the payables project."

A confused look crossed her face. "Thank you."

"You should thank him. And Josh is bringing over pizza tonight at seven, if you'd like to join us."

Lara hesitated before answering. "Sure." A hint of a smile showed as she opened the door and left.

Josh entered less than a minute after Lara had gone and closed the door behind him. "How'd it go?"

"I had to practice that speech for a half hour, and I'm still not sure I got it right. Are you positive this is the right thing to do?"

His strong hands took my shoulders as he looked into my eyes and nodded his answer. "Have a little faith. If the baby bird doesn't get coaxed out of the nest, it never learns to fly."

"I don't know who this is harder on."

He released me and pulled a folder from his bag. "I've got a present for you."

"Not again." He'd been showering me with gifts for the last week.

He put the folder back in his bag. "Okay, if you don't want it…"

My curiosity got the better of me. "What is it?"

Josh handed me the papers with a sly grin. "You might want to sit down."

I returned to my chair and opened it. It was a letter from Benson Corp., signed by him and Harold Snyderman.

"I'm taking Bremmer away from you."

I snorted as I read the paper. "I can live with that."

"She's all yours now. I'm not your boss anymore."

I got to the important part. It was a letter of rescission, canceling the purchase by Benson.

"Rossi's is independent again," he said. "I've made sure the bank will honor your previous loans and credit line, but anything beyond that is up to you to negotiate. And, you can pay me back the money I put in when things settle down."

I sprang up and launched myself at my man. I gave him the passionate kiss he deserved for delivering on my dream, but only for a few seconds, because this thank you wasn't good enough. I lowered my hand to palm his growing erection. "I have a key to a locked closet in the back hallway."

His eyes lit up. "Lead the way, Nickels."

EPILOGUE

IF YOU LOVE SOMEONE, SET THEM FREE. IF THEY COME BACK, THEY'RE YOURS; IF THEY DON'T, THEY NEVER WERE. - RICHARD BACH

NICOLE

JOSH SAT ACROSS THE TABLE FROM ME WITH HIS IPAD IN FRONT OF HIM, JUST AS HE had that first time I'd laid eyes on him. The breeze off the water was warm, and the sun was setting, the same as it had been months ago. The only difference was his expression. He tapped the device again, and concern etched itself across his face. It wasn't cooperating, and the electronics didn't care who he was.

I twisted my water glass. "Checking again won't make it come any faster."

"Yeah," he said dejectedly. "It's just..." He didn't need to finish the sentence. It was hard for him to be this close to learning the truth.

"Give her time," I encouraged him. I knew if I were in Debbie's position, I'd be scared, and that would lead to being careful and slow about my next steps.

Debbie had been in touch this afternoon, finally, and asked Josh for a picture of his face, which he sent right away. He'd been the very picture of excited when he'd found the email in his inbox after all this time.

Debbie had responded that she'd get back to him later but later hadn't been defined.

He rechecked the screen. "It's hard after all this time."

I tore off a piece of bread. "And what did your Dad say about being patient?"

I'd heard the conversation, so I just needed him to repeat it out loud and listen to the advice.

"That women are fickle and can't be trusted."

I threw the bread chunk, and it caught him mid-chest. "He did not." I held out my hand. "Hand it over. You're going electronic cold turkey tonight."

He shut it down, closed the cover, and slid it my way. "I'm all yours, Nickels." His tone conveyed his meaning. He was mine, all mine.

I relaxed into my chair and breathed in the ocean air. Coming back to Barbados, where it all began, had been his idea, and I hadn't required much coaxing. Josh had even invited Sandy, but she'd thought it would be weird, so it was the two of us alone at last. No work, no family, no distractions save the setting sun and each other.

Tonight we didn't have Bad Dad and his boisterous, roughhousing kids, which was a plus. This weekend was our rewind to the way it could have gone the first time we were here—the way it should have gone.

"Two green monkeys," Josh told Diego. "And a bottle of champagne, please."

I tapped my finger to my wine glass. "I don't need more."

Our waiter ignored me and scurried off to rustle up our drinks.

Josh's eyes locked with mine. "Staying true to the memory, Nickels."

His smile grew, and I couldn't help thinking this whole idea was corny as hell —and also sweet. This was starting off perfectly.

I ran my bare foot up his calf under the table. "You know you don't need to get me liquored up tonight. I'll probably say yes to whatever you have in mind."

He returned my wink with a raised eyebrow. "I'm counting on it."

I'd already said *yes* twice—or was it three times?—yesterday after we arrived. And then again this morning and after lunch. We'd given the bed, the floor, the wall, the couch, and the bathroom counter all a try, and were going to run out of surfaces in our suite at this rate. But we did have furniture on the balcony, if we were quiet enough.

"What are you smiling at?" Josh asked, pulling me back to reality.

"Oh, just counting the ways."

"What ways?"

I toyed with my fork and looked up into those blue eyes that mesmerized me. "The ways I adore you. The ways you make me happy. The ways I count myself lucky that I met you here. Those ways."

He leaned forward and took my hands. "I do that too, Nickels. More times a day than you can comprehend."

The words spread warmth through me.

Diego returned with our drinks and the bottle of champagne, which he opened with a flourish before pouring flutes for each of us.

"To us," Josh said, raising his champagne glass. "To us as a team."

I lifted my glass and clinked with his. "To us as a team." As I took in the man in front of me, I knew we'd become a team, both in and out of work.

We sipped and went back to our meals.

I thought about how we'd progressed from antagonism to lovers in the truest sense of the word. I loved everything about this man, from the way he danced as he cooked, to the way he made me feel with every look and every touch, and the little two-line poems he left for me.

I lifted another bite of my penne marinara to my mouth. "How long are they going to hold that table?"

Josh looked over and shrugged. "Who knows? Diego said it was some large family event."

Right next to us, in the direction of the beach, they'd put several tables together for a large group that so far was a no-show.

Josh chewed a mouthful of his steak. He'd fallen behind in the food race while recounting how many times he'd noticed me watching him those few days here before the night where I fell into the pool.

He checked his watch. "It's time."

It was three hours earlier in California, and Ernst was due to be sentenced in the late afternoon. He'd been charged with four murders and had pled guilty already.

It turns out Daddy had uncovered his scheme to siphon money out of the company and confronted him. That started the chain of events that had devastated my family. Ernst had killed Maro, and even Lara's boyfriend, Vern, to keep people away from the trees that hid where he'd buried my parents. And he'd recruited Stephanie Quantell into his scheme after the money he'd stolen from my parents ran out.

Stephanie hadn't been found yet. Her trail had gone cold. But, the Knowltons had managed to stop a wire transfer out of the Caymans that they suspected was on its way to her. With Adam's help, the FBI had started the asset forfeiture process to recover over three hundred thousand dollars from the account. It was only part of what Ernst and Stephanie had stolen, but it would help.

My neighbor Hugo Lenz had been the one to plant the note Lara found. He'd put it in the almond trees, expecting Ernst to find it. Lenz had seen Ernst kill

Vern, but he hadn't come forward back then because of his immigration status. Instead he'd left town.

He'd recently gotten a green card and returned. But his plan to trap Ernst had been thwarted by Ernst planting the bloody glove on Lenz's property and calling in a tip to get him arrested.

I ate as Josh watched his phone.

Finally, it dinged.

"It's done," he said. "Twenty-five to life."

To me, it seemed too little. "I should have shot him." I sighed.

"No," Josh said forcefully. "You did the right thing by not letting him pull you down to his level."

I knew Josh was right. I'd traded regret over that one moment for a lifetime of possibilities with the man across from me.

I pushed my plate away. "I'm full." Even after a full lunch, Josh had insisted I join him for chicken satay and spring rolls mid-afternoon, along with a mai tai. With the mimosa at breakfast, my liver was getting a workout on this trip.

Josh waived Diego over again. "One tiramisu to share, please."

"I'm stuffed," I complained.

"Last time you jumped into the pool to avoid it."

"I was pushed," I corrected him.

"Either way, you're not getting out of it again. You promised dessert with me another time, and this is another time."

I sipped my green monkey. "It's very sweet, but don't you think you're taking this event re-creation thing a little too far?"

"I want the karma to be right, and to get a different outcome than that night."

I knew when we got back to the room, things would end a lot different than that night had. "I think it's worked out pretty well since then."

He nodded. "This time I want your yes to be a real yes, and not *another time*."

Diego returned with our dessert, but it was covered with a paper tent.

It had writing on it. The silly poem was pure Josh.

Roses are red,
Violets are blue.
It was here that I fell
In love with you.

My eyes misted up. "You're still a goofball."

His gaze locked with mine. "I love you, Nicole Marie Rossi. Please say yes."

Diego reached in to pull the paper off our plate.

My heart stopped as I took in the ring set into the top of the dessert.

It was a gorgeous diamond solitaire—the kind of ring every little girl dreams of getting from her man. It was the kind of ring I'd hoped to one day get from my man—and that day had come.

I sniffed and blinked back happy tears. Decisive, snap decisions is what Josh had taught me.

"Yes," I told him. "Hell, yes."

In a moment, we were on our feet and clamped together in a kiss.

Applause broke out behind me, but my eyes were closed as I reveled in the arms of the man who'd delivered on every promise he'd made me, and was now promising to be mine forever.

"Hey, get a room." The voice was Sandy's.

"How come you didn't get down on one knee?" Serena yelled.

We broke the kiss, and I realized the huge group that had been clapping their approval wasn't fellow diners. It was Josh's entire family, pouring into the restaurant area.

We accepted congratulations from the crowd in a never-ending series of hugs.

Everybody was here: all Josh's brothers, sisters, and significant others, his parents, Sandy, Lara, my aunt Rossella, and even Constance, Winston, and Dee.

"What is this?" I asked Josh breathlessly between hugs.

"Your engagement party," Robin answered for him.

"You knew about this and didn't warn me?" I asked Sandy.

She nodded. "Josh promised to line up a date for me if I kept my mouth shut." She pulled herself closer to Winston. "And he came through."

Winston smiled. "Wanna dance, Sandstorm?"

Sandy had already earned herself a nickname.

They wandered off.

I corralled Serena for a moment. "How are things in London?"

Duke joined us.

"Great, except that I had to agree to report to my brother instead of Dad," she said.

"The weather isn't great for riding my bike," Duke added. "And they drink their beer warm."

Serena leaned in. "Thank you for getting me the job."

"I didn't do anything," I protested.

"Whatever you say," she replied.

When I found Kelly, she had her arm around Adam, and they were laughing up a storm with Dennis and Jennifer, which was good to see.

I found Lloyd and Robin off to the side.

"Do I have you to thank for this?" I asked.

Lloyd answered. "You're a part of the family now. This is what we do for each other."

His answer warmed me. As I looked around at all the love, I realized these people truly were my family now.

"I wanted to thank you for that recording you made for me," I told him.

Robin took his hand.

He looked down at his wife, eyes full of love. "It wasn't easy for Robin to get me to see my part in this, but I meant it when I said thank you for being the catalyst for these changes."

"We're going on our first cruise next month," Robin said with obvious excitement.

Lloyd patted his ample midsection. "I don't know if I'm going to be able to handle the all-you-can-eat part of the experience."

Josh joined us. "You'll have to do laps on the upper deck."

"Probably true," Lloyd agreed. "Any news?" he asked Josh.

I held my breath for Josh's answer about Debbie.

"That's a question for tomorrow," Josh answered as he tugged me to his side. "I need to take my fiancée now. Our song is coming up." He pulled me to the dance floor, and just as he predicted, "My Girl" by the Temptations began to play.

I melted into his arms as we rocked to the music, and he sang the song in my ear. The rest of the family rapidly joined us, turning the floor into a mass of swaying couples.

My man had made my happiest dreams come true. I nestled my head against his chest, close to the heart that now was mine, as mine was his.

Tonight, I wouldn't argue. Being his *girl* was perfect.

THE END

THE FOLLOWING PAGES CONTAIN A SNEAK PEEK AT THE NEXT BOOK IN THE SERIES: ***Saving Debbie***.

SNEAK PEEK: SAVING DEBBIE

CHAPTER 1

DEBBIE

I PULLED INTO THE DRIVE AT HOME AFTER MY SHIFT AT THE MINIMART. AS USUAL FOR a Monday, I was the first one home. Reaching the porch, I came face-to-face with the ugly notice tacked beside the door. *Shit*. A tear threatened. I liked it here.

It wasn't the first eviction notice I'd seen, and probably wouldn't be the last.

Turning around, I got back into my car and left.

The notice would put Dominic in an awful mood, and I had no appetite to be around when he saw it.

Two miles away, I parked and lugged my backpack into the Hilltop Diner.

Nell chatted with a customer at the counter and waved as I took my usual seat in the back booth. She came over a minute later. "The usual?"

I nodded. "Please."

A minute later I had a steaming cup of decaf coffee in front of me and tore open two sugar packets to add to it. If I had the money, I'd hang out at the packed Starbucks on the next block, but this coffee was a quarter of the price. Saving money meant freedom someday—a day that couldn't come soon enough. Atmosphere was a luxury that would have to wait.

I pulled my library book out of the backpack and started reading at the dog-eared page. The hero was about to save the heroine, and boy, did she need it. Without him, she was doomed—in more ways than one. At the end of the book, they would embark on their happy future, *happily ever after* they called it. Too bad life didn't imitate these books, not even close. Unfortunately for me, surviving to the next day without anything bad happening was the best I could hope for, and often things didn't turn out that well. Today was a case in point.

Nell came by to top off the decaf coffee I'd been nursing. "Good book?" she asked.

I held it up and showed her the cover with the title printed over the shirtless dude. "Pretty good." I turned it back and admired the image. I'd never had my hands on a chest like that, but a girl could dream.

"I liked that one, and the next in the series too."

Nell and I had similar tastes in escapist reading.

I pulled the next book from my backpack. "Ready to go."

"You know you might run into Willy if you stay too long."

I grimaced. "Chance I'll have to take, I guess." She knew I wasn't angling for any more time in Willy Little's presence. The guy wasn't getting the hint.

"Just thought I'd warn you."

The bell over the door jangled, and another customer entered.

After verifying it wasn't Willy, I went back to my book.

~

Two hours and another cup of decaf later, I packed up my book and waved goodbye to Nell.

My luck had held, and Willy was a no-show. Now I was off to face the real menace, my stepdad, Dom. Dominic Fortuzi was a real piece of work, but then I hadn't picked him—settled for him was more like what Mom had been faced with after Dad's death.

When I pulled back into the drive, both their cars were parked—Mom's Toyota and Dom's pickup.

When I reached the porch, the eviction notice was gone. This house wasn't much to look at, but it was a step up from the last two places we'd stayed.

Dom had the TV on and was watching baseball. "You're late," he barked.

The Red Sox were playing. Even though we lived in Virginia now, he still rooted for his old team. The side table held three beer bottles—two empty, and one halfway there.

"My shift got extended. Nancy was late," I explained. It had happened before when Nancy had daycare issues and was my standard excuse.

"Get dinner ready. Your mom's resting," he said, gulping down more beer. "And make it good." *Good* in his terminology was a hard thing to determine, as it seemed to depend entirely on his mood.

"What do you want?" I asked to avoid a confrontation later.

"Surprise me, but make it quick."

Surprising him was never a good idea.

"How about spaghetti?" It was one of his go-to meals.

"I guess, but less garlic this time." Last week he'd criticized my meal as *not* having enough garlic or pepper.

"I can do that." In the kitchen, I threw ground beef in the skillet and a pot of water for the noodles on the stove before checking on Mom.

I found her in the chair in their bedroom with her cat in her lap and red eyes.

"I'm fixing spaghetti for dinner."

"That's nice. How 'bout a salad on the side?"

Misty, Mom's fluff ball of a cat, ignored me. The cat avoided my room like the plague, which was fine with me. All it had taken was me hissing at it the few times it had ventured in. Getting up in the middle of the night and feeling the wet squish of one of her hairballs underfoot in the dark had soured me on having long-haired cats around.

"Mom, are you okay?" I didn't want to give away that I'd seen the ugly notice on the door.

"Just allergies, dear."

Denial was one of her coping mechanisms.

I closed her door and busied myself in the kitchen.

A half hour later, I had dinner ready—no garlic this time—and served it up on three trays: plates of steaming al dente spaghetti with the salads in separate bowls.

Dom merely grunted when I handed him the tray to balance on his lap. Eating at the table wasn't a dinner-time occurrence for him, as it would cut into television time.

"Less garlic this time," I mentioned.

Mom wanted to eat hers in her room.

I added vinegar to my pasta before sitting down to eat in the kitchen with my book in front of me.

Even as I cleaned up, nobody mentioned the dreaded news hanging over us.

Dom and Mom had argued about this before. He thought nothing of getting a few months behind after a year or two and getting evicted. It saved on rent was his view. The fact that we had to put in the effort to move again and the effect that had on friendships Mom or I had made didn't compute in Dom's world. He didn't seem to have any friends anyway. As a Metrobus driver for WMATA, it wasn't like he spent any time with anyone at work. A solitary job like that fit him —less opportunity to argue.

Later, reading in my room, the argument started, loud enough that I could hear some of it.

"Dominic, I'm fed up with this. I'm not moving again, goddammit," Mom yelled.

"We wouldn't be in this mess if you didn't spend so damned much on that cat."

"I can't help it that she needed the surgery and then got an infection."

"You could help it by getting rid of the ugly thing."

"And what about all the stupid Powerball tickets you buy every week?" she shouted back.

"One of those is gonna win and set us up for life, and you know it."

"I'm not that stupid."

"You calling me stupid? I'm not the one who ruined my car by ignoring the check engine light."

He had her there. Mom had ignored the light and seized the engine of her little car a few months ago.

"I told you about it. You're the car specialist."

"I drive a bus. I don't fix the fucking things."

"Well, then you have to give up Powerball, because I'm not moving again," she yelled.

"There is another way. That thing we talked about."

"Not that again," she complained. "That's too dangerous."

"It'll be easy. You'll see. It would fix all our problems."

After that, the door to their bedroom closed again, and the argument went from yelling to talking, which meant only muffled sounds, and no words for me.

I pushed my nightstand to the side, pulled the heating grate open, and added today's ten dollars to my getaway stash.

After closing up my hideaway, I put my earbuds in and cranked up the music in case the yelling resumed.

Soon, I'll have enough to get away.

CHAPTER 2

Luke

TUESDAY MORNING, THE PHONE WOKE ME.

The clock said a little after nine. "Hey, Luke, I just got a Rocket Three in, if you're interested," Mike said when I answered.

"What kind of damage?" I asked. Mike called his yard a *motorcycle dismantler*, although to me, it was just a muddy junkyard for wrecked bikes—many of which represented the starting point of one of my projects.

"Front end's messed up, and the back too. The frame's a total loss. The idiot got himself sandwiched—hit front and rear. Hope you don't mind cleaning off blood." He laughed. Pretty much all of his inventory came with a history of mayhem.

None of that mattered to me. "And the engine?" At two and a half liters, the Triumph Rocket Three had the baddest motorcycle engine anyone made—bigger and more powerful than any Harley.

"Can't speak to the drive-shaft, but otherwise it looks good to me, 'cept for the blood and guts."

"You already said that. Hold it for me, and I'll be up this afternoon." The drive back from Baltimore in traffic would be a bitch, but worth it if the engine was good.

After we hung up, I rolled out of bed to check the surveillance footage from last night. The cameras were motion-activated, and a quick review showed only a raccoon and two cats, no thieves of the two-legged variety.

"One of these days…" I said to the video monitor before I shut it off and headed for the coffee machine.

I added a heaping spoonful of cocoa powder to the mug and stirred while I walked around the clothes on the floor to the bathroom. The cup came with me into the shower, and I sipped it while hot water ran down my back. Chocolate in my coffee was one of the luxuries I appreciated now that I was on the outside—that and not having to constantly watch my back.

~

THAT AFTERNOON, I ROLLED UP TO THE SIDE ENTRANCE OF MIKE'S YARD AND HONKED. A minute later, his son unlocked the chain on the gate and let me through.

There it was, straight ahead. The once-beautiful masterpiece was in even worse shape than Mike had described. A chain-reaction crash usually totaled a car for insurance purposes, with bodywork front and back messing it up, but it often left the occupants uninjured. That in no way compared to what had happened to this poor bike and rider.

I climbed out.

"See what I mean?" Mike asked as he walked up.

I stepped slowly around it, surveying the damage. "Yup. A real mess."

He'd been right. The black stains of dried blood were everywhere. The key was still in the ignition.

I turned it, and the neutral light on the instrument cluster flickered to life. I shut the power off again, visualizing the scenario.

The poor rider had been idling in neutral behind a stopped car when he got hit from behind and squished up against the car in front of him. The poor fucker never stood a chance. Probably hit by a young girl texting and driving—they were the absolute worst. A few seconds of someone's inattention had cost this rider his bike and his life. Although I didn't know that for sure, the evidence was pretty plain.

After a quick check, and seeing no oil leak to indicate a cracked case, I turned to Mike. "It sure is a mess. How much you want for it?"

We threw a few offers back and forth before settling on a price I could live with. I nodded and turned the key again and pressed the starter button. The engine turned over. Flicking the kill switch on the handlebar grip to on, it rumbled briefly to life before I quickly shut it down again and pocketed the key.

They helped me load the crumpled machine onto a pallet and into the back of my van.

I settled up with Mike for a sum I wouldn't regret when this engine had a new home. Before leaving, I checked for my travel authorization, as I always did. Better safe than sorry.

The drive back to Virginia in the afternoon traffic was boring and annoying. What made it worse was the smell from my cargo in back. Having the air conditioning vent blasting at my face mostly cured it, but the carcass of the bike needed to be hosed down before I let it sit overnight in my garage.

Dinner time was approaching as I left the freeway. I counted down the fifteen stop signs that remained between me and home and rolled down the window to keep the stench at bay.

With eleven intersections to go, I stopped behind a minivan at the four-way stop. I pulled up after it went ahead. A VW came from my left and slowed. The unpainted replacement fender showed it had recently been in an accident.

I went ahead.

The clueless girl looking down surged forward.

I jerked right and slammed on my horn, waking her up.

Miss Clueless screeched to a halt, just missing me. Another stupid girl that shouldn't have a license.

"Fuck you," I yelled. The epithet didn't faze Miss Clueless. I flipped her the bird and drove off. The fact that most traffic accidents happened close to home was almost proven here today. The repaired fender should have clued me in to give her a wide berth—a lesson I'd remember for next time.

At home, I backed up to my garage door and parked far enough away to slide my cargo out. After pulling up the door, I opened the back of the van and maneuvered my ramps into place. The electric winch from the garage provided the muscle to get the pallet out of the van and to the ground.

Without the time tonight to thoroughly clean it, I left it outside and closed the door.

Being set back from the road gave me the latitude to leave it outside without upsetting a neighbor.

If my teenage thieves returned tonight and the weight didn't deter them, the stench surely would.

Inside, I logged today's trip on my travel authorization paper and put it away before I called for a pizza delivery.

~

DEBBIE

DOM'S DRIVING SCHEDULE GAVE HIM TUESDAY OFF, SO HE WAS HOME WHEN I GOT OFF work from Mama's Minimart and parked at the house.

He was kneeling in front of Mom's car—screwing on the license plate, it looked like. "Cleaning things," he said as I passed.

I looked back at my car. The front license plate was spattered with bugs, but I doubted it was a good idea to ask if he'd clean mine as well.

Once inside, I went to my room and changed.

Mom was in the kitchen, putting cookie tins away in the pantry. "How was your day?" Her voice was oddly cheery, given the news we'd gotten yesterday.

"Pretty good. No shoplifting, so that was good." It was a battle we didn't fight every day, but the owner, Mama Garcetti, took it very seriously. If she thought I was slacking off in watching for it, it would be my job, and I needed that job. Nobody else would allow me to split my paycheck like she did. I took part of it in cash, out of Dom's reach.

When I'd worked at McDonald's, the pay had been a little better, but my entire paycheck had been auto deposited, and Dom took it all and doled out a tiny allowance in return. The day I'd complained had been a lesson never to be that insolent again.

"Paying us back for all the years we've supported you," he'd said.

Nobody else's parents treated their kids this way, but complaining wouldn't fix it, only escape would.

Mom was now cutting broccoli on the board. "Want to get the broiler pan for me?"

"Sure." I pulled it out from under the oven and rinsed it off in the sink. "What are we having?"

"Steak. Oh, and if you could wash three potatoes and put 'em in the microwave to preheat, that would help. We're having baked potato as well."

I knew the meal well. It was Dom's favorite, and one we couldn't afford every week. "What kind of steak?"

She continued chopping. "Filet mignon in the fridge. Three nice pieces."

That was a definite change. New York strip was as fancy as we normally got, unless it was his birthday.

I finished drying the broiler pan and located three potatoes for us. "Mom, is everything okay?"

She almost floated, moving to the other counter and sweeping the broccoli into the pan. "Of course it is."

I scrubbed the first potato, unsure how to bring up the elephant in the room. By the second potato, I couldn't hold it back. "Mom, are we going to move again?"

"No. Why would you ask that?"

I finished the third potato, turned off the water, and faced her. "I saw the notice."

She waved my concern away like a fly. "Oh, that's handled. It's not a problem anymore."

I snapped my mouth closed—it had dropped open at those words. "How?"

"It finally happened. Your father won at Powerball last night."

The news floored me. I jumped into her arms and hugged her. "I really didn't want to move again."

She hugged me back. "Me either, dear."

I put the spuds in the microwave and started it.

She opened the freezer. "Oh, shucks. We don't have any ice cream to celebrate."

"I can run and get some," I offered.

She pulled her wallet from her purse and handed me a crisp, new bill. "Get two gallons of rocky road, and hurry."

I pocketed the cash and picked up my purse on the way out. "Going to the store for ice cream," I told Dom, who'd finished outside and taken up residence in his normal chair in front of the television.

A grunt is all I got in return.

On the way to the store, I stopped at the stop sign and looked down to change the radio station. I refused to listen to another second of the song Willy had labeled *our song*. I'd already deleted it off my phone.

I punched another button on the radio and started again.

A horn blared.

I slammed on the brakes.

The horn continued, and the van driver's tattooed arm came out of his window with the middle finger I deserved. He sped off. At least he didn't stop and berate me or pull a gun on me for my distracted driving.

Fuck, that had been close. I already had one dull black fender on this car. Saving up for my escape was more important than getting the fender painted to match the red.

Past the intersection, I pulled over and closed my eyes. Trying to stop the shaking of my legs, I rested my head against the wheel to get my breath back. I'd almost doomed my prospect of escape by not paying attention. If I'd wrecked the car, I'd be stuck here for God knows how long.

Twisting the radio off, I made a new rule: no music in the car—none.

After a cleansing breath and a check of my mirror, I resumed my trip to the supermarket, slowly this time. Rocky road ice cream coming up.

Concentrate on what was important. No car, no escape. It was as simple as that.

Once inside the store, I had to decide between two brands and chose the Breyers rocky road.

At the checkout counter, I handed the man the brand-new hundred Mom had given me. He held it up to the light and ran a counterfeit-checking pen across it before counting out and handing me my change. For once, lady luck had favored my family.

CHAPTER 3

Debbie

Wednesday morning, Mom already had breakfast cooking when I got to the kitchen. "Good morning," she said with a sing-songy voice.

The sun shone in through the window.

I poured water into a mug. "It is. Anything special today?" I added a teabag to my mug and started it in the microwave.

Mom was staring distractedly at the cupboard. "I'm sorry, dear. What was that?"

"Anything special going on today?" I repeated.

She pulled bread from the toaster and checked her fingers. "I think I'll get my nails done today."

I didn't ask what had come over my Mom. The hundred-dollar bill last night answered that question.

Yesterday we'd been thirty days from being kicked out of here, and this morning she had lottery winnings to fix things money-wise—at least for a time.

She glanced at the far wall again.

Dom appeared, rubbing his chin. "Morning, Deborah."

Surprised, I struggled to get the word out. "Morning." It was the first time in at least a year that he'd used my full name. "Got pretty lucky, huh?"

He looked at Mom and smiled. "It's skill, not luck."

Famous last words of a compulsive gambler.

Mom smiled back and nodded.

THAT AFTERNOON AT THE MINIMART, ANNIE WAS IN THE BACK, PULLING CASES OF soda to restock the refrigerator, when he came in—over three hundred pounds of angry man with a scar on his cheek.

Scarface had been in before, and never with a good attitude. Today the mustard stain on the front of his shirt said he'd recently lost a battle with a hot dog or two.

After a trip down the aisle, he came to the register with a twelve-pack of beer, a box of Ritz crackers, and a jar of peanut butter.

"Will that be all?" I asked. Treat all customers with respect and a good attitude, I'd been taught.

Annie came from the back with three cases on the hand truck.

"Yeah," he grunted.

I rang his items up.

Scarface pulled a SNAP food stamp card from his wallet.

"You can't buy beer with that. Sorry," I told him.

His eyes narrowed. "Yes, I can."

Annie rushed over.

"The rules say no alcohol," I told him again.

His face twisted up in anger that made the scar look even meaner. "Just do it."

"Sure," Annie told him, reaching over to hit the button on my register. She shot me a don't-ask-questions-just-do-it look.

The reader beeped after a few seconds, and he retrieved his card.

I bagged the crackers and peanut butter for him with a smile he didn't deserve, and he lugged his purchases away.

After the door closed behind him, I turned to Annie. "What the hell?"

"He's bad news."

"It's still not right," I insisted.

Annie went back to the hand truck. "Just keeping you alive. He nearly twisted Jerry's arm off a few days ago over the same issue."

CHAPTER 4

Debbie

(Three weeks later)

I got off my shift early and returned home to get changed for pizza night with Annie. The lack of cars meant I was the first one home.

Upstairs I shucked off my black work pants and pulled on jeans and a better blouse.

Downstairs in the kitchen, I started a load of laundry and unloaded the dishwasher. Getting these chores done before I left was the price of pizza night.

While putting cups back in the cupboard, I noticed the lid off one of the cookie tins on the upper shelf that Mom had rearranged the other day. It felt heavy when I slid it to the side to reach the lid that had fallen.

I pulled it down.

And gasped.

It was filled with cash—bundles of bills with paper wrappers around them like in the movies. One had been torn open. I picked up an intact bundle. It felt heavier than I would have guessed—a big stack of one hundred dollar bills, all stiff and fresh.

Why didn't Dom have his winnings in the bank like everybody else? Leaving this much money lying around the house was stupid. But then Dom's middle name was either *mean* or *stupid*, depending on the day.

The wrapper of the bundle I held said ten thousand dollars—more money than I'd ever seen before, and the tin was half full of them.

The temptation was almost too great to resist. That much money would make my escape plan a breeze, and I could leave this minute and be free of Dom tonight.

I put the bills back in the tin. After replacing the lid, the cookie tin went back up on the shelf. I closed the door to the cabinet and shivered for a moment at what I'd done. I'd actually contemplated taking the money and leaving.

It wouldn't be fair. The money wasn't mine. It was theirs. I couldn't take it from Mom. Or subject Mom to Dom's wrath when he found out.

She wouldn't leave him and come with me; that much I knew for certain.

I vowed I'd never be that woman—the one who'd settle for someone who landed on the scale between *disappointing* and *bad*. I'd be sure to have more respect for myself than that. I couldn't make her see it, but maybe someday she'd come to the realization on her own.

A few months ago, I'd heard about a bus driver shooting on the radio, and I'd wished for it to be him while I drove home. Did that make me a bad person? If it would keep Mom safe, I'd accept that label.

The shooting had been on his route, but another driver had been the victim. The incident had only resulted in him telling us every week how he risked life and limb to bring home the money to support us.

I kept my eye rolls to myself on that one.

~

Luke

It was Tuesday night, and that meant wings at Pete's Country Club, which was a lot country and zero club. No golfers in polo shirts here. The outside screamed seedy, and the inside matched, but the peanuts were free.

Pete had died years ago and left the place to his son, Jules. Pete's didn't have big-screen TVs with sports playing or happy hour for the business weenies getting off work. The place was more old school: three pool tables in the back, an assortment of guys nursing beers between the tables and the bar, and always a few smokers out by the door if it wasn't raining too hard. Pete's was the kind of place that didn't mind customers like me to keep the hipsters away. As an ex-con who worked with his hands and had no college education, I fit right in with this crowd.

After surveying the scene at Pete's, I grabbed a bowl of peanuts from the bar and found my usual table near the pool tables.

"The usual?" Cindy, my waitress, asked after she swooped by and dropped a refill at a nearby table. She wore a top that was even more low-cut than usual. She made a point of leaning over when she talked to the customers, me included, and I got an eyeful of good-tip-inducing cleavage as a result. She was tougher than she looked and perfectly capable of keeping most of the customers' hands in line.

"Sure, Cyn."

She winked and scurried off.

Early on, there had been a time I'd considered hooking up with Cyn, but after seeing the caliber of the customers she left with, I lost my appetite for dipping my wick in that particular petri dish.

Mike, one of the regulars, spotted me. "Hey, Wrench, ready for a re-match?" I worked on his bike on occasion, hence the nickname.

"Not unless you got a twenty to put up."

"How about ten?" he countered.

"Not worth it. Twenty."

He shuffled his feet and pulled out a bill. "Okay, but I'm ready for ya this time."

I pulled out my wallet and added my bill on top of his.

Mike was always challenging me to arm-wrestle him. I let him win one time in four so he'd keep coming back and supplying me with beer money. This wasn't due to be his night.

He pulled up a chair.

As we settled into a grip, a small crowd formed.

Cindy came back with my order and was smart enough to keep it off my table until we were done.

"On three," he said. "Three... Two... One..." And we started.

I grunted and groaned for an appropriate time before forcing him over onto the table. Just like that, I was twenty bucks up for the night.

"I wasn't ready," Mike complained. "I want a rematch." He made too much of my groaning.

I swiped the money off the table. "You know my rule, Mike. Only once per night."

"I'll take a piece of that action," Cliff said as he set down his pool cue.

Cliff was an unpleasant vision from my past. He'd transferred to my cell block a week before my release and had been in two nasty fights in that short time—and that was just what I'd seen.

"I'm done for tonight," I told him.

Several of the onlookers stepped back as Cliff approached.

He was big in all dimensions, with a hell of a belly, thick arms, and a neck wider than his head. The scar running down his left cheek spoke to one of the fights he'd been in. He took the chair Mike had vacated.

"I only take one person's money a night," I said before grabbing a wing. "Sorry." I smiled and started eating.

He placed his elbow on the table, his hand up in the air. "Won't be a problem, because you're not taking mine."

I shrugged. "Not interested."

Cliff stood quickly, and the chair fell over behind him. "No balls?" His fists clenched at his side.

From the side of my eye, I caught Jules rushing our way.

Only an idiot would take on a guy his size, but my time behind bars had taught me there were times when backing down was the more dangerous alternative.

I stood and pulled down my fly.

That action caught him by surprise.

I lifted a wing. "I said I only wrestle once a night. Now, you wanna share some wings or kiss my balls to see how big they are?"

Jules arrived with his ax handle in hand, ready to break both our heads if anything started.

I offered Cliff the wing.

He stared at me for a second before breaking out into a laugh. He took the wing. "You got brass ones. I'll give you that."

I zipped my fly back up, and we both sat.

That had been a close one. The last thing I needed was a fight in here. Fighters stood out, and I wanted to blend in.

The crowd dispersed, and Jules took his battle club back behind the bar.

"Cliff," he said, offering his hand.

I shook it. "Luke. I left Augusta just after you got there."

No hint of recognition crossed his face. "I don't remember you."

"I don't try to be remembered."

He grunted and chewed his wing.

"How long you been out?" I asked.

"Three months or so," he said between chews.

"Passin' through?"

He nodded. "Checking places out, ya know."

"Hey," the guy at the pool table yelled. "We finishin' this or what?"

Cliff stood. "Yeah, yeah, I'm not done beatin' your ass." He grabbed two more wings. "Thanks for the eats."

I lifted my beer to him. "Later." I was hoping for a lot later. Cliff was not going on my Christmas card list.

I spent another two hours at Pete's shelling peanuts, chewing on wings, and sipping my one Corona. Getting buzzed was not on the agenda. It made it harder to catch the conversations going on around me.

Nobody paid me any heed, which was exactly how I wanted it. I was here often enough that I was like a piece of worn furniture—present, but unnoticed.

CHAPTER 5

Debbie

Wednesday afternoon, Dom wasn't home yet, and I couldn't take it any longer. I had to know the truth. The money in the cookie tins didn't make sense.

I found Mom at the table in the kitchen nook, looking out the window.

"Mom," I said as I pulled up a chair and sat. "Can we talk?"

Her hands were clasped tightly around the mug of tea in front of her. "The goldfinches have found the feeder again," she said. She loved her birdfeeder when we had the money to keep seed in it, and she'd recently refilled it.

I looked outside at the gaggle of birds attacking the feeder. "Mom, I want to know about the money."

"The cardinals are back too."

"Mom. The money?"

She shifted her gaze from outside to me. "What money?"

"The cash," I said.

"I don't know what you're talking about, dear."

"The money for the rent, to start with."

"Dominic won at Powerball, I told you." She looked outside again. "They're very pretty, don't you think?"

I cocked my head and sighed. "Mom, I checked. He couldn't have won anything on Powerball Monday night."

Without looking at me, she picked up her mug and went to the sink. "He won at Powerball." She started to rinse the mug with her back to me. "Now let it be."

I wasn't letting this become another thing we didn't talk about, like the hitting. I walked to the cupboard, opened it, and pulled down one of the cookie tins. It felt heavier than before.

She rushed over. "Leave that be."

I spun around, took it across the room, and emptied it onto the table. "They pay lottery winnings this big in a check or a wire transfer, not cash. I checked. And, they only do drawings on Wednesday and Saturday."

Some of the packets had fallen to the floor. "I said to leave it be," she yelled. She knelt and started to pick up the money on the floor.

The front door opened and closed.

"Quick, help me get this back where it belongs," she whispered.

"I'm home," Dom called.

I started to shovel the money bundles back into the tin.

"Be out in a minute," Mom yelled back.

They wouldn't all fit without reorganizing the stacks.

Dom appeared at the door before we finished. "What's going on in here?"

Some of the money still lay on the table.

I gathered up my nerve and faced him. "Where did this come from?" I stood tall.

"None of your business. Now get to your room," he bellowed, pointing toward the hall.

I stood my ground. "No."

He moved toward me with fury in his eyes. "I said, get in your room before I put you there." I knew that look. It was the one that came right before violence.

"Yes, sir." I scooted around him and went to my room.

Dom's voice boomed from the kitchen. "What did you tell her?"

"Nothing."

"I don't believe you."

"Nothing, I swear."

I grabbed my purse from my nightstand and started for the door. I didn't make it.

Dom's meaty hand held the door closed as I reached for the handle. "Where do you think you're going?"

"Out… We need groceries." It was the best I could think of.

He grabbed my purse away. "No. Get back in your room. You're not going anywhere."

I couldn't overpower him, there was no way around him, and even if I did get past him, he had my purse with my keys. I turned, speed-walked to my room, and slammed the door.

The sound of his pacing came through the door.

"She knows," Mom said quietly.

Dom's pacing continued. "What do I do now? What do I do now?" he said.

Mom didn't answer him. The question wasn't meant for either of us.

I was trapped.

A HALF HOUR LATER, MY DOOR OPENED.

It was Dom. He laid cold eyes on me. "We're going out."

I didn't move. "I'm fine here." My bedroom was my one safe haven in this house.

"Now." He moved forward and pulled me up. "Get in the car with your mother."

I didn't fight him. It would have been futile. "Where are we going?" I walked out toward the cars.

"Out."

Mom was already in the driver's seat of her car, which was odd. Normally if it was the three of us, Dom would drive.

Dom carried a black satchel with him and locked the door behind us. He got in the front with Mom, but only after I climbed into the back seat and closed the door.

We started heading toward town.

"Where are we going?" I asked, hoping for but not expecting an answer.

"Taking Dominic into work," Mom said.

I didn't expect to like the answer, but I asked anyway. "Why do I have to come along?" It was probably because I'd said I wanted to leave, and they didn't trust me.

"Just because," Dom said. Which confirmed what I'd suspected: He didn't trust me to be in the house when they got back, and he was right.

Mom stopped for a red light in town.

I could have opened the door and bolted, but what good would that have done me with no car to escape in and not enough money?

We drove through town, still heading east toward DC.

I hadn't saved as much as I'd planned to, but now I knew I'd take the first chance after we got home to get free.

He was up to something that wasn't good. He hadn't won the lottery, and God only knew what he was into that got him that much cash all of the sudden. If he'd robbed a drug dealer or something, being in the same house with him wouldn't be safe.

That thought sent a chill down my spine. How would I get Mom to safety if it was something like that?

She turned onto the beltway north, which seemed odd, but I'd never driven Dom into work.

Getting into DC would take time. All I could do was watch out the window and try to think of a plan that would get us both away from Dom.

We crossed the river into Maryland, and Mom got off the beltway heading south.

Soon after I saw the sign saying we'd entered Bethesda, Mom pulled into an alley off the main street we were on.

I sat up.

Dom turned back toward me. "Now, you and I are going to work."

I scrunched up my face in confusion. "What?"

He offered a black thing over the seat.

It was a gun.

"No," I said.

"Take it," he demanded. "It's not loaded."

I grabbed the heavy thing and put it down on the seat next to me. "What the hell?"

He had another gun, this one pointed at me.

I froze.

"This one is loaded. Now listen to me and do exactly as I say. Pick up the gun."

I put my hand on the beast and pulled it into my lap. I felt as cold as the steel of the gun.

"You're going with me into the bank."

I put the gun on the seat again. "I am not."

"Yes, you are." He cocked the pistol. "Or I'm going to shoot you."

My breathing stopped. All I could see was the black barrel of the gun pointed at me. I was in a nightmare. That had to be it. This couldn't be happening. This didn't happen to normal people.

Mom looked at me through the rearview mirror. "Dear, you have to do this." Fear laced her words. "For me."

With Mom begging me, I had no choice. I picked up the cold, evil gun.

"Good girl," Dom said, grinning. "Now that we understand each other, here is what we're going to do."

I tried to gulp, but my mouth was so dry I couldn't.

"Your mother is going to drive us around the corner to the bank," he said. "You and me are going in and making a withdrawal. You don't say a thing. I'll do all the talking."

I nodded.

He tossed the black duffle bag over the seat to me. "The teller counters are on the righthand side. You'll go back there and put the money in the bag. Understand?"

I blinked and nodded.

"What are you going to say?" he asked.

"Nothing."

"That's right. It'll be over in less than thirty seconds. You try to run. I shoot you. You say a word, and I shoot you. You hesitate for one second, and I shoot you. Do you understand me?"

I wrapped my arms around myself and nodded again.

"Say it," he demanded.

"I understand," I squeaked out.

I'd seem him ignore us. I'd seen him angry we were out of beer. I'd seen him dismissive about Mom's cooking. I'd seen him angry that dinner was late. But I'd never seen this version of Dom, the *I'll kill you* version.

Mom had refused to leave the few times I'd broached it years ago, saying he'd find us. She'd joked that he'd never let her leave. This Dominic pointing the gun at me was the Dominic she feared, the one who would hunt her down and kill her if she left. It hadn't made sense until now.

Now I understood her fear of leaving him. I had no doubt he was deadly serious, and an angry, armed Dominic was not one to tangle with.

"We go in," he said. "You get the money. You don't say anything. We get out. That's the whole plan. Don't follow the plan, and I shoot you—simple as that."

"But—" I started to object.

Dom pointed the ugly gun at me again. "But what? You want to live or not? You'll follow the plan or not?"

I took an unsteady breath. "I'll do it." Right now, I would agree to anything to get away from this madman, the version of Dom I'd been shielded from until today.

Dom put the gun away. "Let's go." He pulled a mask over his head.

Mom added a mask as well and started the car. She pulled around the corner to the main street and stopped in front of the bank two blocks down.

"Do I get a mask?" I asked.

"Not this time," Dom said. He looked up and down the street. "Let's go."

I got out of the car and followed him inside.

"Everybody on the floor," he yelled before firing a shot into the ceiling. "Back from the counters," he added, waving his gun at the tellers. "Open the gate."

After that, it was a blur as a dribble of pee ran down my leg.

The customer's faces were even more panicked than I felt.

"Get the money," he said, pointing to the right.

A teller pulled open the gate to the back.

I went down the line on shaky legs, not looking at the scared employees, who didn't understand I wasn't the one to be afraid of. I pulled cash from the drawers into the duffel, and after getting to the end, ran back to the gate and out.

Dom pointed the gun at me and waved me to the side.

I moved over.

Bang!

His gun went off, and I looked back to see one of the tellers slump to the floor, a red splotch on her shirt.

He'd fucking shot her.

My lunch started to come up with the realization that he'd just killed a lady here, and he might kill me too.

He nodded toward the door and ran for the entrance.

I followed him and put my hand to my mouth to hold back the vomit. I swallowed it down and spit the wretched taste out of my mouth. I got out the door a few seconds behind him and launched myself into the back seat of the car.

Mom drove off.

I shook uncontrollably. "What the hell?" I yelled.

I couldn't hold it back any longer, the vision of the blood blooming on that lady's shirt came back to me, and the awful smell of the gunpowder. My lunch came up and decorated the floorboards.

Dom had already taken his mask off. He turned back to me. "I just winged her. Get a hold of yourself."

"What?" Mom asked.

My barf smelled as bad as I felt.

Dom rolled down his window. "You'll clean that up when we get home."

"He shot a lady," I told her.

"Why, Dominic? Nobody was supposed to get hurt."

"Shut up and drive," he told her.

He turned back to me again. "You can't leave now unless you want to face attempted murder. We're in this together, little girl."

That's what this had been about. He'd intentionally cut off my ability to leave and start a new life.

Printed in Great Britain
by Amazon

45787799R00210